PAPERS AND CORRESPONDENCE
OF
WILLIAM STANLEY JEVONS

Volume I

William Stanley Jevons, aged 22
from a photograph taken in Australia, 6 February 1858

PAPERS AND CORRESPONDENCE
OF
WILLIAM STANLEY JEVONS

Volume I

BIOGRAPHY AND PERSONAL JOURNAL

EDITED BY

R. D. COLLISON BLACK

AND

ROSAMOND KÖNEKAMP

MACMILLAN
IN ASSOCIATION WITH THE ROYAL ECONOMIC SOCIETY

First published 1972 by
THE MACMILLAN PRESS LTD
London and Basingstoke
Associated companies in New York Toronto
Dublin Melbourne Johannesburg and Madras

SBN 333 10256 8

Printed in Great Britain by
R. & R. CLARK LTD
Edinburgh

CONTENTS

A complete index to the Papers and Correspondence will be contained in Volume IV.

LIST OF PLATES AND MAP

MAP

PREFACE

William Stanley Jevons has long been recognised as a leading figure in the development of economic thought and for that reason, perhaps, the general impression has tended to be that there is little more to be known about his life and work than has long been established and accepted. This impression was fostered by the fact that after his early death in 1882, his widow, aided first by H. S. Foxwell and later by Henry Higgs, brought out a series of volumes which appeared to incorporate virtually all of Jevons's completed economic papers, including both those already published and those left in manuscript. These were *Methods of Social Reform* (1883), *Investigations in Currency and Finance* (1884) and *The Principles of Economics* (1905).

Mrs Jevons also published, in 1886, the *Letters and Journal of W. Stanley Jevons*, a selection from her husband's letters and private papers 'which would give, to those who knew [him] only by his writings, the best idea of his character as a man in the different relations of life'. This became the main source of biographical information, used extensively, for example, by Keynes in his 'Centenary Allocution' on the life and work of Jevons, read before the Royal Statistical Society on 21 April 1936, and later reprinted in *Essays in Biography*.[1]

With these volumes available it is not surprising that it should come to be accepted that, whatever might be said by way of commentary, nothing new could emerge in the way of primary sources for Jevons's life and work. This certainly was the view which I held when, late in 1958, Mr Alfred MacLochlainn, of the Manuscripts Department of the National Library of Ireland, invited me to inspect the papers of John Elliott Cairnes which had then just been placed on deposit there. I was interested and surprised to discover among them a series of letters from W. S. Jevons, which appeared to place the relationship between this pioneer of marginalism and the 'last of the classical economists' in a new light.

In order to prove or disprove this point, my first task was clearly to locate the letters written by Cairnes to Jevons. I anticipated no difficulty in this, for with so well known a figure as Jevons I felt sure that his papers would be preserved and catalogued in a major library either in London or Manchester. Enquiries made to the Librarians of

---

[1] *Journal of the Royal Statistical Society* (hereafter *JRSS*) 1936; *Essays in Biography* (ed. Geoffrey Keynes, 1951), 255–309.

University College, London, and Manchester University revealed that neither had custody of any Jevons papers or could make any suggestion as to their possible whereabouts. However, the then Librarian of Manchester University, the late Dr Moses Tyson, mentioned my query to Dr Wolfe Mays, of the Philosophy Department of Manchester, who was interested in Jevons's work as a logician. Dr Mays kindly suggested that I should contact Jevons's surviving daughter, Miss Harriet Winefrid Jevons, and provided me with her address. Miss Jevons, then in her eighty-second year, replied promptly and helpfully to my queries, telling me that her father's papers had been kept by her brother, the late Professor Herbert Stanley Jevons, and at his death in 1955 had passed into the care of his daughter Rosamond Jevons, now Mrs Friedrich Könekamp.

Mrs Könekamp, approached in turn, kindly provided me with copies of the letters from Cairnes to Jevons which she possessed; so I was able to build up the two sides of the correspondence, and to publish my discovery.[1] In addition, however, Mrs Könekamp sent me a copy of a letter from Alfred Marshall to W. S. Jevons which had not been included in *Letters and Journal*.[2] I began to realise that the unpublished material was of considerable extent and potential importance and as a result of further enquiries was invited to see it and to meet Mrs Könekamp and Miss Jevons at the latter's home in Hillingdon in July 1959. This visit amply confirmed the fact that a large volume of correspondence and papers which had not been included in *Letters and Journal* existed and stood in need of collation and editing. Both Miss Jevons and Mrs Könekamp were anxious to see the papers properly preserved and to give facilities for their editing. Consequently I approached Mr C. F. Carter, then Stanley Jevons Professor of Economics at Manchester University, and he took up the matter with Lord Robbins. The outcome was a decision that the Jevons Papers, while remaining the property of his descendants, should be deposited at Manchester University and that the Royal Economic Society should sponsor the preparation and publication of an edition of them.

The material in the papers could be divided into two main categories – personal and professional. The personal papers included much correspondence with other members of the Jevons family, as well as Jevons's personal Journal and diaries – from which his widow had published only small selections. The professional papers included the manuscripts of most of Jevons's published books and articles, but the only major item not published was a set of notes of the lectures on economics given by Jevons at Manchester in 1875–6 as taken down by

---

[1] R. D. Collison Black, 'Jevons and Cairnes', *Economica*, **xx** (August 1960) 214–32.

[2] A. Marshall to W. S. Jevons, 4 February 1875 published in Vol. III, Letter 416.

one of his students, Harold Rylett. Apart from this there were many notes from which it was possible to trace the growth of Jevons's economic ideas from his early days in Australia, and, perhaps most important, many letters discussing those ideas with his contemporaries, from the most famous to the most obscure. Nearly all these letters related to economic subjects, but a few touched on logic and scientific method. Most of Jevons's logical papers had, however, been given into the care of Dr Wolfe Mays by Professor H. S. Jevons.

At the outset, then, a natural division of labour suggested itself – that Mrs Könekamp should undertake the editing of the personal papers of her grandfather, while the editing of the professional papers was to be done by me. I have confined myself in this to items with an economic character, including those which deal with Jevons's logical studies only where they serve also to throw light on his general approach.

Unfortunately, towards the end of 1968, when the editing of both parts of the papers was well advanced, Mrs Könekamp found that her state of health would not permit her to continue with the work. She had completed the editing of the Journal, and prepared the Biographical Introduction which precedes it, but there remained a considerable volume of personal correspondence, about the editing or publication of which no final decision had been taken when Mrs Könekamp handed her part of the work over to me to complete. Some of this correspondence throws light on the development of Jevons's ideas, some of it, especially the letters written from Australia, provides remarkably fresh insights into the economic and social history of Jevons's time. In the end, I have taken these two points as my criteria for deciding whether a personal letter should be published or not. Those letters which cast light on Jevons's thinking or the public affairs of his time I have included, those which deal purely with family matters I have not.

Hence the layout of the volumes developed into the form in which they are now being published. Volume I comprises the Biographical Introduction and the text of Jevons's personal Journal, to which has been added as an Appendix his diary of a visit to the Sofala goldfields in 1856. This seemed to belong with the Journal, in which Jevons's accounts of his other tours in Australia were directly written. Volumes II and III contain the whole of Jevons's correspondence, Volume II running up to 1862 and Volume III from 1863 until 1882. The correspondence is arranged chronologically, so that personal and professional correspondence are intermingled. However, the great bulk of Jevons's professional correspondence developed in and after 1863 and consequently family and personal letters predominate in Volume II, letters to fellow economists and other colleagues in Volume III. Volume IV contains, first, the complete set of notes of the lectures which

Jevons gave at Owens College, Manchester, in 1875–6, as taken down and transcribed by Harold Rylett; second, a collection of all those articles and papers published by Jevons which were not collected into either *Investigations in Currency and Finance, Methods of Social Reform* or *Principles of Economics*. While these show a variety of aspects of Jevons's economic thought, many of them are now scarce and not easy of access. Finally, this volume includes a selection of items which cast light on the development and reception of Jevons's economic ideas – extracts from his early diaries showing his reading on economic subjects and the early development of his utility theory; then the examination paper of 1860 which led to his 'sad reverse' in political economy to be 'fully avenged' 'when I bring out my *Theory of Economy*',[1] and finally the reviews which that theory secured when it did appear in full in 1871.

It cannot be claimed that either the letters or the papers contain theories or ideas of major significance which have never previously been published. Foxwell, Higgs and H. S. Jevons were expert and thorough in their editing of the manuscripts which Jevons left at his death and they did not omit any of his work which was sufficiently complete to be publishable. What, then, is the justification for publishing these additional papers now? One justification is that the generation of economists which Foxwell and Higgs knew is no more, and many items of correspondence with Jevons which they might have thought it undesirable or unnecessary to publish now can and should be published, so that economists of today can learn more of how that generation thought of, and talked to, each other. A more significant reason, perhaps, is that the works of Jevons, published during and after his lifetime, display the finished products of his mind. The papers published here enable the reader, for the first time, to see the workshop in which they were produced – the personal and public environment in which Jevons lived and the professional contacts and discussions he had, all of them contributing to shape his ideas. So they afford an opportunity to study the formation of a mind and the making of a reputation – an opportunity which may have value not only for the student of Jevons's economic work, but for all who are interested in the intellectual and academic life of the mid-Victorian era.

In the course of the ten years which I have spent in editing the Jevons Papers, I have accumulated many debts to those who have helped me, which can only be inadequately acknowledged here. I owe a special debt to Jevons's granddaughter, Mrs Rosamond Könekamp, for her kindness in making the papers available to me and her constant co-operation throughout the editing process, as well as for the very

---

[1] W. S. Jevons to Herbert Jevons, 25 July 1860, Vol. II, Letter 145.

great amount of work which she carried out prior to 1968, not only in writing the Biographical Introduction but also in editing the text of the Journal. I am also much indebted to the Librarian of Manchester University, Dr F. W. Ratcliffe, who has willingly continued the arrangements made by his predecessor, the late Dr Moses Tyson, for housing the Jevons Papers, and done everything in his power to facilitate my work on them.

Since Jevons kept no copies of letters which he wrote, I had to make protracted searches for correspondence surviving in other collections, during the course of which I received much help from more people than I can cite individually here. Thanks are especially due, however, to Professor William Jaffé for his assistance with the Walras–Jevons letters; to Professor A. W. Coats, who brought to my notice the Jevons–Palgrave correspondence at King's College, Cambridge, and Mr A. N. L. Munby, Librarian of King's College, who made this material available to me; to Miss Audrey Foxwell, who kindly searched her father's papers for Jevons material and gave me valuable leads to further sources; to Dr Wolfe Mays, who, in addition to putting me on the track of the Jevons Papers in the first place, gave me access to those papers which the late Professor H. S. Jevons had passed over to him.

In the course of editing the papers I have benefited from discussions with many colleagues, for whose suggestions and criticisms I am grateful – the late Professor Jacob Viner, Professor Lord Robbins, Professor R. S. Howey, Professor Ross Robertson, and Dr D. P. O'Brien.

In making arrangements for the publications of these volumes Professor E. A. G. Robinson and Mr C. F. Carter, of the Royal Economic Society, and Mr T. M. Farmiloe of The Macmillan Press Ltd have done a great deal of work and I am very much indebted to them for their patience and assistance.

During the course of preparing this edition I have been facilitated by the Senate of the Queen's University of Belfast, through the grant of a term's study leave, financial assistance from the Research Fund, and especially their making available to me the services of a Research Assistant during the last five years. This post has been held successively by Mr C. Pohl, Mrs Then Bee Lian and Mrs J. Wright, and I owe much to the help which I have received from them. Mrs Wright, in particular, has done much valuable work in preparing the typescript of the Journal and family letters for the press.

The process of converting the material from manuscript to typescript has inevitably been a protracted and difficult one, and I am grateful to Mrs M. Hughes and Mrs E. Larkin, who have carried the main burden of this work.

A complete index to *Papers and Correspondence of William Stanley Jevons* will be included in Volume IV.

Last, but most certainly not least, I am grateful to my wife and family for accepting without complaint the many hours of silence and absence which the completion of this project has necessarily involved.

For any errors and imperfections in editing which remain, the responsibility is mine alone.

R. D. COLLISON BLACK

Queen's University,
Belfast
22 December 1970

LIST OF ABBREVIATIONS
used throughout the volumes

Relating to Jevons material

LJ   *Letters and Journal of W. Stanley Jevons*, edited by his wife (1886).

LJN   Previously published in LJ; manuscript not now in Jevons Papers, or other known location.

LJP   Previously published in LJ, but only in part; fuller text now given from the original manuscript in the Jevons Papers, or other indicated location.

WM   From a manuscript made available by Dr Wolfe Mays, University of Manchester.

Investigations *Investigations in Currency and Finance*, by W. Stanley Jevons. Edited, with an Introduction, by H. S. Foxwell (1884). All page references to first edition.

Methods *Methods of Social Reform and other papers*, by W. Stanley Jevons (1883).

T.P.E. *The Theory of Political Economy* by W. Stanley Jevons (1st ed. 1871, 4th ed. 1911). All page references to fourth edition, unless otherwise stated.

Relating to other material

BM   British Museum, London.

FW   Fonds Walras, Bibliothèque Cantonale de Lausanne.

HLRS   Herschel Letters, Royal Society, London.

JRSS   *Journal of the London* (later *Royal*) *Statistical Society*.

KCP   Palgrave Papers in the Library of King's College, Cambridge.

LSE   London School of Economics, British Library of Political and Economic Science.

MA   Archives of Macmillan & Co. Ltd.

NYPL   New York Public Library.

TLJM   Isabel Mills, *From Tinder Box to the 'Larger Light'. Threads from the Life of John Mills, Banker* (Manchester, 1899).

Walras Correspondence *Correspondence of Léon Walras and Related Papers* edited by William Jaffé (3 vols, Amsterdam, 1965).

Figures following any of these abbreviations denote page numbers.

BIOGRAPHICAL INTRODUCTION

I

The Journal of W. Stanley Jevons records the development of his thoughts, his feelings, his purposes and his struggles during the fifteen most vital years of his life. It is an intimate and even a moving document. Jevons started this journal in 1852 when he was almost seventeen, and he continued to write in it until just before his marriage in 1867. After that there is only one entry, made in 1869.

The full text of the journal has never been published. Numerous extracts were published in *Letters and Journal of W. Stanley Jevons*, edited by his wife in 1886, four years after his death.[1] These extracts were interspersed amongst the letters in date order to provide a chronological story of his life 'as far as possible in his own words'. The unpublished portions, though not perhaps of equal importance, are nevertheless interesting. The work too, when seen as a whole, has a consistency of its own.

The journal, whilst primarily of interest to those engaged in Jevons's own fields of work, would seem to have a wider appeal. The obstacles he had to overcome in his personal life were more formidable than have so far been revealed. He had '. . . qualities not always found in men of science, which make his character as unique as his intellect', wrote R. H. Hutton. 'Moreover, there was a deep religious feeling at the bottom of his nature which made the materialistic tone of the day as alien to him as all true science . . . was unaffectedly dear to him.'[2]

The journal covers four phases of Jevons's life. First, his two years at University College, London, from 1852 to 1854, before he broke off his university studies and emigrated to Australia; next his career as Assayer to the Royal Mint in Sydney, from 1854 to 1859; then the years in London again after his return from Australia, from 1859 to 1863, when he resumed his studies at University College and then struggled to earn a living by writing; and finally his first four years on the staff of Owens College, Manchester.

When Jevons was in Australia he did not keep the journal in quite the

---

[1] *Letters and Journal of W. Stanley Jevons*, edited by Harriet A. Jevons (1886). This book is still the source of almost all published biographical material.
[2] Obituary notice in the *Proceedings of the Royal Society*, quoted LJ, p. 450.

same intimate way as before and afterwards. Australia was in an exciting period of her history, with the recent gold discoveries fermenting the colonies, and the Continent still largely unexplored. The grant of 'responsible government' to New South Wales in 1855 was also a landmark. There was too much to record. Jevons's daily activities were entered in day-to-day diaries at this time. Other diaries were filled with descriptions of his various journeys and social studies of the colonies. His rapidly expanding mental powers are shown in the long letters he wrote to his family at home. These letters, especially those to his two sisters, also confided his deepest thoughts and feelings. The journal entries for this period are therefore more miscellaneous, and they consist largely of descriptions of his explorations of the Blue Mountains and other parts of New South Wales.

It has seemed best to present the journal as it stands without any interspersed biographical data, and to give the main facts necessary to an understanding of the journal in a short biographical introduction. To put the Australian entries in their setting rather more detail is given about these years than about the other periods.

The original of the journal is a single leather-bound volume of parchment, of which Jevons has written inside the cover 'This book I believe to have been a Law Common Place Book belonging to my Uncle Henry Roscoe'. A number of pages of this volume have been torn out. The book contained entries relating to the law and some of these pages were no doubt unusable; others, however, were part of the original manuscript and were presumably torn out by Jevons himself, though there is no way of knowing this.

II

Jevons was born on 1 September 1835, at No. 14 Alfred Street,[1] Liverpool, into a well-to-do and cultured home. The family fortunes and position had been built up by his two grandfathers, both men of modest origin and dissenting opinions who rose to success in the great commercial expansion which accompanied the industrial revolution. Jevons's father, Thomas Jevons, was an iron merchant in Liverpool. His mother, Mary Anne, was the daughter of the well-known William Roscoe of Liverpool. Both parents were brought up as Unitarians and had connections with many of the leading intellectual families of the time.

The Jevonses were from Staffordshire. *William Jevons* (1760–1852), the grandfather of Stanley Jevons,[2] moved to Liverpool in 1798, to act as agent for the sale of nails and iron for his employer in Staffordshire.

[1] The house is still standing.   [2] W. S. Jevons was known as 'Stanley' in the family.

After a few years he founded his own business as an iron merchant with the help of capital lent by the Reverend John Yates, the minister of his chapel, who shared in the profits of the firm.[1] The business prospered, and when Thomas, the eldest of William Jevons's three sons, grew up he was taken into partnership, the firm being known as Jevons & Son: the second son, William, chose an intellectual career, and was for a time a Unitarian Minister and the third son, Timothy, joined Thomas as a partner in the family business. For the last few years of his life William Jevons – who has been described as being endowed with a great deal of good sense, and as a man of strong affections and much religious feeling[2] – was a member of Thomas Jevons's household, and he died there at the age of ninety-one in the same year that Jevons began to write his journal.[3]

In the journal Jevons refers to his father, *Thomas Jevons* (1791–1855), as 'the most humane of men' and as being remarkable for a 'calm clear mind'. He combined the practical sense of a man of business with a lively interest in many other fields, and a flair for invention. Though not able to carry many of his inventions into practice, he was a modest innovator in the use of iron for the construction of ships, being in advance of his time in believing in iron for this purpose. In 1815 he launched on the Mersey a small iron pleasure boat built to his design in which he sailed, this, he claimed, being the first iron boat to sail on salt water. He wrote an account of this boat and of a second, a ribless

[1] The Reverend John Yates (1755–1826), was minister at the chapel at Paradise Street, Liverpool. When his third son, Richard Vaughan Yates (1785–1856) became old enough to enter business, the Reverend Yates ceased to be a sleeping partner in the Jevons business and Richard became an active partner with William Jevons. This partnership lasted some few years, and then Richard Yates set up business as an ironmonger. Thomas Jevons, the father of Jevons, served his own apprenticeship with Richard Yates before becoming a partner with his father in Jevons & Son. The Yates family were friends of the Martineaus and Richard and his sisters were particular friends of Harriet Martineau. The Reverend Yates was also the father of James Yates (1789–1871), the well-known Unitarian and antiquary who took a leading part in the preparation of the plans for the foundation of University College, London.

[2] LJ, p. 1.

[3] When he was in London after his return from Australia, Jevons did a considerable amount of research into the history of the Jevons family. He established beyond doubt that the name was of Welsh origin, being Jevan or Jevon – the final 's' was added by Stanley's grandfather. The family had, however, been settled for many centuries in South Staffordshire in the districts of Sedgeley, Coseley, where Jevons's grandfather was born, Tipton, Old Swynford, West Bromwich and Wolverhampton, in which areas the Jevonses were chiefly living at the time when Jevons was making his investigations (1861–2). These districts were all near to the family seat of Sedgeley Hall, which was in the recorded hereditary possession of the Jevan family from about 1500, although Jevons did not succeed in tracing the links of his particular branch of the family, for which the pedigree was known for six generations, with other and earlier pedigrees he traced. When the South Staffordshire coalfield was developed, and later the ironworks were built, the landed estates were broken up (half the Sedgeley Hall estate was sold in 1792) and the area was for generations the centre of the nail-making industry.

iron lifeboat, built in 1822, which is included as a footnote in the book *Iron Shipbuilding: with Practical Illustrations* by John Grantham, Consulting Engineer and Naval Architect, Liverpool (London, John Weales, 1858). He also designed a movable iron landing stage for steamers. Two iron coasters later built to Thomas Jevons's design are described in a letter written to Jevons on 18 April 1855.[1] Another hobby was designing houses.[2] His interest in the 1851 Palace of Glass, the structure of which was of iron, is shown in his early letters to Jevons. Both of Jevons's parents were musical and Thomas was a connoisseur of organs. In view of Jevons's passion for the organ it is interesting to note that he was following a Liverpool tradition of the love of music and of organ playing.[3]

Thomas Jevons published a small book, in 1834, on the reform of criminals, a subject upon which William Roscoe had written – entitled *Remarks on Criminal Law; with a Plan for an Improved System, and Observations on the Prevention of Crime* (published anonymously, London: Hamilton Adams & Co.; Liverpool: D. Marples & Co.). He advocates the establishment of reformatories of different grades for reforming instead of punishing criminals, to be partly on the 'open-system'. In 1840 he joined in the controversy on the future of the Corn Laws, publishing a pamphlet, *The Prosperity of Landlords not dependent on the Corn Laws* (Longmans & Co., 68 pages), expressing the view of the enlightened commercial classes – arguing against protection and that the best interests of landlords, agriculture and the country as a whole lay in increased trade and a rise in the general purchasing power of the population. He strongly supported the idea of a decimal coinage as being an aid to increased trade, actually introducing the system in his accounts in 1855.[4]

In *William Roscoe* (1753–1831), his maternal grandfather, Jevons had an ancestor of quite exceptional talent and character. An almost self-educated man, who became a solicitor and later a banker, he achieved an immense reputation in his day, mainly as an historian – the author of the *Life of Lorenzo de' Medici* and the *Life and Pontificate of Leo X*. He is now best remembered for his collection of early Italian and Flemish paintings – a part of which is the pride of the Walker Art Gallery in Liverpool – and as one of Liverpool's greatest citizens. In a modern assessment of Roscoe's life and work Dr Chandler has written:[5]

---

[1] See Vol. II, Letter 58.

[2] See his letter of 8 June 1852 to Jevons, Vol. II, Letter 18.

[3] George Chandler, *Liverpool* (1957) p. 432.

[4] See his letter of 17 June 1855 to Jevons, Vol. II, Letter 63.

[5] George Chandler, *William Roscoe of Liverpool*, with introduction by Sir Alfred Shennan (1953) p. 2. This volume also contains the first complete edition of Roscoe's poems.

He was Liverpool's cultural pioneer *par excellence* and there is hardly any movement or institution in modern Liverpool which does not owe some part of its existence or tradition to his work. Whilst taking a prominent part in many of the important movements of the day, Roscoe led, in some cases, not only Liverpool and England, but also the world. Look at his record: first well-known Liverpool poet; organiser of the first art exhibition of its kind in Liverpool; leader of the movement against the slave trade (although this was believed to be the foundation of Liverpool's prosperity); successful lawyer and banker; writer of idealistic political songs which swept the country; historian of world reputation; Member of Parliament; connoisseur and collector of international significance; one of the earliest writers of poems for children, some of which are classics; author of a book on botany which is still a collector's piece; advocate of prison reform and political freedom; patron of fine printing of quite outstanding beauty; devout Christian who would not abate one jot of his beliefs as a dissenter to secure preferment.

This is a formidable catalogue and to it may be added that Roscoe was a patron of living artists, notably of the painter Fuseli. Roscoe's character also, was on the grand scale: '. . . There was about his outlook something universal and godlike . . . nothing humane, enlightened, tasteful and tolerant appealed in vain for his fearless support . . . both as lawyer and banker he must daily have handled the affairs and finances of townspeople whose wealth was founded upon slave trading, privateering and perhaps even smuggling also . . . yet Roscoe throughout life preserved a Blake-like innocence and simplicity.'[1] Success in business brought Roscoe wealth and luxury, but in the commercial crisis of 1816 his bank had to suspend payments and he faced ruin. He sold his valuable collections of books and paintings and his country home at Allerton Hall, where his daughter Mary Anne was brought up, but could not avoid eventually being declared bankrupt in 1820. Roscoe had seven sons and two surviving daughters, Mary Anne being the eighth child. Her younger sister Jane (1797–1853) is the 'Aunt Jane' referred to in the journal.

Mary Anne Roscoe (1795–1845), Jevons's mother – also a poetess, author of *Sonnets and other Poems, chiefly devotional* (1845) editor of *Poems for Youth, by a Family Circle* (3rd edition, 1841) and editor of *The Sacred Offering*[2] – shared the intellectual and artistic milieu of her father's home until her marriage at the age of thirty. A miniature portrait of her

[1] *William Roscoe of Liverpool*, Introduction, p. xv.
[2] '. . . a collection of poems which came out in yearly volumes for several years, and the contents of which were chiefly written by members of Mr. Roscoe's family . . .' (LJ, p. 3).

in the Walker Art Gallery, Liverpool, by John Hargreaves, reveals both her beauty and her serious disposition. Even in youth she was deeply religious and the many trials of her life only served to strengthen her faith. Study, a quiet domestic life and social work meant more to her than luxury and ordinary society. Her 'Literary Diaries', which have survived,[1] show how earnestly she studied and reflected in the years before her marriage. Her many subjects included logic, chemistry (she shared her younger brother Henry's lessons in the laboratory) and at least some political economy, for she records having read Mrs Marcet and Adam Smith's *Wealth of Nations*. So necessary was the subject of political economy considered that it was taught even to the young and Jevons received his first lessons at the age of about eight, from his mother, using Archbishop Whately's textbook, *Easy Lessons on Money Matters for the use of Young People*.[2] She also taught him botany, to the study of which he later attributed his success in logic. She was a lifelong friend of the authoress Emily Taylor.

Jevons's parents were married in November 1825, and they had eleven children in quick succession. William Stanley was the ninth child to be born in less than ten years of marriage. He was, however, only the fourth child to survive. The first-born, a girl, Jane Emily, born in January 1827, died the same year; a stillborn son was born later that year. The three next children, Roscoe, born in 1829, Lucy Anne, born in May the following year and Herbert, born in 1831, all lived. A twin son and daughter born in 1832 both died of influenza when a year old and another son born in 1834 died in the spring of 1835, a few months before William Stanley was born. Three and a half years after his birth came his sister Henrietta, in 1839, and his younger brother Thomas was born in 1841. Jevons was the only 'solitary' child in the family – the three eldest children being close together in age and the two youngest also.

The home was a happy one until Mrs Jevons died in 1845, when Jevons was ten. His sister Lucy, who from that time became the 'mother' of the family, has described this loss in some memories noted down in 1884:

> Nothing in my earliest years seemed more dreadful to me than to think I might lose my Mother ... Alas! the day came when I knew He (God) would take her, for she became ill – not suddenly but gradually, and gradually the truth came to me – and gradually it was as if all the sunshine, all the joy, all the happiness of this world had passed

---

[1] Unpublished, in the possession of Mrs R. Könekamp.

[2] *An Introductory Letter on the Importance of Diffusing a Knowledge of Political Economy*, p. 31; cf. below, Journal, p. 157. The full text of this lecture is reprinted in Vol. IV of this edition, Part II.

away from me for ever. I was but 14 – when the world lost its happiness for me – 15 and a half when she was gone. My grief was not simple grief, it was agony . . . In the extremity of our grief we clung to each other, and in that way a new affection sprung up that had laid dormant. I now knew that my father was better than I had ever known before – the little ones – had they not lost their Mother even before they knew how to value her? Was not their loss greater than mine? And there was my elder brother (Roscoe), had he not rejoiced in his Mother's love for a year at least longer than I? He was nearly seventeen – how could he bear such a loss? I was well drawn out of my own grief when I watched him swaying himself on a chair with a book before him (Cowper's poem on his Mother) for hours together. . . .[1]

Roscoe Jevons (1829–69), named after his maternal grandfather, played a role in Jevons's life which the full journal reveals for the first time. A streak of tragedy runs through the Jevons family history – of which Jevons's own accidental death is an instance. And Jevons carried a secret burden from early youth. Roscoe became insane at the age of about eighteen, shortly after his mother's death, and never recovered. It was this loss which drove Jevons to work with such remorseless passion. Roscoe was a poet who showed brilliant promise as chemist and mathematician. Unfortunately his poems and diaries, which meant so much to Jevons, have not survived. His insanity was kept secret even in the family, until after the death of Jevons's son, Professor Herbert Stanley Jevons, in 1955,[2] and his papers were no doubt destroyed. There is thus not a great deal of information about him, apart from the journal. He was educated at the Mechanics Institution High School in Liverpool, which Jevons and his brother Herbert also attended. He was one of the school's 'best pupils'.

He had his own laboratory in an old coachhouse: Jevons 'worked under him as a younger brother'.[3] Harry Roscoe also experimented there:

> Another of my experimental delights [he wrote in his autobiography[4]] was firework-making under the guidance of my elder cousin, Roscoe Jevons. We used to spend every half-holiday in the summer and autumn preparing our fireworks for the 5th November. We worked in

[1] MSS in the possession of Mrs R. Könekamp.
[2] This explains why J. M. Keynes had not access to the complete text of the Journal when he wrote his 'Centenary Allocution on William Stanley Jevons, 1835–1882', read before the Royal Statistical Society, on 21 April 1936. See *Essays in Biography* (1951) p. 308. Keynes sensed some 'deeper cause' of Jevons's ill-health, see p. 306.
[3] See Journal entry for 23 May 1864, p. 194 below.
[4] *The Life & Experience of Sir Henry Enfield Roscoe . . . written by himself* (1906) p. 19.

an old stable which had been converted into a laboratory, near the house of my uncle by marriage, Thomas Jevons, the father of Stanley Jevons. On one occasion we were drying in front of a fire a quantity of rockets, squibs, and Roman candles which had been packed moist in their cases when one of them ignited and set some of the others off. Our presence of mind in throwing the burning ones out of the window saved a catastrophe, for there were several pounds of blasting powder lying uncovered on the table, and if this had ignited the roof would have been blown off and we boys probably sent into eternity.'

Roscoe was taken away from school at the end of 1845, when almost seventeen.[1] He must have gone straight into a foundry in Liverpool to learn the iron business, the intention no doubt being for him, as eldest son, to follow in his father's trade. Jevons describes how duty and his inclinations conflicted, and this, at a time when he was still suffering from the death of his mother, must have proved too much for his sensitive nature.[2]

A letter of March 1847, from Herbert to his father, is the first reference to Roscoe and his prospects of recovery, so that his breakdown probably occurred in the early part of 1847. His condition appears not to have been so serious as to preclude hopes of recovery, and a letter of 17 January 1850, from Herbert to his father refers to the fact that if old William Jevons were not a member of Thomas Jevons's household – then Roscoe might be at home and a very great expense saved. He was, at this time, at Crown Street near to the Jevons home, and Thomas Jevons visited him every Sunday to take him for a walk. In a letter of 17 May to his father, Herbert wrote: 'I believe Roscoe's present state of health arises more from a diseased conscience than anything else. Its effects have been more and more upon him because he has so much more sensibility, genius and powers of mind than myself. . . . You should read his diary which you will find in his desk.'

Later Roscoe was at Birmingham. Thomas Jevons mentions a visit to him in his letter of 14 July 1855, to Jevons.[3] Jevons visited him in Birmingham in 1859 on his return from Australia: Roscoe appeared to recognise him. There is no further information until 1866, when

[1] A letter (unpublished) written on 10 January 1846 to Thomas Jevons by the Headmaster, W. B. Hodgson, reads: 'I much regret that your son Roscoe will not be with us this half-year. Had he remained, I have no doubt that he would have closed his career by gaining in the Science Department Life Membership, which by the kindness of Mr. George Holt, we are enabled to award to the best pupils, whether in that, or in the Literature Department.'

[2] See Journal entry for 19 March 1869, p. 212 below.

[3] See Vol. II, Letter 67; also Jevons's summary and comment in the Journal, p. 120 below.

Roscoe's state had deteriorated: Jevons wrote to his brother, Herbert: 'I saw Roscoe not very long ago and will see him again in a week or so. We now have a special attendant always with him, though the man has to be changed every few months as one man cannot stand it. His condition is rather more sad even than it used to be . . . he is more restless and has to be watched lest he should swallow things'.[1]

Roscoe had not much longer to live. Apparently he was moved to Liverpool. He was taken ill with a bad cold and died on 18 March 1869 at the Liverpool Hospital, Ashton Street. He was quietly buried in the cemetery of Toxteth Park Chapel. On 23 March Jevons wrote to inform Herbert adding:

> I saw what remained of poor Roscoe at the asylum where he lay at last calm and placid and with signs of peace and rest upon a face which so often distressed me. It seems that there was no return of anything like reason . . . This will remove a sad weight from our minds and though it must revive many painful memories we need not hesitate now to dismiss them as far as possible for the future. From what Lucy now writes to me she seems to have been filled with unhappy remembrances of Roscoe's illness more than I had supposed and you will doubtless also remember more than I do, though I can remember enough that is painful. Mary Bentley[2] tells me that my mother seemed aware of Roscoe's danger, for she said one day 'Poor Roscoe, I fear he will have much to suffer' and we know that few have suffered what to us seems worse . . . This letter tells you the end of a sad chapter in our history and now I hope we may close our minds to its memory . . .'[3]

These last words were to prove ironic. Jevons's elder brother, *Herbert Jevons* (1831–74), was another source of anxiety to his father and later to Jevons. As a young man he was dogged by ill-health, with a passion for metaphysical thought, permeated by the kind of doubt expressed by the poet Arthur Hugh Clough.[4] Sociable and voluble, he was a complete contrast to Jevons. Many of his long letters, especially to his father, which survive, show his intelligence and his constant struggle to overcome his weakness and it is impossible not to feel much sympathy for him. He was unable to settle to any career for many years, but eventually he did find his own feet as an employee of the Bank of New South Wales in New Zealand, as gold-buyer in the new gold fields, then assayer and finally as Manager of the branch bank at Grahamstown,

---

[1] See letter of 24 March 1866, Vol. III, Letter 239.
[2] One of the family servants.
[3] See letter of 23 March 1869, Vol. III, Letter 313.
[4] See Journal entry for 23 October 1852, p. 65 below.

where he died at the early age of forty-two in 1874.[1] Jevons named his son, born the following year, after him. A few years later, when mentioning Herbert's death to a friend, he could write philosophically:

> If any one has had cause to doubt the benevolent government of human affairs, it is I and my brothers and sisters; and yet nothing can eradicate from my mind the belief that there must be a brighter side to things, and that we do not see all. It may be very unscientific, and 'exact thinkers' like Mill may have proved the opposite. In that case I must consent to remain among the unscientific.[2]

Herbert studied at University College, London, in the Medical Faculty, and attended the lectures of Thomas Graham, in the session 1850–1, when Jevons was at University College School. He then became seriously ill and to recover his health went abroad in September 1851, to Natal and then to India, returning home on 1 December 1852.[3] For the next three and a half years he worked in the office of the family business to learn the iron trade, but his cousins Henry and George Jevons were in charge and Herbert may have given up hope of being taken into partnership. In the summer of 1858 he emigrated to Wayzata, Minnesota, to farm. The life of a log-cabin pioneer farmer proved impossible. He returned to England in 1861, found no employment, and then emigrated again in August 1862 to try his fortune in Australia, from there going to New Zealand, causing Jevons much anxiety about his future as the Journal shows.

Jevons's young brother, *Thomas Edwin* (*Tom* or *Tommy*) (1841–1917), aged only four when his mother died, was the closest friend of his later life. He became a successful businessman after emigrating to New York in 1865, but made frequent visits to this country. After attending University College School and studying at University College, London, where he took his B.A. in 1860, the same year as Jevons, he entered the Liverpool firm of Rathbone Bros. & Co., for an agreed period of five years. After this he was to join the firm of Jevons & Co., but he remained with Rathbones and became a partner of their New York agent in the firm of Busk & Jevons in 1868. He married an American, Isabel Seton, a descendant of Blessed Mother Seton, and built a house and settled in Long Island. Ferdinand Jevons, the last of Tom's children to survive, died there in November 1967. Tom did not exert himself as Jevons did; but of his gifts his elder brother had a high opinion. 'His memory is very good,' Jevons wrote to Herbert on 25 July 1860, 'and he can learn

---

[1] For Jevons's thoughts about his brother after his death, see letter of 19 April 1874 to his brother Tom, Vol. III, Letter 369.

[2] See letter of 7 April 1878 to E. J. Broadfield, Vol. III, Letter 527.

[3] See Journal entry for 12 December 1852, p. 76 below.

anything which he chooses with great ease, so that I am confirmed in my opinion that he has the best natural abilities in our family. It is only from his not applying himself with sufficient force to any one or more subjects that he fails to get prizes.'[1]

Lucy Ann Jevons (Mrs John Hutton) (1830–1910), Jevons's elder sister, was not only a substitute 'mother' to the younger children; she gave Jevons the moral support, understanding and encouragement so necessary to his intellectual development. It was she who counselled him, in his darkest period at the end of 1862, to stay on in London – advice which resulted in his writing *A Serious Fall in the Value of Gold*. Possessed of an extrovert and believing nature, artistic gifts and much discernment, she lived at home until her father's death and was his companion on his last fatal journey abroad. She was engaged to marry Russell Martineau, son of James Martineau,[2] but broke off the engagement in 1859. In January 1862, she married, as his second wife, *John Hutton* (1824–94), civil engineer and quarry-owner, the brother of Richard Holt Hutton, and son of Reverend *Joseph Hutton*, the Unitarian preacher. John Hutton was manager of Penmaenmawr Quarry and Lucy and he went to live in Beaumaris. He was a widower with five children. The family moved to Clynnog on the mainland in 1865 and to Ludlow in 1869. Lucy had two children, a son and daughter, but the son Grindal died at the age of thirteen in 1875. Even after her marriage Jevons kept closely in touch with Lucy, spending most of his vacations near her home until his marriage, and he corresponded with her throughout his life. After his death Lucy was also of much support to his widow. She provided material for Mrs Jevons for *Letters and Journal*, two interesting manuscripts being still extant.[3]

It was, however, to his younger sister *Henrietta* (*Henny*) (1839–1909), that Jevons freely showed his affection. He felt a special nearness to her. She was musical, a pianist and interested in religion. The letters he wrote to her from Australia are the warmest and most lively of his letters, full of music, and of brotherly solicitude. This solicitude was very necessary; she found life difficult because there was a conflict she was not able to resolve. Her fate was tragic. She lodged with Jevons on his return from Australia, except when paying long visits to relatives, when he was in London and in Manchester, until his marriage. She attended Roscoe's funeral in March 1869. A few months later she herself lost her mental balance, suffering from delusions, and she died in 1909 without recovering.

Keynes remarked that Jevons had good hereditary cause for not

[1] See below, Vol. II, Letter 145.
[2] See below, p. 80.
[3] In possession of Mrs R. Könekamp.

overlooking the phenomenon of business fluctuations, both his grand-father Roscoe and his father having been bankrupted following com-mercial crises,[1] (his grandfather Jevons and two uncles, Timothy and William junior as well). As the son of an iron merchant, indeed, he was reared in the teeth of the phenomenon, fluctuations in the iron trade being the most severe of all. It was the year following the start of Roscoe's illness, in January 1848, that the firm of Jevons & Sons failed, following the railway boom crisis of 1847.

The bankruptcy drastically affected the lives of all the members of the Jevons family. Thomas sold his house at Park Hill Road and moved to a smaller one nearer the centre of Liverpool – No. 125 Chatham Street. The house, since renumbered No. 173 and now scheduled for demolition, is the first house on the right after Falkner Street. Here the family were living at the time Jevons started his journal. Thomas became the Manager of the Liverpool house of the South Wales ironmaster, Sir John Guest, of the Dowlais Iron Company, at a salary and profits. After being his own master for so long, and an ironmaster in a small way himself in South Wales with his two brothers and a cousin, Townshend Wood, in the firm of Jevons & Wood which was also bankrupted, he suffered in his new position. He remained excluded from the family business, reconstituted by his nephews Henry and George Jevons, until April 1854, just a year and a half before his death, although Timothy was taken back as a partner much earlier. He had no time to regain his fortune. Consequently, the effect of the bankruptcy was permanent. Jevons's financial stringency, which worried him for many years in later life, dates from this time, and he and his brothers and sisters became the 'poor relations'.

These various troubles had the effect of drawing the family very close together. William Stanley, like Lucy, had to shoulder family responsi-bilities at a much earlier age than would have otherwise been the case. On 28 June 1851, when he was only fifteen, his father wrote: '. . . I shall begin now to look to you for assistance in family affairs by consultation and advice . . . I need the help of a friend in whom I can trust, and I must bring you forward to take part in the battle of life, young as you yet are . . .'[2] Again, in a letter dated 26 September 1851, 'Deprived as I am of the society of your two elder brothers you may readily conceive that I think the more of you . . . I cannot lose sight of the promise your already acquired powers give of future fame and usefulness and if I have been doomed to disappointment in my cherished hopes of my first born I cling the more to my fond desires for your success in life . . .'[3] After the death of their father, when the youngest

[1] J. M. Keynes, *Essays in Biography* (1951) p. 257.
[2] See Vol. II, Letter 12.　　　　　[3] See Vol. II, Letter 13.

children were still only fourteen and sixteen, the sense of responsibility and solidarity of the brothers and sisters developed still more strongly, and it lasted all their lives.

Although by the age of fifteen Jevons had given his father hopes of his future fame – and his sister too, for on 31 January 1849, Lucy made the following entry in her diary: 'In Stanley I see the dawning of a great mind,'[1] – he was never in the usual sense a precocious child. Till the age of ten he was educated at home by a governess. In January 1846 he went to school at the Mechanics Institute High School in Liverpool, where he worked easily and did well – though his quietness and shyness were remarked upon by one or two masters as being in his way. The headmaster, Dr Hodgson – later to become Professor of Political Economy at Edinburgh – was disappointed when Thomas Jevons took his son away from the school and sent him in Autumn 1847 to Mr Beckwith's private school in Lodge Lane, Liverpool. In the autumn of 1850, being then just fifteen, Jevons went to University College School in London. He left at the end of the following summer, after having received three first and two second prizes, and in October 1851 entered University College as a student at the age of sixteen.

When Jevons first went to school in London he lived in lodgings with his brother Herbert who was then an undergraduate at University College. After about three months, however, Herbert decided to stay with his uncle – Dr Richard Roscoe – at Richmond, and Jevons had to go into a 'gloomy house in Gower Street' where boarders from the school were taken and where he was most unhappy. When he returned to London in autumn 1851 to go to college he lived with his aunt, Mrs Henry Roscoe, in Camden Town. Her son, Harry Roscoe (later to become the chemist, Sir Henry Roscoe) was two years older than Jevons and they became lifelong friends.

Jevons began his journal after he had been at college for one year, after he had matriculated (June 1852), for 'students commonly matriculated in the university from college rather than before entry, and normally took two years for the B.A.'[2] There was no science degree at this time, science being part of the General Department.[3] In 'a considerable part of the area of its activities, the middle years of the century were for the college a period of stagnation . . . In two departments alone, those of Chemistry and of English, was new work of the first importance being done.'[4] In chemistry, which was Jevons's main interest, the teaching was outstanding. Thomas Graham was Professor of Chemistry and A. W. Williamson was Professor of Practical Chemistry.

---

[1] LJ, p. 8.
[2] H. Hale Bellot, *University College, London, 1826–1926* (1929) p. 298.
[3] Op. cit., p. 124.   [4] Op. cit., p. 252.

Williamson – schooled in the famous laboratories of the continent, an exponent of the Atomic Theory and himself a contributor to its development – was a particularly brilliant treacher just at this time.[1] Sir Henry Roscoe, who studied under him and was later his assistant for a time, has described his effect on his students in the laboratory:

> His was a mind of great originality, and his personality a most attractive one. Ardently devoted to his science, he infected all who worked under him with the same feeling. And his pupils willingly own that much of the success that they may have met with in after years was due to his teaching and example. I well remember the feelings of interest he aroused as he each day came down to the laboratory brimful of new ideas. First it was his explanation of the theory of etherification . . . Next it was his well-known paper on the constitution of salts, in which he enunciated principles which have since been generally adopted. Then came his views on atomic motion and interchange. . . . All this was the work of a very few years.[2]

Thomas Graham was one of the great pioneers of chemistry through his work on molecular motion.

> If along the highroad of chemistry temples were erected to the memory of the master minds who moulded and guided the science forward into the unknown future, one of the greatest of these would be to the memory of Thomas Graham. Like all great men his mind turned towards fundamental ideas. The movements of the ultimate particles of matter was the problem that he attacked, and his discoveries in this field of research are of an importance that cannot receive too high praise.[3]

It is scarcely surprising that a mind like Graham's aroused an interest in fundamental laws in Jevons. In the journal he says that molecular philosophy interested him most (entry for 4 November 1855);[4] that he himself speculated concerning the ultimate molecular constitution of matter, doing a little original research in 1852 and 1853 (entry for December 1862);[5] and he even believed like Graham in 'a general ultimate property of matter to mix with all other matter of a similar nature' (entry for 7 November 1852.)[6] He retained a lifelong interest in the subject of the movement of particles (Brownian Motion),

---

[1] W. A. Tilden, *Famous Chemists* (1930).
[2] *Life and Experiences*, pp. 36–7; quoted Bellot, op. cit., pp. 284–5.
[3] J. Norman Collie, *A Century of Chemistry* (1927), quoted Bellot, op. cit., p. 127.
[4] See p. 114 below.   [5] See p. 101 below.   [6] See p. 70 below.

PLATE 1   No. 14 Alfred Street, Liverpool – the birthplace of W. S. Jevons
(corner house in picture)

PLATE 2   No. 173 (formerly No. 125) Chatham Street, Liverpool (on left of picture)

PLATE 3   'Diggers at Dinner', taken at a gold-diggers' camp by W. S. Jevons

publishing two papers, in 1870 and 1878.[1] Dr. Mays of Manchester University has drawn attention to the relevance of this theory to modern statistical mechanics.[2] Jevons's future work in all its branches shows this same search for the underlying identity of properties and of 'ultimate' particles and the laws of their movement: in logic, the principle of 'sameness', in scientific method, the theory of probability; even in economics, his marginal utility theory hinges on the ultimate, infinitesimal particle or 'degree' of utility, the changes in 'utility' or price, corresponding to the 'laws of movement'.

Augustus De Morgan (1806–71), Cambridge trained logician and mathematician, was Professor of Mathematics from 1828, when he was only 21, until 1831, and from 1836 to 1866. Brilliant in intellect, profound in thought, stimulating and eccentric, with a wide range of interests, he was a brilliant teacher: 'the outstanding figure in the first quarter century of the life of the college . . .'[3]

Jevons studied under De Morgan from 1851 to 1853 and from 1859 to 1861 – there is no mention of his having taken mathematics in the 1862 session – longer than under any other teacher, and he worked harder at mathematics than at any other subject, not finding it easy. It was in Australia that he came to realise the fundamental nature of mathematics. De Morgan's classes were the ones he remembered, and it was in order to study further under de Morgan that he was to return again to University College to take his B.A. Many accounts of De Morgan and his classes have been written; he was a profound influence on some of the greatest alumni of the college, and especially upon Jevons.[4] He was concerned to reconcile logic and mathematics and his classes were as much a training in logic as in mathematics. There would seem no doubt that Jevons's approach to scientific method, involving verification by exact mathematical calculations and the use of probability and Jevons's approach to economics, using the differential calculus as the basis of theory and statistics for exactitude, combined with probability, were influenced by De Morgan. The underlying unity of thought behind all Jevons's work has been discussed in an article by Dr W. B. Mays on 'Jevons's Conception of Scientific Method.'[5]

[1] 'On the so-called Molecular Movements of Microscopic Particles', *Manchester Literary and Philosophic Society* (1870); 'On the Movement of Microscopic Particles suspended in Liquid', *Quarterly Journal of Science* (April 1878).

[2] *The Manchester School*, xxx, 3 (September 1962) p. 239.

[3] *Bulletin of the Institute of Historical Research*, iv, 1926–7, 183, quoted Bellot, op. cit., p. 80. In the article on De Morgan which he wrote for the ninth edition of the *Encyclopaedia Britannica* (1877), Jevons declared that 'as a teacher of mathematics De Morgan was unrivalled . . . [his] mathematical writings contributed powerfully towards the progress of the science'; but 'it is probably as a logical reformer that De Morgan will be best known to future times' (vii, 64–7).   [4] See Bellot, op. cit., p. 83.

[5] *The Manchester School* (September 1962).

Jevons did exceptionally well at chemistry, gaining the silver medal at the College examinations in this subject in 1852 and the gold medal in 1853, but he had no intention of taking up a career in chemistry like Harry Roscoe, or an academic career of any kind. He never considered the question of his staying on at University College a third year to take his B.A. His intention was to leave at the end of the 1853 session and to become a businessman in Liverpool – though not in the family concern, where Herbert had priority. In his spare time he would complete his education and, upon making a fortune, retire.[1] No doubt the example of William Roscoe was in his mind. He had no plans to give any subject special attention at this time, yet one can plainly see that in the three years 1850–3, before he went Australia, the seeds of his future direction were firmly sown. De Morgan's influence, which was to lead him to logic, mathematics and a preoccupation with the fundamental philosophy of science, had been established. London itself invoked his application to the social sciences.

The predisposition towards the study of economics he owed to Liverpool: to the non-conformist intellectual and family background and to the city's traditional struggle against poverty. In Jevons's youth poverty and its attendant problems were worse in Liverpool than in any other city, largely because the rapid expansion of the port and its geographical situation led to the immigration of vast numbers of the poor of Ireland and Wales. Because of this Liverpool was a pioneer in many social services;[2] the first medical officer in the country, for instance, was appointed there in 1846.

But it was in London in the early fifties that the problems of the growth of towns coupled with rising prosperity were present in all their magnitude. Public health was a matter of much public concern. Major cholera epidemics occurred in 1849 and 1854. Edwin Chadwick and Southwood Smith were working for improved public water supplies, sewage disposal, street improvement and other services necessary for hygiene and health throughout the country. Charles Dickens threw his strength into a personal campaign for sanitary reform. In his novels the London poor were made real in scenes in *Oliver Twist* (1838) and *Bleak House* (1853). Jevons was influenced by Dickens's writings. Charles Kingsley wrote *Alton Locke* in 1850 and he and his Christian Socialists secured legality for co-operative and friendly societies in 1852. The poor of London and their way of life were documented by Henry Mayhew and Charles Knight. In and out of Parliament Lord Shaftesbury sought measures to improve the worst slums, the common lodging-

[1] See letter from Thomas Jevons to W. S. Jevons of 9 February 1853, Vol. II, Letter 21.

[2] For details see Chandler, *Liverpool*, Chap. VIII, 'The Poor and Underprivileged'.

houses. Model lodging houses, built by private enterprise, had been immune from cholera. In 1851 Shaftesbury secured the passage of a bill to make the licensing and inspection of all common lodging-houses compulsory; a second, though ineffective bill of the same year empowered local authorities to raise a rate to build model lodging-houses. The Unitarians had established a Domestic Mission in Spitalfields, where the silk industry was dying, as early as 1832.

Jevons investigated London at first hand. His chief spare-time occupation, as the journal shows, was to make long walks through the commercial and manufacturing districts and the poor and squalid districts, like Dickens before him and like Marshall a few years later.[1] But he was not concerned only with poverty. In 1851 he became interested in 'the industrial mechanism of society'.[2] This was the year of the Great Exhibition at the Crystal Palace,[3] which Jevons visited several times, and where the national wealth, the new machines and the products of the expanding colonies must have contrasted pointedly with the wretchedness of the slums. Also in 1851 the census was taken; this census being the occasion when fuller information about occupations was collected for the first time, on the basis of Dr William Farr's classification of occupations.

Jevons's interest appears to have centred upon the subject of the classification of trades, and the growth and structure of towns, especially London. He continued to study towns, both statistically and by observation in Australia. In his uncompleted *The Principles of Economics* he wrote: 'My own early studies of economics may be said to have commenced with this subject (classification of occupations). Starting with Dr Farr's system of statistics of the 1851 census, I made an elaborate investigation in the years 1856 and 1857 of the trade portion of the *London Directory*, and compiled statistics intended to be the foundation of . . .' The note is incomplete but a manuscript title page amongst Jevons's manuscripts shows that the work contemplated was to have been *Notes and Researches on Social Statistics, or the Science of Towns, especially as regards London and Sydney. Commenced November, 1856.*[4]

---

[1] '. . . in my vacations I visited the poorest quarters of several cities and walked through one street after another, looking at the faces of the poorest people. Next, I resolved to make as thorough a study as I could of Political Economy.' Marshall, writing of his life circa 1867, quoted Keynes, *Essays in Biography*, 'Alfred Marshall' (1951) p. 137.

[2] W. S. Jevons, *Principles of Economics* (1905) p. vii. A fragment of a note left by Jevons reads: 'It was in 1851 that I first began, at the age of sixteen, to study the industrial mechanism of society, purchasing for the purpose some of the . . . By the year 1857 . . . I had achieved a careful study of the London Directory.'

[3] *Punch* gave the building this name (*Punch*, Vol. xix, p. 183). See C. R. Fay, *Palace of Industry, 1851* (Cambridge, 1951) p. 15.

[4] *Principles*, p. 107.

Behind the efforts to ameliorate social conditions in the early 1850's, lay the political struggle. This Jevons also followed and it centred on an economic question. It was the struggle of the new commercial and industrial classes and the Liberals under Gladstone to complete the introduction of Free Trade against the opposition of the conservative and landed interests who strove to retain Protection.

III

Jevons did not have the opportunity to carry out his plan to leave college and make a fortune in business, which his father regarded as somewhat illusory.[1]

In his last term at University College, when he was seventeen, Jevons was offered, and accepted, the post of assayer to a new mint to be built at Sydney to coin the gold resulting from the Australian gold discoveries of 1851. He describes the circumstances in his journal; but not the pain it cost him to accept, and which a sentence written much later reveals – ' . . . that dreadful week which passed a sentence of transportation upon me', he called it.

A decisive factor was undoubtedly the financial position at home. However, misunderstanding also played some part. A few years later Jevons wrote in the following terms about his father: '. . . he could not have been aware, as I was both reserved and but little conscious of it myself, of my entire devotion to serious views and studies . . . I am certain that if at the time [of being offered the post in Sydney] I had stated my wish for further study and a different start in life, he would have immediately agreed. . . .'[2]

The new mint was to be a branch (the first) of the Royal Mint, working under its direction. Its establishment was authorised by an Imperial Order in Council on 19 August 1853. It was formally opened on 14 May 1855. 'The Home Mint appointed and promoted the personnel, administered their activities, furnished their master dies, and tested their work by sample coins taken from circulation', and the chief officer was to be considered as a Deputy Master of the Royal Mint. Captain Ward (later Major-General Sir Edward Wohlstenholm Ward, K.C.M.G.) of the Royal Engineers, 'deputy master of the branch till 1877, saw to construction, equipment and first staffing appointments. Most of the first appointments were Royal Engineers with a few technicians from Tower Hill. . . . The personnel were organised as an

---

[1] 'I know that your idea is, like many others before you, to amass a fortune in a short time so that you may afterwards devote your whole time to science, but in this you indulge a fallacy. . . .' See letter of 9 February 1853 from Thomas Jevons to Jevons, Vol. II, Letter 21.
[2] See letter of 14 October 1858 to his sister Lucy, Vol. II, Letter 123.

overseas edition of Tower Hill and were paid and pensioned as members of the Imperial Civil Service, not of the State of New South Wales.'[1]

At first this did not apply to the assayers. Two assayers were appointed, the second being F. B. Miller. They were each to have their own assay offices independent of the mint and to undertake assaying for private banks and private persons as well as for the mint on piece rate. In addition the mint was to pay a fixed salary of £100 per annum.

Jevons had to undertake the planning of his assay office, to buy all the necessary equipment and arrange for its shipment to Australia, and was responsible for setting up the office himself when he got to Sydney. He at once started to learn assaying. He worked all through the summer vacation in London in the private assay laboratory of Professor Graham. Captain Ward must have felt doubt about him on account of his youth, for he then asked that he should also go for a probationary period to the assay office of Professor W. A. Miller, Professor of Chemistry at King's College, London, and Non-Resident Assayer to the Royal Mint and to the Bank of England.[2] Both professors signed a joint testimonial on 13 October 1853, stating that he was qualified to carry out 'at once and without further preparation all the various duties of Assayer to a Mint.'[3] He expected to leave for Sydney in November. However, the building of the mint was delayed. Jevons therefore returned to Liverpool. In February 1854 he went to Paris to take a two months' course at the Paris Mint and took their Diploma. At home again, he waited for the sailing date to be fixed and completed his arrangements.

One year after being selected, Jevons sailed; on 29 June 1854, from Liverpool. His official appointment dated from 1 July 1854. He took with him a young man to be his assistant for his office, called Charles Bolton, the younger brother of Anne Bolton who was the Jevons's family nurse. They sailed on the 1272-ton clipper of the Black Ball Line *Oliver Lang*, owned by the Liverpool company of James Baines & Co.; an emigrant ship with nearly six hundred souls on board, Jevons travelling first class and sharing a cabin with a Scottish youth.

He describes the journey in detail in the journal, in what was presumably the draft of a letter to his father, written as the voyage neared its end. Much of his time on board ship he spent studying the weather, and clouds especially.

When the ship reached Melbourne Jevons went ashore for a short while. He landed at Sydney on 6 October and was met at the ship by Mr

[1] Sir John Craig, *The Mint. A History of the London Mint from A.D. 287 to 1948* (Cambridge 1953) p. 386.

[2] See Thomas Jevons's letter of 17 September 1853 to Jevons on this issue, Vol. II, Letter 28.

[3] See below, Vol. II, Letter 29.

Miller and by Sergeant Trickett, who was also to be on the Mint staff.[1] The journey had lasted one hundred days, which was exceptionally long. He found that the building of the mint had only just begun.

He had difficulty in finding premises for his office: rents were 'enormously' high and accommodation scarce. He took a two-roomed cottage at No. 8 Charlotte Place, Church Hill, standing in a yard behind a warehouse in the centre of the town, 'an old tumbledown place with lots of cobwebs and rats' as he described it. Here Jevons and Charles Bolton lived, slept and cooked in the two rooms, one of which was the laboratory and the other a storeroom. They built the melting and cupel furnaces, made the work-bench and laboratory table, installed the apparatus, etc. Jevons suffered from boils and occasioned his father some anxiety.[2] On 5 January 1855, at Church Hill, he made his first journal entry in Australia and the first, apart from the description of the voyage, since January 1854. He had already made up his mind not to stay on in Australia.

When the office was complete Jevons had very little work. Apart from preparing some exhibition coins there was no official work. He was short of money and had to pay his assistant. He tried to obtain private orders, but found this both difficult and uncongenial. It therefore suited Jevons, when, in January 1855, Captain Ward made the two assayers an offer of full-time employment on the mint staff.

This new arrangement disappointed Jevons's father greatly. It is referred to in the journal – not directly, but in Jevons's comments on the letters of his father of 3 June 1855 and 29 October 1855.[3] There is no direct mention of his work at the mint in the journal.

The mint had to refine gold and it was restricted to coining sovereigns and half-sovereigns identical in weight and fineness with the home coins, but different in design. The assayers fulfilled their task well: '. . . it is not impossible that our coin might be rendered legal in England ultimately', wrote Jevons in January 1857.[4] 'This is partly because our coin has turned out so satisfactorily, especially as regards *assay* or fineness, that it is much superior to the English coinage itself.' Jevons made some improvement in the assay process himself.[5] He was also trained in the much more difficult task of assaying silver and other metals, and at the mint was often given unknown ores to assay. It was anticipated that the mint would serve all the Australian colonies.

---

[1] See letter of 31 January 1855 to Jevons from Thomas Jevons, Vol. II, Letter 53.

[2] See letter of 1 August 1855 to Jevons from Thomas Jevons, Vol. II, Letter 69.

[3] See pp. 120 and 121 below.

[4] See letter of 18 January 1857 to Herbert Jevons, Vol. II, Letter 97. MS now in the Mitchell Library, Sydney.

[5] For details, see article on 'Gold Assay' by Jevons in Watt's *Dictionary of Chemistry* (1864).

However, the State of Victoria refused to accept the Sydney coinage until July 1857, so that until that date they were legal tender in New South Wales alone. The Victorian gold was exported to England. Although, therefore, Jevons's work at the mint was at first hard and exacting,[1] entries in his diary show that from April 1856 it slackened off. The assayership became more or less a sinecure, and Jevons was able to spend a great deal of his time at the mint on work of his own, especially on meteorology. 'I should not wonder if several days of each week I am not occupied over the assays more than half an hour per day; but I nearly always attend the full five hours, and fill up the time by preparations for larger numbers, or various things of my own', he wrote in January 1857.[2] After the State of Victoria proclaimed the Sydney coins legal the gold intake at the mint recovered and Jevons must have become somewhat busier. The circulation of the coinage was subsequently extended outside Australia; a second mint was opened at Melbourne in 1869 and the Sydney mint was closed in December 1926.

When the mint opened Jevons left Church Hill and went to live with Miller and his wife at their house at Petersham near Sydney on the road to Parramatta, Annangrove Cottage. He wrote to Harry Roscoe on 11 July 1855:[3]

> I live out here very comfortably with Mr. and Mrs. Miller having a little sittingroom and bedroom and everything in fact as well as I could wish it. It is four miles from Sydney, therefore regularly in the country and surrounded by woods, but upon a turnpike road on which omnibuses run continually to Sydney. By these we go a greater or less part of the distance, have a good day's work in town at our offices, from about ten to five o'clock and then return to dinner.

Jevons was now feeling more established in Australia, and goes on to tell his cousin

> a fellow must stand on his own bottom here, in fact I am getting *colonial* (an expressive term not to be understood in England) which means being up to everything and everybody. You will be surprised what tricks we shall play on honest Englishmen, after living a few years among the thieves and convicts of New South Wales. This is not all joking either, for in living here you necessarily become acquainted with numbers of convicts, particularly in the gold trade, who you know are not better than they were before but more cautious.

---

[1] See letter of 16 July 1855 to his father, Vol. II, Letter 68.
[2] See letter of 18 January 1857 to Herbert Jevons, Vol. II, Letter 97.
[3] See Vol. II, Letter 66.

Jevons lived with the Millers all the time he was in Sydney. In March 1857 they moved to a new house which Miller had built on the beautiful shore of Double Bay.

Being settled on a fixed salary and in a comfortable home, the few years which followed were carefree and abounding in activity, both mental and physical. Freedom, wealth, and the stimulus of the new continent drew out his powers of observation and a host of ambitious schemes. But the future was his deeper preoccupation. 'It is a perfectly decided thing in my mind to be at home again in from five to ten years, and as I have no intention of being nothing better than an assayer or chemist all my life, I shall have to begin life again on a new bottom', he had written in his journal on 5 January 1855. To carry out the plans for study broadly as he had outlined these in his journal when in London was his object. On 29 July 1856, he wrote: 'My principle of action, indeed of life is this, and it has been growing more and more defined for some time; I aim at qualifying myself for any object I desire in life, I aim not at it and try no means to obtain it but those of being fit for and worthy of it' (Journal entry for 29 July 1856).

The context in which his future would be worked out was made plainer by the death of his father after he had been in Australia only one year. Thomas Jevons died, suddenly, at Pisa, on 8 November 1855, and was buried in the Protestant cemetery at Leghorn.[1] Jevons, who had found the keeping of his journal decidedly tedious, now turned to it to record this event.

IV

Jevons made a systematic study of Australia and New South Wales – its climate, geography, geology, topography, flora and social and economic character and policy. He began with the climate. In mid-January 1855 he started to take twice daily meteorological observations at Church Hill; they were comprehensive, covering air pressure, temperature, moisture, rainfall, and cloud and wind conditions. He continued the observations until mid-1858 when they were recorded officially by the Sydney Observatory. For about a year Jevons was the only meteorologist in Sydney and his records for this period were incorporated in the official meteorological record.[2] 'It was by his meteorological work that Jevons was best known in Sydney', writes Professor J. A. La Nauze, in his study of *Jevons in Sydney*.[3] 'It is mature

[1] A memorial tablet was placed in Renshaw Street Chapel.
[2] LJ, p. 112.
[3] Chapter II, Essay on *Jevons in Sydney* in *Political Economy in Australia*, by J. A. La Nauze (Melbourne, 1949).

and complete in itself – a distinct and impressive phase of his varied life's work.' His published work in these years was mainly but not exclusively on meteorology, the dramatic character of the climate, with violent and frequent thunderstorms, hot winds and the alternation of flood and drought, calling forth some vivid writing. In September 1856 he became unpaid Meteorological Observer for the newspaper the *Empire*, run by Henry Parkes, the poet who later became one of Australia's leading politicians, many times Premier of New South Wales. From 3 September 1856 the *Empire* published his weekly meteorological reports, sometimes with extended special remarks appended. He also wrote special articles for the paper on meteorological subjects. From June 1857 to June 1858 he also provided elaborate monthly reports for the *Sydney Magazine of Science and Art*, and two yearly summaries.

He interested himself in the 'science of clouds' or the theory of their formation and wrote a long paper entitled *On Clouds; their various Forms, and producing causes, with experimental illustrations* [etc.], which was read before the Philosophical Society of New South Wales on 9 December 1857, after extended work and observation. Most of the work he did in his office at the mint, where he began his experiments early in 1856 and built an apparatus for making different kinds of clouds in miniature. The Philosophical Society of New South Wales met monthly to hear and discuss papers on scientific and technical subjects under the active presidency of the Governor-General, Sir William Denison. It was inaugurated in May 1856, and Jevons was elected a member on 13 June. The proceedings were published in the *Sydney Magazine of Science and Art*.[1] Jevons's paper on Clouds was prefaced by the introductory remarks. '. . . the following interesting paper was read by Mr. W. S. Jevons, whose contributions to the Meteorology of this country have been so numerous and so highly esteemed. The paper we here publish will add largely to his reputation, and will, we are sure, excite the earnest attention of Meteorologists in England.'[2] At the mint he also constructed an Actinometer or sun-gauge, described in a shorter paper read to the Philosophical Society on 8 July 1857, entitled *On a Sun-gauge, or New Actinometer*.

After a few years in Sydney Jevons was able to assemble a great mass of material, statistical and descriptive, about the climate of all Australasia and to incorporate this into his major study – *Some Data Concerning the Climate of Australia and New Zealand*, published in Waugh's *Australian*

[1] Issued monthly from June 1857 to June 1859, by James Waugh, a Sydney bookseller and publisher, who also published *Waugh's Almanack*.
[2] Vol. I, January 1858, pp. 163–76. An abbreviation of the paper 'On the Forms of Cloud', was published in the *Philosophical Magazine, London* (April 1858).

Almanac for the Year 1859 (50 pages). It has been described as 'the most valuable contribution to the meteorology of Australia that had been made up to the time of its publication . . .'[1] It took six months of prodigious labour to complete and contains a chapter on the Periodicity of Droughts. Indeed, as Professor La Nauze has noted, Jevons was invariably searching for 'laws' and 'uniformities' to simplify large masses of otherwise incomprehensible data. Even as early as 1853 he recorded in his journal Faraday's reference to the periodicity of sun spots.[2]

The years Jevons spent in Australia were at a turning point in the history of the continent. The shipment of convicts to New South Wales was prohibited in 1840. Gold was found in the Turon River area north-west of Bathurst in New South Wales in 1851 and caused an immediate gold rush and a flood of immigrants from the Mother Country. The gold discoveries of Victoria followed soon afterwards, and with this sudden source of wealth Australia's economy ceased to be purely pastoral and the rise of commerce and manufacturing industry in the following century was dramatic. The seeds of the future economic development in the Northern and Southern Coalfields were just visible when Jevons visited these areas. Meantime, the problem of expanding and new towns was present in Australia as in England.

It was not long before Jevons was engaged upon making a study of Sydney. He often made long walks through different parts of the town on his way home from the mint to Annangrove Cottage, and on Sundays sometimes longer trips in the neighbourhood with Maurice O'Connell, brother-in-law of Mr Miller. He made four tours of New South Wales while he was at the mint. The first and longest, was, not surprisingly, to the gold diggings at Sofala on the Turon River. He wrote up a detailed day-by-day account of the excursion in a special notebook (7 in. × 4½ in., 83 pages, with register of meteorological readings for each day – sometimes as many as six recordings at intervals throughout the day – and illustrated by small interspersed sketches). The other tours Jevons wrote up in the journal itself: indeed, they comprise the greater portion of the Australian section (about 41 out of 70 pages). After Jevons left the mint, in January of 1859, he visited the goldfields at Braidwood about 160 miles south of Sydney, where Charles Bolton and Maurice O'Connell were digging; walking most of the way there and back. There remains no written-up account of this, only some notes in a small field notebook.[3]

---

[1] H. C. Russell, 'Astronomical and Meteorological Workers in New South Wales, 1778 to 1860', in *Report of the First Meeting of the Australian Association for the Advancement of Science* (Sydney, 1889), quoted in La Nauze, op. cit., p. 30.

[2] See entry for 23 January 1853, p. 82 below.

[3] Some account is given in a letter written in February 1859 to Lucy, see Vol. II, Letter 129.

On his way home to Europe Jevons travelled the long and difficult journey, six hundred miles overland, by coach from Sydney to Melbourne. He then toured the goldfields and towns of Victoria. On board ship bound for South America he worked on writing up accounts of these journeys, but unfortunately he lost his 'Australian journals' at Havana. The accounts of the four tours of New South Wales are therefore the only ones which survive, and it seems unreasonable not to publish the first account, written in the separate notebook, along with the other three. It is therefore included here as a separate appendix.[1]

Jevons's interest in the subject of geology, which he started to study before leaving England, is clear from the detailed geological observations he made on all his trips in New South Wales. He published three articles on geological subjects in Sydney, all in the year 1858.[2]

The University of Sydney, founded only in 1852, had a staff of three at this time. The Reverend John Woolley, M.A., D.C.L. was the Principal and Professor of Classics. He was a highly accomplished scholar who took a prominent part in the social life of the colony and in the running of the Sydney Mechanics School of Arts, an institution with a reference and lending library and reading room and where public lectures and educational classes were held. Professor Morris Birkbeck Pell was Professor of Mathematics and Natural Philosophy, and Dr John Smith, M.S., graduate in Arts and Medicine of Aberdeen, where he had conducted classes in chemistry for many years, was Professor of Chemistry and Experimental Physics.[3]

Dr Smith, with whom Jevons was friendly, read both Jevons's papers, on 'Sun-gauge' and 'Clouds', before the Philosophical Society, of which in 1857 he was Secretary.[4] Dr Smith took a prominent part in the colonial life, especially in education. He was elected a member of the Legislative Council for New South Wales in 1874 and died in Sydney in 1885.[5] Jevons kept in contact with him after leaving Australia. In 1861, on a visit to England, Dr Smith read a paper to the British Association at Manchester and met Jevons who was reporting the Association meetings, and a few months later Dr Smith visited Jevons in London.[6]

Jevons, on his tours, gained first-hand experience of the primitive state of Australian communications. He took part in the public debate on the introduction of railways into New South Wales. At the Inaugural

[1] p. 213 below.   [2] See La Nauze's bibliography, op. cit., p. 43.

[3] H. E. Barff, *A Short Historical Account of the University of Sydney, 1852–1902* (Sydney 1902).

[4] Jevons's diary entry for 8 July 1857 reads: 'In evening to Philosophical Society, where I put a very good face upon the matter and heard my paper read by Dr. Smith; no question being asked I got through the evening with great composure'. Regarding the paper on clouds, see La Nauze, op. cit., p. 28, footnote 10. See also journal entry for 31 December 1862, p. 187 below.   [5] Barff, op. cit.

[6] See letters of September 1861 and 3 March 1862 from Jevons to his sister Henrietta, Vol. II, Letters 154 and 157.

Meeting of the Philosophical Society in May 1856, the Governor-General read a paper on the subject of 'Rail Roads', which aroused Jevons's interest.[1] On 11 July 1856 Professor Pell read a paper to the Society entitled 'On the Application of Certain Principles of Political Economy to the Question of Railways'; a theoretical paper (quoting Mill) on the question of whether railways would be 'economic'. A week later, on 18 July, Jevons wrote in his diary: '. . . I have lately become much interested in a discussion on the Introduction of railways into this colony'. He published his views in a series of letters and articles to the press. On 10 February 1857 he contributed a long letter to the *Empire* on the subject of the Western Railway Line and the General Policy of Government Railway Extension.[2] The question of land values and Government policy in the sale of the Public Lands was an essential factor in the economics of railway development, and Jevons dealt with this in his article 'Comparison of the Land and Railway Policy of New South Wales',[3] and in a further article 'The Public Lands of New South Wales'[4], in which he quotes Mill on rent. A third letter, on 'Railway Economy', was published in the *Empire* of 29 December 1857.[5]

These first publications on economics may not be of any permanent importance in themselves.[6] It is clear from Jevons's letters from Australia and from the journal that his reflections on capital and on the time element largely arose from contemplating his own personal situation and his plans for the future. His studies were for the future, the money he saved for travel and further study was capital investment in himself. Money in itself did not interest him: time concerned him, and money to buy time. Lord Robbins, referring to Jevons's *Theory of Capital*, has pointed out that 'It is . . . time which is the central figure in the picture'.[7] He notes that Jevons's discovery of his theory of capital was antecedent to his discovery of his marginal utility theory, the 'whole doctrine' being 'anticipated' in the passage in the letter to his sister Henrietta of 30 January 1859,[8] also referred to by La Nauze, relating to

---

[1] Diary entry for 1 July 1856, records: '. . . commenced letter concerning the Governor's lecture on Railways'.

[2] Diary entries for 7 and 9 February 1857.

[3] Published in the *Empire* of 8 April 1857.

[4] *Empire*, 24 June 1857. Both articles are summarised by La Nauze, op. cit., pp. 40–41.

[5] La Nauze, op. cit., p. 41, attributes this letter to Jevons, it being 'From a Correspondent' and signed 'An exact Thinker'.

[6] La Nauze, op. cit., p. 32, writes: '. . . These articles contain some acute and vigorously worded criticisms; but I do not suggest that they are of enduring value. There is nothing in them to compare in interest with the reflections on the nature of capital contained in a letter written in January 1859.'

[7] Lionel Robbins, 'The Place of Jevons in the History of Economic Thought', *The Manchester School*, VII (1936), pp. 11 and 12.

[8] See Vol. II, Letter 128.

'the proper relation of preparation and performance'.[1] However, it is also clear that consideration of the question of the introduction of railways into New South Wales caused Jevons to give serious study to economics. This classic example of capital expenditure raised fundamental problems of economic and financial policy, involving rent, labour and interest. And it is to be noted that the passage on capital referred to is illustrated by an example drawn from railways.

It was in the first half of 1857, when he published his first three articles on railways, that Jevons began to study economics seriously.

Jevons read the *Wealth of Nations* in the first three months of 1856. We can follow his reading from his diaries. It is mentioned in the text; and he also lists the books read or partly read month by month at the back of the diary. In November and December 1856 he read Burton's *Political Economy* and the volume on *Railway Statistics* in Weale's Series. Mill's *Principles of Political Economy*, published in 1848, was the work to which he devoted most attention in the first half of 1857, starting with Volume II and going on to Volume I later.[2] In April and May he read the book on railways, Lardner's *Railway Economy* (1850), which first gave him the idea of investigating economics mathematically.[3]

Jevons also read Malthus's *Essay on Population*, and Archbishop Richard Whately's *Introductory Lectures on Political Economy*. The latter he bought on 26 March 1857, and on 5 April he set down some remarks upon it in his journal. They illustrate the wider context of Jevons's interest in economics as part of anthropology.[4]

Here and in several other of the journal entries, e.g., remarks on *My Novel* (entry for 10 June 1855), Jevons appears to have been much occupied with the motives behind his own and human behaviour in general. In his remarks on Whately's *Lectures* he makes reference to his own conception of 'the principle of Individual Competition' or 'selfish competition'.

His general views on 'selfishness' he elaborated in the journal for 13 September 1856, after hearing a lecture on 'The Selfish Theory of Morals' by Professor John Woolley at the Sydney Mechanics School of Arts. He states here the hedonistic thesis, which was to become the basis, when joined to 'utility' and the differential calculus, of his subjective or marginal theory of value: '. . . I regard man in reality as essentially

---

[1] Robbins, op. cit., p. 10, footnote 4.

[2] His diary records that he 'drew from library Mill's *Political Economy*, Vol. II' on 4 February 1857 and finished it on 6 March. He started Vol. I on 18 May and finished it on 20 June.

[3] He bought a copy on 22 April 1857, for 14s. 0d. Jevons acknowledged his indebtedness to this book in his Preface to the *Theory of Political Economy*, 4th ed., 1931, p. xviii.

[4] Viz. diary entry for 21 May – '. . . proceeded with the Introduction of my book on Anthropology or the general consideration of Man in the concrete, comprising Political and Social Economy, Moral Philosophy and parts of Ethics and Metaphysics'.

selfish, that is as doing everything with a view to gain or enjoyment or avoid pain' (p. 133 below). It was, therefore, in Australia that Jevons first adopted the utilitarian approach to man's economic behaviour, which was to be formally set out in his 'Brief Account of a General Mathematical Theory of Political Economy' in 1862 and later and more fully in *The Theory of Political Economy*.

According to the list of 'Work to be done in 1857' at the beginning of his diary for that year Jevons was to write 'Work on "Formal Economics"'. No trace of the work has survived. Some of his work on classification of occupations which he began in London in 1851 (see p. 17 above), and on towns has, however, survived. On 31 July 1856, he wrote in his diary: 'Commenced reading Mayhew's Great World of London in which my idea of a Science of Poliography or a Topographical Description of the districts of a city seems to have been anticipated'. In November 1856 he commenced a work entitled 'Notes and Researches on Social Statistics or the Science of Towns, especially as regards London and Sydney'.[1] His purpose is more precisely described in a letter of 9 June 1858:[2]

> . . . I have even had for many years the idea of a work on 'Towns and Cities', to analyse their constitution, and causes, the relative character of their parts, and the relative character of particular cities and thus eventually lead to such knowledge of their nature as shall ensure their improvement, as any scientific knowledge is eventually reduced to practice.

For the analysis of their constitution he laboured at the statistics of occupations. 'Working hard at *Division of Labour*', he wrote in his diary on 13 October 1857, 'and engaged adding up the totals of returns of employment from the British Census. These total results when finished will be quite complete giving the number of persons, male and female separately, for every order of every section and class. The trouble, however, is very great.' A fragment, consisting of a coloured chart representing these results, is described in the Preface to *Principles of Economics*.[3] On the topographical side he worked at his 'Social maps of Sydney' as he described them, and made a detailed study of the nature and topography of the town. The results were incorporated in a manuscript which La Nauze has called the 'Social Survey of Sydney' and which he describes as 'the most interesting work in political economy done in Jevons's Australian years'.[4] This seems to be a fragment of the 'Notes and Researches on Social Statistics, etc.' project. The survey –

---

[1] *Principles of Economics*, Editor's Preface, p. vii.
[2] To his sister Henrietta. See Vol. II, Letter 117.
[3] p. vii.   [4] Op. cit., p. 33.

which amounts to a one-man Social Survey – is described by Professor La Nauze in his article 'Jevons in Sydney'.[1] The survey is descriptive, and is organised on a geographical basis (ten areas). Information was obtained through observation on walks and from the Sydney Directories. Jevons classified the inhabitants by social class, there being three social classes based on occupational groupings, and recorded the distribution of their residences in each area. He also classified businesses by type of product and recorded their geographical distribution. The results were indicated upon a map, which appears to have been lost. Each geographical area is also described in detail. The only portion of the work which Jevons published was an article entitled 'The Social Cesspools of Sydney. No. 1 The Rocks', in the *Sydney Morning Herald* of 7 October 1858.[2] It was not until 1929 that the greater part of the manuscript was published, in instalments in the *Sydney Morning Herald*.[3] Jevons also started similar surveys of some other Australian towns.

Jevons's interest in Man as a social being in the widest sense and his belief in Man's capacity to improve himself and his environment without limit through his own efforts were traditionally Unitarian. The youthful religious opinions he expresses in the journal for 28 January 1857 go almost as far as deifying Man. The last entry in the journal in Australia was made only a few months later (account of the trip to Wollongong), and the last entry in his diaries there is for 13 October 1857. After this date only his letters remain to show the further development of his belief and purposes. Fortunately the letters are long and illuminating, especially those to his sister Henrietta. Deprived of the support of her father, finding difficulty in making her own life after leaving school, and seeking a firmly based religious philosophy, Henrietta turned to Jevons for guidance. Through this shared feeling of being seekers after the truth he gained confidence in Henrietta's understanding; whilst of his elder sister, Lucy's, intelligent interest and support he was certain. The result was that Jevons was able to confide to his sisters his most secret thoughts and hopes. Such revelations are possible in letters, especially when written from a great distance, whereas only to the most intimate of friends could they ever be spoken face to face. When he was back in England it was to his journal that Jevons turned as the 'friend' or recipient of his most cherished confidences.

The letter in which Jevons disclosed to his sisters his aim in life was written on 17 November 1857:[4] 'I have a second nature within me hidden to the world, yet directing all my behaviour towards the world',

[1] Op. cit., pp. 33–7.

[2] La Nauze, op. cit., p. 42, writes: 'This is . . . evidently an expanded version of the section of the Social Survey. . . . No second article appears to have been published.'

[3] La Nauze, op. cit., pp. 33–4.

[4] See Vol. II, Letter 111.

he wrote. '. . . My whole second nature consists of one wish, or one *intention*, viz. to be a *powerful good* in the world. . . . To be *powerfully good*, that is to be good, not towards one or a dozen, or a hundred, but towards a nation or the world, is what now absorbs me.' What Jevons is expressing here is 'charity', and indeed, he had earlier written: '. . . If I may call myself a Unitarian it is for this reason, that of all sects I believe they alone are *charitably* disposed towards others. . . . If I gave any creed for my own belief, I should give it from the Bible, and say that I have Faith, Hope and Charity, but most of Charity . . .'[1] Through charity of spiritual love the world would be redeemed and man reach perfection.

Jevons considered that the possibility of his being able to become a powerful good lay in the type of mind he possessed; in its capacity for originality: the rare mind was the one capable of reflection and reasoning.

Jevons did not then foresee that formal logic would be the purest field for the exercise of his mind in 'reflection and reasoning'. He read Mill's *Logic* in 1857, after he had finished Mill's *Political Economy*; in his journal for December 1862 he says he perhaps partly understood this, but that he 'knew little or nothing about logic then'. But he did envisage the application of scientific method to the social sciences, as is clear from references in letters of 1858 and 1859 to his sister Henrietta.[2] The task Jevons set himself, and the cultivation of his powers to achieve it, demanded discipline and loneliness.

In the journal for the Australian years there is but one entry referring to this question of sociability: an indirect one in the form of some extracts or quotations from two authors upon the subject of 'visiting' and mental isolation.[3] Jevons's letters show that these reflections were stimulated by concern for his sister Henrietta as well as by his own situation. He was disturbed by her constant visits to friends and relatives, seeing in the distraction a threat to her seriousness and stability; and in making the extracts he seems to have had her in mind as well as himself: '. . . I very much fear that a gay unsettled life is just what would rub off from your mind many buds of truth of which I caught a glimpse', he wrote to her on 4 August 1858.[4] '. . . No one can rise above the common level if he do not cherish within him an almost secret soul to animate or guide him.' For Jevons himself, the problem was to be a continuing one as the journal for the following years shows and these words find an echo in the entry for 3 December 1865, when he wrote: '. . . One of my chief reasons for the little love of society is that

---

[1] See letter of 4 January 1857 to his sister Henrietta, Vol. II, Letter 96.
[2] See letters of 4 August 1858 and 30 January 1859, Vol. II, Letters 120 and 128.
[3] Mrs Gaskell and George Hogarth. See undated entry, p. 178 below.
[4] See Vol. II, Letter 120.

in most company my hopes and feelings seem snuffed out.' The solitariness of his life in Sydney is a subject to which Jevons's letters refer with increasing frequency as the years go by.

On the superficial level he was by no means without companions and acquaintances and by no means always 'stay-at-home'. This is clear from his diaries. He was friendly with the Millers and with his colleagues at the mint. He took an enthusiastic interest in all the affairs of the colony, including its politics under 'responsible government'. Photography became a hobby and one shared with others at the mint, especially E. R. Hunt. Some of Jevons's photographs are of historic interest.[1] His work is described in an article 'Australia's First Pictorialist' in the *Australian Photographic Review*.[2] It comprised not only views of Sydney and nature but also portraits and self-portraits, interior scenes, photographs of the mint apparatus, the goldfields, etc. He went to many performances of plays, operas and concerts during the years 1856 and 1857, as his diaries show. He was a member of the Unitarian Chapel of which the Reverend Stanley was minister. There were boating and walking expeditions with others from the mint. Altogether Jevons gained a position of some eminence in the colony. Yet it was not an entirely satisfactory one, for his scientific knowledge was not accompanied by an academic degree. He wrote to his cousin, Harry Roscoe, that if he had had the B.A. 'before coming to this colony I should vastly have improved my position in, as well as outside, the mint.'[3]

But of all his spare-time occupations, music was the most important. By temperament he was a musician.

> You say [he wrote to Henrietta[4]] that I seemed from my last letters not so much occupied with *music*. This can scarcely have been the case for music is always to me the same, a condition of my existence, a part of me. I believe I could live a *life of Music*. If our physical nature did not interfere, I can almost conceive it possible that a man might play music *ad infinitum* and still never tire'.

And again

> To love music I regard as one of the most blessed things in the world ... the simple, intense and enduring pleasure which music affords me gives me some slight conception of what a universal harmony might

---

[1] *The Australian Photo Review* presented his son, the late Professor H. Stanley Jevons, in 1954 with a Special Recognition Medal 'In Recognition of Achievement in Photography, to mark the centenary of W. S. Jevons's arrival in Sydney on 6th October, 1854, and in recognition of the excellence of his photography during the years 1857 and 1858'.

[2] By Iris Burke, January 1955.

[3] See letter dated January 1859, LJ, pp. 118–19.

[4] In an unpublished letter of 27 September 1858.

be in Heaven where the harmonies of sound, sight, and mental feeling are of course merged into something infinitely purer.

He bought a harmonium in 1855 soon after going to live at Annangrove Cottage, and spent evening after evening playing for himself music he bought and music sent from home. Henrietta was a pianist and many of his long letters to her are entirely concerned with musical subjects. In 1857 he wrote a book about music, and invented a new system of notation. He sent the manuscript home to Henrietta chapter by chapter but no trace of the work remains.

V

After four years in Sydney, Jevons was determined upon returning home. In what he had described to Henrietta as 'the scientific investigation of *man*' he had found the field in which he wished to work and he had also realised the fundamental importance of mathematics to the further development of his ideas.[1]

Knowing that he had accumulated sufficient capital for the purpose, he planned to return to University College for a year and possibly take his B.A., then to earn his living as a writer. The decision was nevertheless a burdensome one to take. It involved not only his own future but that of his two sisters, both still unmarried. Herbert was at this time a struggling pioneer farmer in Minnesota, having left the family business. Tom had just started to study at University College. Jevons was the only one earning. To give up his post meant sacrificing any possibility of offering financial help to his sisters for years to come.

It is scarcely surprising that his relatives at home were grievously opposed to Jevons's plans. In many letters he patiently and logically explained his motives to them.

Though some of my English friends may think this step rash and foolish [he wrote to Harry Roscoe[2]], and though you will perhaps shake your head and wish that 'something certain' should turn up first, yet I am sure you will not misjudge me. To explain all my motives is more than I could profess to do, or think necessary, but my main argument in favour of leaving is this – Every year I spend here is so much cash in pocket, but curtails by so much the time yet open to me for improvement and for qualifying myself for any position I may desire. My actions now will influence me for life, and a few hundred pounds weigh very light in the balance of my mind against the

[1] See letter of 30 January 1859, Vol. II, Letter 128; also Jevons's letter dated January 1859 to Harry Roscoe, LJ, pp. 118–19.
[2] See letter of 9 October 1858, Vol. II, Letter 122.

satisfactory employment of the many future years I look forward to . . . of all enervating employments perhaps a wellpaid Government post is the worst, and adding to this the isolation of colonial life the many difficulties in the way of study, and the few other pleasures which present theselves, and you have the sum of what I object to in my residence here. . . .

The burden of the decision was increased when Jevons was offered a lucrative post worth up to £2000 a year at Melbourne, but his reasons for refusing are given in a letter to his sister Lucy of 9 December 1858,[1] and at the end of December he left the Mint. He did not leave Sydney immediately, but made the long trip south to the goldfields at Braidwood. He had decided to return home round the world, visiting his brother in the United States on the way. In March 1859 he left Sydney for Melbourne. After visiting the goldfields he took a steamer to Peru; went from there to Panama, crossed the isthmus by railway, made his way by steamers to New York, travelled thousands of miles inland to visit Herbert in his log hut, and finally returned to Liverpool on 17 September 1859. He had been away almost five and a quarter years; he was just twenty-four years old.

The gap in the journal continues for more than four and a half years. The first entry after Jevons's return home was made on 8 December 1861.

Jevons returned to University College in October 1859, to complete his B.A. degree. His younger brother, Tom, had entered the college in 1857 and was also in his last year of study for the B.A. His two sisters came to London, and with them and Tom, Jevons took lodgings at No. 8 Porteus Road, a small street near what is now the Paddington Recreation Ground, conveniently situated for Gower Street. He lived at this address until he left London in May 1863.

Although for more than two years Jevons made no entries in his journal a fairly full picture of his activities during these years can be gained from the letters of this period. On his return to college in the winter of 1859–60 he not unnaturally felt 'rather strange' and found that 'the charm is rubbed off a few things'.[2] But his correspondence reveals his determination to acquire a greater mastery of mathematics, and the rapid growth of his interest in, and understanding of, philosophy and the theory of political economy. The letters recount the now well-known story of his 'sad reverse' in political economy when he was placed equal third in the college examination of June 1860 in that subject; in the

[1] See Vol. II, Letter 127.
[2] See letters of 15 October 1859 and 27 January 1860, to Herbert Jevons, Vol. II, Letters 141 and 143.

mental philosophy examination, the only other college examination he took, Jevons was placed joint first.[1] Nor did his 'sad reverse' in the political economy examination prevent him from winning the Ricardo scholarship in December 1860, as at one time he had feared it might.

Jevons had already decided to stay on at University College for another two years to take his M.A. in philosophical subjects. Meantime, he took his B.A. in October 1860. The 'catalogue of work' for this, he gives his brother in his letter of 25 July 1860: 'viz. Latin, history, mathematics, Roman history, Greek history, English history, French, animal physiology, logic, natural philosophy, moral philosophy, all of which', he comments, 'require looking up seriously, and many to be learnt from the beginning'.[2] He passed the B.A. in the first division; his brother, Tom, in the second division. Jevons wrote to him: '. . . I suppose that you more or less expected first, but if you really calculated the chances, from your leaving London for four or five weeks, losing your cramming by toothache, etc., and also leaving Natural Philosophy so entirely to the end, I think you have no need to be particularly vexed or at all discouraged'.[3]

The letters of 1861–2 show vividly the range and depth of the studies which Jevons undertook for his M.A. degree;[4] in June 1862 he passed the examinations for it, and was awarded the gold medal for the best candidate 'in the third branch', which included logic and moral philosophy, political philosophy, history of philosophy, and political economy.

During all these years at University College, Jevons also spent a great deal of time on his own work. Political economy occupied him from the start, and a fragment of a diary for February 1860 shows him working intensively at both this subject and mathematics. On the evidence of the entries in this, Professor La Nauze has inferred that it was on 19 February 1860 that, after one or more false starts, Jevons felt himself to have arrived at the conception of the marginal utility theory.[5]

As already noted, Jevons had adopted the 'subjective', hedonist approach in Australia. It can scarcely be a coincidence that, on his return to University College, he 'started right away in differential calculus' with De Morgan, and that soon afterwards he used the calculus as the basis of his mathematical theory of Economy – 'to treat Economy

---

[1] See letter of 25 July 1860 to Herbert Jevons, Vol. II, Letter 145.

[2] See Vol. II, Letter 145.

[3] Unpublished letter of 30 October 1860.

[4] See, for example, his letters of 28 November 1860 to Herbert and of 3 December 1861 to Tom, Vol. II, Letters 147 and 155.

[5] J. A. La Nauze, 'The Conception of Jevons's Utility Theory', *Economica* (November 1953).

as a Calculus of Pleasure and Pain – as he later wrote in the Preface to the *Theory of Political Economy*.[1]

The first entry which Jevons made (on 8 December 1861) in his journal after his return to London shows not only his sense of achievement in 'political economy and the social sciences', but also the way in which his mind was ranging over philosophical problems and moving towards the ideas about the 'likeness of things' which he was later to develop in his logic. Yet the entry also shows another field of work in which he had made great progress during 1860–1. This was the field of historical statistics or the collation of time series.

Jevons had decided in Australia that if economics and the social sciences were to develop, an essential factor must be the assembly of exact basic data, suitably analysed. Theory and carefully marshalled facts were meaningless without each other. The manner of collecting, working up, interpreting and presenting large quantities of statistics he had learned in Sydney where he had also 'hit upon' his method of 'pricking off curves' on squared paper.

Although the statistical atlas which Jevons projected at this time was never published,[2] the fruitfulness of his work on the diagrams for it he was to demonstrate in a whole series of works which were to stem from it, notably his studies of short-term commercial fluctuations, cyclical fluctuations and secular changes in the price level. Moreover, as Dr Wolfe Mays has pointed out, it seems unlikely that Jevons's statistical researches in economics did not influence his views as to the important part probability played in science in general.[3]

Apart from the great labour on the diagrams and his college work, Jevons wrote a number of articles during the year 1861. Between January and August, he contributed nine articles to the *Dictionary of Chemistry*, edited by Henry Watt, F.R.S., assistant professor of chemistry at University College from 1846 to 1857 and translator of Gmelin's *Handbuch der Chimie*. His article on 'Gold Assay' has already been mentioned (p. 20 above); the others were on 'Cloud', and on the measuring instruments 'Balance', 'Barometer', 'Hydrometer', 'Hygrometer', 'Thermometer' and 'Volumenometer'. In July 1861 he published an article 'Light and Sunlight' in the *National Review*. In September 1861 he reported the meetings of the British Association at Manchester for the *Manchester Examiner*, writing seven articles. He also presented a paper at this meeting, his first to the British Association,

---

[1] Preface to the 1st ed., p. vi.

[2] Only the two coloured diagrams referred to in his letter to R. H. Hutton of 1 September 1862 (see Vol. II, Letter 164) were published by Edward Stanford. See journal entry for 8 December 1861, p. 181 below.

[3] Mays: 'Jevons's Conception of Scientific Method', *Manchester School*, xxx, 3, p. 246.

'On the Deficiency of Rain in an Elevated Rain-gauge as caused by Wind', before the Mathematics and Physics Section; the paper being read by his college friend and later colleague at Owens College, Professor R. Clifton.[1] At Manchester Jevons met again Dr Smith, of Sydney University, who read a short paper on the separation of gold from quartz. The President of the Economics and Statistics Section was the economist and statistician William Newmarch, whom Jevons was also shortly to meet.

In contrast to his intellectual pursuits, Jevons was a keen member of the Volunteer Movement, the 'home guard' formed in 1859 to meet the threat of invasion by the Emperor Napoleon III of France. He joined the Queen's Own Rifles, a Corps of the Westminster Brigade, to which two of his Roscoe cousins, Frank and Fred, also belonged. He collected information for writing a history of the volunteer movement, but did not complete it.[2] He won a prize of an Enfield rifle in a shooting competition, was promoted a sergeant and continued in the volunteers until he left London in 1863.

When his studies were finished, in June 1862, Jevons set out to earn his living. He was still dependent upon his savings and a small personal income. The ease with which he had written and published articles in the Australian press led him to aspire to be a writer, contributing articles to intellectual periodicals and newspapers. It would also seem that he had before him as an example *Richard Holt Hutton* (1826–97), nine years older than himself, who, in 1861, had left the *Economist*, of which he was joint editor with Walter Bagehot, to begin his long career as editor of the *Spectator*. Richard Hutton was the son of Joseph Hutton the Unitarian divine, contemporary and friend of William Caldwell Roscoe, Jevons's cousin, and of Walter Bagehot at University College. The Huttons were old friends of the family;[3] Richard Hutton is often mentioned in family correspondence, and became connected with the family through marriage, first to Jevons's cousin Mary Ann Roscoe[4] (sister of William Caldwell) and later to his other cousin Eliza Roscoe. Lucy was married to his brother John. Jevons had met Richard personally in July 1860. In a letter to his brother Herbert of 25 July 1860 he had written: '. . . R. Hutton is now much the same sort of literary and scientific hack as I am looking forward to being, he is sub-editor of the *Economist*, editor of the *National Review*, Examiner in

[1] See p. 41 below.

[2] See journal entry for 21 December 1862, p. 186 below; also Jevons's letter of 28 December 1862 to his brother Tom, Vol. II, Letter 168.

[3] Information kindly supplied by Professor J. H. Hutton. See note 3 to journal entry for 23 January 1853, p. 80 below.

[4] See journal entry for 23 January 1853, p. 80 below; also Thomas Jevons's letter of 28 June 1851 to Jevons, Vol. II, Letter 12.

Political Economy at the University and so on, but he has of course been a long time in reaching what he has. Of course I should expect to strike out more original ideas than he favours the world with, although he may be a good student and writer.'[1]

Jevons also decided now to make known the results of his reflections and researches over the previous years. In June 1862 he published the two statistical diagrams already mentioned above. In September he sent two papers to the British Association, the first entitled 'Notice of a General Mathematical Theory of Political Economy', and the second 'On the Study of Periodic Commercial Fluctuations, with five diagrams'. The meeting opened on 1 October, at Cambridge; both papers were read and Jevons recorded that the Secretary of the Association informed him that 'the second was approved of'.[2] Neither was printed in full, but summaries of both papers were included in the Report of the Association for 1862 (Transactions of Sections, pp. 157-8, and 158-9), the synopsis of the 'Theory of Economy' occupying the equivalent of one full page. In his journal for 31 December 1862 Jevons commented bitterly on the lack of interest with which these papers were met, and this episode in the history of economic thought is now well documented.[3]

There is a certain irony in the papers having been read at Cambridge in view of the later attitude of Alfred Marshall, in 1862 an under-graduate studying mathematics at Cambridge. Whether Marshall attended the British Association meeting or took an interest in the published proceedings is not known, but the central idea of the sub-jective value of exchange and of the co-efficient of utility is clearly set out in the printed summary. Fawcett – to whom Marshall was later an assistant in the Department of Economics – and Cairnes may have been present, for Fawcett invited Cairnes to be his guest for the meeting.[4]

Jevons's efforts as a writer were no better appreciated, and he made little progress. He felt himself to be without influence; he had changed his subject; the memory of William Roscoe had faded; connections, which, ten years earlier, might have been useful, probably were so no longer.[5] Richard Hutton endeavoured to assist him. On 14 September 1862 he told his brother Herbert: '. . . I am beginning some articles in the *Spectator* – one in this week's number. I am also finishing some very laborious statistical calculations – what, in fact, you copied out for me, the bank returns, and shall probably offer them to the *Economist*. I

---

[1] See Vol. II, Letter 145.

[2] See Vol. IV, Part III.

[3] Cf. Keynes, *Essays in Biography*, p. 284; R. D. Collison Black, 'W. S. Jevons and the Economists of his Time', *Manchester School*, xxx, 3 (September 1962) p. 205.

[4] Leslie Stephen, *Life of Henry Fawcett*; 4th ed. (1886) p. 200.

[5] See Thomas Jevons's letter of 18 March 1851 to Jevons, Vol. II, Letter 11.

may also undertake some other articles.' Of the articles which he was asked for by Richard Hutton for the *Spectator*, only one would appear to have been published, and this on a meteorological subject, since Jevons's notebook in which he recorded his publications mentions only the following: 'September 13–Clerk of the Weather Office – in *Spectator*'. His other published articles for 1862 were also on scientific subjects.[1]

The period in London after he left college was one of great unhappiness for Jevons. He had just reached the age of twenty-seven. The journal shows that disappointments in his work were made doubly bitter by a disappointment in love. The identity of the girl he fell in love with is not known. He was lonely, for since Lucy's marriage Henrietta spent most of her time away visiting friends and relations. Herbert's lack of success in making a career after his return from America and subsequent decision to emigrate again gave Jevons further cause for anxiety.

The tone of the journal changes; becomes serious, more introspective, the confidante of his disgust and discouragement. The number of entries increases. Bitterness entered into his letters as he wrote to Herbert, struggling to find a living in the Antipodes.

Our family [he wrote on 17 August 1862] enjoy some blessings, but also lie under certain curses – one of which is a certain stupid simplicity of character which continually mars their undertakings. A little wiliness, a rather thicker skin, would make us succeed far better in this world – and I really cannot believe that success in this world is always to be sacrificed. We have between us so much good-nature and inflexible honesty, that it sometimes seems as if we can none of us ever be of the least use to friend or foe. . . .[2]

A few weeks later, after the journal entry for 6 September 1862, he wrote:

. . . Our family have not half enough humbug. One part of our composition with five of humbug would make a first rate character. If I had even a small percentage of H.E.R.'s ways, I should by this time have been soaring up in the regions of fame, ease and fortune, instead of labouring away in obscurity and without a half penny of profit. . . ."

He then quotes from Shakespeare's sixty-sixth Sonnet – to which he refers again in his journal entry for 25 April 1863.[3]

Meantime, Jevons continued to take part in some college activities and struggled to cure himself of one of his weaknesses – his fear of

---

[1] 'Spectrum', *London Quarterly Review* (April 1862). 'Notice of Kirchhoff's Researches on the Spectrum', *Philosophical Magazine* (July 1862).
[2] LJ, p. 167. [3] See p. 191 below.

public speaking – by joining the College Debating Society, the most important of the rallying points for social intercourse in the student life of the college and founded in about 1843 by Bagehot, R. H. Hutton and William Caldwell Roscoe.[1] He himself revived the Literary and Scientific Society, which had existed from 1853 to 1855, and was chosen as its first president, in 1862.[2]

In December 1862 Harry Roscoe – Professor of Chemistry at Owens College, Manchester, since 1857 – had suggested that Jevons should go to Owens College as a tutor. The post was a humble one; his sister Lucy counselled him not to give up his research in London; he decided not to accept the post for the time being. He started a literary agency, being prepared to undertake research in the Libraries and Collections of the Metropolis, for 3s. an hour, but the response was slight. 'I . . . as yet have had only one job, and that not the right sort', he told Herbert on 18 January 1863, 'I am much inclined to fear it will not do. It is regarded as too dubious and irregular an occupation, as is apparent from the notes of the few who have applied to me . . .'[3]

In this same letter to Herbert, Jevons mentions for the first time his interest in the change in the value of gold, a question which had occupied economists and statisticians ever since the Californian gold discoveries of 1848. His pamphlet *A Serious Fall in the Value of Gold ascertained and its Social Effects set forth* was published on 16 April 1863, and quickly gained the approval and acceptance which the British Association papers of 1862 had failed to achieve. In this single tract Jevons had, by devising his own means of measuring price changes and sorting out the cyclical factors affecting them, solved one of the great questions of the day. His proof that there had been an important fall in the value of gold 'met with general acceptance', wrote Foxwell in his Introduction to *Investigations in Currency and Finance*[4] and '. . . . by its singular success placed its author at once in the first rank of living economists'.

Nevertheless, Jevons still had no employment. He was having second thoughts about the tutorship at Manchester. Owens College was the only English college besides University College which could employ a Nonconformist. As early as February 1863, Jevons had written to Herbert: 'There is no doubt, I think, that the professorial line is the one for me to take. I have given up all notion, for the present, of hack-writing, as it seems to me it must be destructive of any true thinking and, unless to a person with a very ready and popular style, must be an occupation full of hardship and disappointment . . .'[5] In April Jevons

[1] Bellot, op. cit., pp. 359 and 296. [2] Bellot, op. cit., p. 297.
[3] See Vol. III, Letter 169. [4] 1884 edition, p. xxviii.
[5] See letter of 19 February 1863, Vol. III, Letter 171.

visited Manchester 'to arrange or consider the tutorship affair'. He talked to Mr Greenwood, the Principal, and to some of the other professors. The prospects and his duties are described in a letter to his sister Lucy dated 20 April 1863, written from Manchester, and he ends by saying, 'You may, then, I think, conclude that I shall tomorrow agree with Mr Greenwood. about it, and the minor arrangements may then be considered as a matter of course.'[1] He was to take up his duties in October. In May he left London and spent the summer in the country getting up his subjects for the tutorship, and also working much at logic.

In December of 1862, Jevons refers more than once to the subject of logic, and from this time onwards he gave as much, if not a good deal more, time to logic than to political economy.

On 31 December Jevons records in the journal:

My atlas of monthly commercial statistics progresses satisfactorily but my logical speculations give me most confidence. I cannot disbelieve, yet I can hardly believe that in the principle of *sameness* I have found that which will reduce the whole theory of reasoning to one consistent lucid process – I can hardly confess to myself the value of such a work. . . .[2]

This principle of sameness forms the basis of his first book on logic. 'My logical system is at last clear from farther doubt', he wrote to his brother Tom on 15 May 1863.[3] A letter written the following month to Herbert shows that he had started working on his own at logic as early as 1861: '. . . . just at present', he writes, 'I am chiefly working at my logical system. It has only of late taken a definite form, but I have been more or less at work upon it for some two years. I think I shall have a paper ready in the course of a few weeks, of a very complete character. . . .'[4] By the end of August his book was finished. It was published at the end of 1863 as *Pure Logic, or the Logic of Quality apart from Quantity, with Remarks on Boole's System and the Relation of Logic and Mathematics.*[5]

A slip of paper pasted into the front of Jevons's own proof copy of this book suggests that it may have been in May 1862 that he discovered the principle of sameness. The note, dated 7 May 1862, reads: 'The original principle of this theory is that *sameness is the one great relation* which the mind deals in when constructing science.' Of the need for simplification in logic Jevons was convinced: he found the subject in as confused a

---

[1] See Vol. III, Letter 173.   [2] See p. 186 below.
[3] See Vol. III, Letter 176.
[4] See letter of 22 June 1863, Vol. III, Letter 185.
[5] Stanford, London, December 1863.

state as political economy before he set out to 're-establish the science on a sensible basis'.

In the lifetime of a generation still living [he wrote in a later work on logic[1]] the dull and ancient rule of authority has . . . been shaken, and the immediate result is a perfect chaos of diverse and original speculations. . . . Modern logic has thus become mystified by a diversity of views, and by the complication and profuseness of the formulae invented. . . . No inconsiderable part of a lifetime is indeed needed to master thoroughly the genius and tendency of all recent English writings on logic. . . .

VI

In October 1863 Jevons took up his duties at Owens College, and so began an association lasting thirteen years which was permanently to link Jevons's name with the University of Manchester.

Owens College, founded in 1851, was housed in Richard Cobden's former house in Quay Street. There was a staff, in 1863, of six professors and two language lecturers; pupils were taken from the age of fourteen, and in the 1863-4 session numbered 110 day students and 312 evening students.[2] The Principal from 1857 until 1889, Joseph Gouge Greenwood, B.A. (1821-94), was also the professor of Greek and Latin Languages and Literature, and he was already known to Jevons, since he had been on the staff of University College School, London. In addition to Harry Roscoe, the Professor of Chemistry, Jevons also knew the Professor of Natural Philosophy, Robert Bellamy Clifton (1836-1921), 'a favourite college friend' as he called him. Clifton, who was slightly younger than Jevons, had studied at University College from 1851 to 1855, was appointed professor at Owens College in 1860 at the age of twenty-five. He resigned in 1865 to become Professor of Experimental Philosophy at Oxford, to pioneer the systematic teaching of experimental physics in that university. The professor of English Language and Literature, of Comparative Grammar and of Logic and Mental and Moral Philosophy, was the Reverend J. A. Scott, who, after a long and remarkable spiritual ministry noted for the revival of 'the gift of tongues', was appointed to the chair of English Language and Literature at University College, London, in 1848; he was appointed the first Principal of Owens College in 1851, but was succeeded by Greenwood as principal in 1857, whilst keeping the professorships.

---

[1] *The Substitution of Similars* (1869) p. 6.
[2] For this and subsequent information about Owens College I am indebted to Joseph Thompson's *The Owens College: Its Foundation and Growth* (Manchester 1886).

Ill-health caused much interruption of his academic work, however, and early in 1866, he died. The Professor of History, of Political Economy and of Jurisprudence and Law, Richard Copley Christie, resigned the chair of Political Economy in 1865, and Jevons, who resigned his tutorship, took his place for one year. The Professor of Mathematics, Archibald Sandeman, M.A., resigned in 1865 and was succeeded by Professor T. Barker, M.A., Fellow of Trinity College, Cambridge, and senior wrangler, who became a friend of Jevons.

The appointment of Jevons to the staff as a tutor was an experiment. 'He was to be prepared to aid the students in any of the branches of knowledge then taught at the college'; though he was evidently to assist specially in the department of the Professor of History, Professor Christie, who had accepted the Faulkner Chair of Political Economy and Commercial Science in 1854. The post carried with it the obligation of giving tuition to backward students, the standard of the students being very low.[1]

Jevons took a house with his aunt, Mrs Henry (Maria) Roscoe,[2] at 9 Birch Grove, Rusholme, his sister Henrietta being also of the household. Harry Roscoe had married in the summer of 1863.

That Jevons realised there would be many advantages in moving to Manchester is clear from the letter he wrote to his sister Lucy on 20 April 1863,[3] but during the early years of his stay there the tone of the journal entries vacillates markedly between hope and acknowledgment of success, and anxiety and depression. He was endeavouring to establish himself both in his career and in his personal life. The entries are introspective; some are short prayers. At times of emotional strain and conflict an intimate journal may provide much solace, and so it is that Jevons wrote more frequently when he was feeling most gloomy, the entries concentrating especially during the spring of 1866 when he passed through a very severe depression. The journal alone, if not taken together with a more objective picture of his circumstances, might well be misleading, and it would seem advisable to study the background in so far as it is possible: certain of the facts we shall never know fully, but some may be mentioned.

His college work 'entailed great labour for a very inadequate reward'.[4] He took the teaching and lecturing work seriously and spent much effort on preparing written work for his students.[5] His fear of lecturing he overcame. This is the first subject he mentions in the first entry he made at Manchester, on 9 January 1864:

---

[1] T. S. Ashton, *Economic and Social Investigations in Manchester, 1833-1933* (1934), Ch. VII, 'The Work of Stanley Jevons and Others', p. 87; Thompson, *History of Owens College*, p. 254.
[2] See p. 74 below.　　　　　　　　　[3] See Vol. III, Letter 173.
[4] LJ, p. 193.　　　　　　　　　[5] *Vide* his textbooks on logic.

Though still capable of taking a very gloomy view of affairs [he begins], there is much on which I may congratulate myself. My first college term has convinced me that I can be a lecturer, a passable if not a good one. One intolerable fear and weakness, that of public speaking, is removed from my way. Moreover my pamphlet on the gold question has had a degree of success that must surely be allowed to be beyond my highest hope . . .

At the end of the first session he also looked back with satisfaction as the journal entry for 4 June 1864 shows.[1]

Jevons went to London in June 1864 to work on the project for his book on coal and remained there until the British Museum closed on 1 September, despite feeling languid and unwell in the heat, and finished the work in Lucy's home at Beaumaris until the beginning of the next College session.[2] He had worked all through the previous summer getting up his subjects for the tutorship and writing his *Pure Logic* at Beaumaris. It is scarcely surprising that his health suffered. The college work with his private work was too much for him; 'the attempt to do both by degrees injured his health, and he never wholly recovered from the effects of the strain upon it', wrote Mrs Jevons later.[3] Jevons refers to the matter in his journal for 14 December 1865, concluding with the remark, 'I may well be glad it did not destroy my powers'. The college evening classes were a particular strain – not only because of the difficult type of student, but because of the unhealthy conditions of the overcrowded gas-lit classrooms.[4] In the first session he had evening classes three times a week, in the second session twice.[5]

This theme of overstrain continues unabated through the entries of 19 November 1865 and 3 December 1865.

The book on coal was completed and handed to the publisher before the end of the year, and published in April 1865 with the title *The Coal Question: An Inquiry concerning the Progress of the Nation, and the Probable Exhaustion of the Coalmines*. It created a nationalscare about the 'progress' of Great Britain, drew Jevons's name into political affairs and into touch with Gladstone, and brought him success with successive editions. But the impact was not immediate. By November 1865 it 'had not made much way', Jevons reported to his brother Herbert.[6] On 14 December he was able to record the encouragement of a letter from Sir John

---

[1] See p. 196 below.

[2] See his letters of 12 and 16 August 1864 to Lucy, LJ, p. 201.

[3] LJ, p. 193.

[4] See Thompson, op. cit., pp. 244–9; and R. Könekamp, 'William Stanley Jevons, Some Biographical Facts', *Manchester School*, xxx, 3 (September 1962) pp. 265–6.

[5] See his letter of 16 October 1864 to Lucy, LJ, p. 202.

[6] See letter of 18 November 1865, LJ, p. 213.

Herschel[1] and in March 1866 came 'reassurance . . . nothing less than providential' in the shape of the letter from Gladstone which Jevons copied into his journal on 6 March.

Gladstone (1809–98) was Chancellor of the Exchequer (under Lord Russell), second in succession to the leadership of the Liberal Party. A few days prior to writing his letter he had become Leader of the House of Commons also (19 February).[2] He had made his reputation and greatly increased the power of the Treasury through his financial policy and rigid insistence on economy in public expenditure and reduction of the National Debt. Jevons devoted a special chapter of *The Coal Question* to the subject of 'Taxes and the National Debt', suggesting that reduction of the Debt was the only means 'towards compensating posterity for our present lavish use of cheap coal'. He praised Gladstone's efforts in this direction, adding: 'Could a minister be found strong and bold enought to carry out a permanent and large measure towards the same end he would have an almost unprecedented claim to gratitude and fame' (3rd edition, 1906, pp. 448 and 452–3).

This is the background to the entry of the 20 April, 1866 in the journal:

> What is this poor mind of mine with all its wavering hopes and fears, that its thoughts should be quoted and approved by a great philosopher in the parliament of so great a nation? Do not grant me intellectual power, O God, unless it be joined to awe of Thee and thy Truth, and to an ever present love of others. For two whole days I have hung about at Westminster . . .

The remainder of this last sentence has been cut off the page. The 'great philosopher' was John Stuart Mill (1806–73), who was Radical Member of Parliament for Westminster from 1865 to 1868. He had drawn attention to *The Coal Question* in the House of Commons on 17 April in a debate on a motion proposing the reduction of the Malt Duty, citing both the title of the book and Jevons's name. He urged, for the sake of posterity, the reduction of the National Debt rather than the further reduction of taxation; his arguments being based upon Jevons's conclusions as to the probable exhaustion of the coalmines and relative decline of the nation. The speech impressed the House; Gladstone promised to deal with the question in his forthcoming Budget speech.[3]

The Times reproduced Mill's speech next day, commenting upon it in the first leader. The following day 19 April, the day before the journal

---

[1] See journal entry for 14 December 1865, p. 200 below.

[2] Queen Victoria had written to congratulate him on the way he had begun his task. It will be noted that Gladstone's letter was written from Windsor Castle. See journal entry for 5 March 1866, p. 203 below.

[3] Hansard CLXXXII, 1866, 17 April, Commons.

entry, *The Times* carried a long leading article dealing exclusively with the subject of coal exhaustion and National Debt reduction, supporting Mill's lurid picture of the future.

Presumably Jevons 'hung about Westminster' in case his advice were needed, but there is no information about this.

By 14 May, Jevons was writing 'the last week or two I have had enough of newspaper fame. I know it is no slight thing to be quoted in the Budget of a Minister when he announces a change in the policy of the country he leads. But', he adds, 'what poor mortals we are! I feel as if I would readily give it all for a few kind words from a loving girl . . .' Gladstone had introduced his Budget on 3 May, interrupting the debates on his bill for Electoral Reform. Half his speech was concerned with the National Debt. The 'change of policy' refers to Gladstone's agreement with J. S. Mill's view that greater attention should be paid to reducing the Debt as opposed to taxation. Jevons's arguments on exhaustion of coal supplies were quoted in support. He proposed reducing the debt by instalments over the next thirty years by a scheme for converting perpetual annuities into terminal annuities.[1]

The Times, in leaders on the 4, 5 and 7 May, was critical, finding the effects of the scheme to be so small as to cause doubt as to whether Gladstone really felt the alarm which he voiced over the future of coal supplies.

Nevertheless, as Jevons wrote to his brother Herbert on 13 May 1866, he had gained his end 'of getting the subject investigated'[2] and the entry in his journal for 23 May records his meeting with Gladstone, 'a great minister in the height of his power'. Gladstone introduced his Terminal Annuities Bill on 24 May 1866, and it may be presumed that he wished to see Jevons before the debate.

For the 1865–6 session at Owens College, Jevons was appointed lecturer in Political Economy for both day and evening classes, R. C. Christie having resigned his Chair of Political Economy in May 1865. Jevons, who at this time held a part-time position as Professor of Logic, Moral Philosophy and Political Economy at Queen's College, Liverpool, was also appointed to act as substitute lecturer in logic at Owens in place of Professor Scott, who was given leave of absence for 1865–6. Jevons's financial position was thus improved and he was able to resign his tutorship.

None the less, Jevons's journal shows how much he still suffered from the feeling of not being appreciated and from his relative poverty. Not only did his sisters need his financial help: Henrietta was unmarried; Lucy's position was chronically on the verge of disaster because of the constant financial difficulties of John Hutton in his quarry business at

---

[1] Hansard, CLXXXIII, 1866, pp. 366 *et seq.*   [2] See Vol. III, Letter 255.

Penmaenmawr. (Jevons had to devote much time to helping John Hutton.) Marriage for Jevons himself seemed out of the question, for he was unable to afford it.

From the very first entry at Manchester it is clear how much marriage occupied his thoughts. It was not only a matter of money but of his work – how to fit this in with marriage. It is not possible to say whether any special person was giving Jevons 'cause to debate' marriage at this time. On 4 June, however, he deals with the problem of his lack of sociability, recalling his letters upon the same subject written from Australia. But he now determined to overcome his shyness. At a party he arranged he mentions a Miss Boyce as being present. This was Miss Alice Boyce of Tiverton (1837–1922) a first cousin of Jevons's future wife, Harriet Taylor. It is not known how long Jevons had known her. There are, however, in existence small day-to-day diaries kept by Jevons during the four months March to June 1864, and in these appear four entries relating to Miss Boyce. It would therefore seem possible that Jevons was interested in her at this time.[1]

It is known that Jevons had proposed marriage in one case. At this period he spent his holidays with Lucy's family as far as possible. He fell in love with the eldest of John Hutton's daughters by his first marriage, Susan Katherine Hutton. Although she was only fifteen or so at the time, Jevons proposed marriage to her as she was advanced for her age. However, the girl felt too young to be able to accept. This must have happened probably around Christmas of 1865.

The crisis which Jevons passed through in the spring of 1866 coincided with his success with *The Coal Question*, and its occasion was the decision in March 1866 to found a new chair of logic and mental and moral philosophy at Owens College for which he applied, but about the outcome of which he had the deepest uncertainty. Jevons was desperately anxious to get the professorship and, as Mrs Jevons has written:

> There was never much reason to doubt that he would obtain the appointment; not only had the whole course of his studies prepared him for it, but he had also been undertaking the duties of the professorship for some time . . .[2] He was still feeling the effects of overwork and this, no doubt, made him less cheerful than usual, and more inclined to exaggerate the chances against his appointment than he would otherwise have been . . .[3]

The disappointment and sense of failure were so intense, however, that one is led to wonder whether Jevons had not expected some hint or reassurance that the public advertisement of the professorship would be

---

[1] See journal entry for 4 June 1864, p. 197 below. In April 1867 she married Mr G. Peter Allen of the *Manchester Guardian*. [2] LJ, pp. 221–2. [3] Ibid., p. 221.

a formality. A hint had been given to him earlier, as he mentioned in a letter dated 20 April 1863 to his sister, Lucy, written just after his return from a visit to Manchester to discuss with the principal of the college, Mr Greenwood, whether he would accept the tutorship. 'Even Mr. Greenwood', he wrote, 'hinted that I might look fairly forward to a professorship in Owens College.'[1]

After Jevons became professor his work was 'more easy, familiar and congenial', and towards the end of 1866 he able to save money. By May 1867 Jevons was contemplating marriage and early in October 1867 he became engaged to Harriet Ann Taylor, the third daughter of John Edward Taylor, the founder and proprietor of the *Manchester Guardian* (*Guardian*) newspaper. John Edward Taylor (1791–1844) had two sons and one daughter by his first marriage,[2] to a Miss Scott, and three daughters by his second marriage, to a Miss Boyce. Harriet Taylor was the second of the three daughters of the second marriage. Her half-brother, John Edward Taylor the younger, who succeeded his father as proprietor of the *Manchester Guardian*, and converted the paper into a daily in 1855, was also a man with a great interest in education and in 1864 he became a Trustee of Owens College, and later a Life Governor.[3]

Jevons had first met his future wife at the wedding of his cousin Frederick Jevons to Harriet Taylor's sister, Sarah (the eldest of the daughters of the second marriage) in 1865.[4] On hearing of his engagement, his sister Lucy wrote to Harriet Taylor about her brother, 'a wife's love will be . . . a love on which his *whole heart* will rest . . . I think you will have one on whom your whole heart may also rest and so make your married life what it should be . . .'[5] The marriage took place on 19 December 1867, when Jevons was thirty-two and his wife twenty-nine.

After his marriage Jevons and his wife lived at No. 36 Parsonage Road, in the Withington district of Manchester. The house is still standing, though owing to renumbering of the houses in the road the number of the house is now No. 33.[6]

[1] See Vol. III, Letter 173.

[2] The children of the first marriage were: Sophia, who married Peter Allen, Manager of the *Manchester Guardian*; Russell, who, after a brilliant start on the paper after the death of his father, died in 1849; and John Edward, born in 1830, who on the death of his brother became sole inheritor of the *Manchester Guardian*.

[3] John Edward Taylor, the younger, was also from 1854 a Trustee of Manchester College, and founder, with Edward Brotherton and others in 1863, of the Manchester Educational Aid Society. On his death he left a legacy of £20,000 to Owens College, and a valuable collection of art treasures, including Turner watercolours, to the Whitworth Art Gallery at Manchester.

[4] The youngest sister, Mary Anne, was later on also to marry a Jevons, William, the brother of Frederick Jevons. [5] Unpublished letter of 6 October 1867.

[6] The information about the renumbering has kindly been supplied by Mr W. H. Shercliff, Local History Librarian of the Manchester Public Libraries.

VII

Of Jevons's life after the journal ends, with his marriage, it is only necessary here to give a very brief summary. He lived to see his work recognised and to achieve public eminence and success, but his life was tragically cut short at the age of forty-six. He was drowned when bathing near Hastings on 13 August 1882, leaving his wife with three young children, one son and two daughters. His *Theory of Political Economy* had been published in 1871 – 'The first modern book on economics, it has proved singularly attractive to all bright minds newly attacking the subject; simple, lucid, unfaltering, chiselled in stone where Marshall knits in wool.'[1] For some years after its publication this book was scarcely noticed in England, though it almost at once aroused the interest of numerous leading continental economists. Jevons then turned again to logical and philosophical subjects, and in 1874 published *The Principles of Science – a Treatise on Logic and Scientific Method –* a book which still has its place and has only recently been reprinted.

In 1875 Jevons took his studies of commercial fluctuations a stage further by exploring their relationship to the cycles of sunspots in three papers written between 1875 and 1879. At the same time he published a series of articles strongly attacking the logic and philosophy of John Stuart Mill, from whose dominance in the examination system he had suffered so long and so intensely.[2] These articles show that Jevons had achieved a masterly command of writing. He had also solved the probem of writing simply about difficult subjects. It had always been his belief that logic and economics were subjects, which could, in suitable form, be understood by the general public. In his lifetime he succeeded in putting the study of logic on to a new and comprehensible basis. His clear textbooks on logic and political economy were an immense success, and as Keynes has remarked, 'for a period of half a century practically all elementary students both of Logic and of Political Economy in Great Britain and also in India and the Dominions were brought up on Jevons'.[3] The books were also translated into six or seven foreign languages and had large sales in America. Towards the end of his life

---

[1] Keynes in *Essays in Biography* p. 284.

[2] The series of four articles under the title of 'John Stuart Mill's Philosophy Tested', appeared in the *Contemporary Review* between December 1877 and November 1879, and are reprinted in *Pure Logic and other Minor Works*, ed. by Robert Adamson, M.A., LL.D., and Harriet A. Jevons (Macmillan, 1890).

[3] *Essays in Biography*, p. 299. Keynes gives the sales of Jevons's elementary textbooks up to 1935 (apart from American and foreign language editions) as follows:

Elementary Logic	130,000 pub.	1870
Primer of Logic	148,000 ,,	1876
Primer of Political Economy	98,000 ,,	1878
Money and the Mechanism of Exchange	20,000 ,,	1875

Jevons could write with authority on the various social subjects which were being debated, and in some of the lighter subjects, such as the article on 'The Use and Abuse of Museums' – reprinted in the volume *Methods of Social Reform and other Papers* (1883) – we see flashes of his strong sense of humour. He gave much thought to the role of the government in economic and social affairs, to the working of the various state-run services, and to the attitude which the government should take towards organised labour – the latter being the subject of his last completed book, *The State in Relation to Labour* (1882).

In 1876 Jevons resigned from Owens College, Manchester, where he had become a loved and valued figure not only because of his academic work and public reputation, but because of his character and of his wise counsels concerning the government and future planning of the College, which was rapidly growing in importance. He became Professor of Political Economy at University College, London. His new professorship involved very little lecturing so that Jevons had more time for his own work. In 1881, however, he resigned this professorship in order to devote himself entirely to literary work, and especially to the writing of a large treatise on Economics 'which will go over the whole field of the subject'.[1]

Jevons disliked lecturing. In the early days at Manchester the difficulties of teaching often depressed him, as they sometimes depress all who take teaching seriously. In later life, when so much literary work was pressing upon him and his health was not so good, he found lecturing and teaching a very great strain and interruption of his thoughts. It would be an error to think, however, that Jevons was not a good teacher. The impression he made on some of his students was profound and lifelong.[2]

His colleague at Owens College, Professor A. W. Ward, has said of Jevons:

Always master of his subject, he was always at the same time in command of his audience – a very different thing. His extraordinary

[1] See letter of 20 July 1881 to Léon Walras, Vol.III, Letter 692.

[2] In 1934, Jevons's daughter, Miss H. W. Jevons, met by accident the Reverend Harold Rylett of Belfast, who had been one of Jevons's students at Manchester. The following is a quotation from a letter which he wrote to Miss Jevons after this meeting, at the age of eighty-four: 'Your dear father was in the truest sense a great friend to me as he was to all the young men who had the great privilege of being taught by him. For he was a real teacher – a really Great Teacher. He was of course a profound student and thinker, a lucid writer, but to me it has always seemed that he was greatest as a teacher. There was such a wonderful personal charm about him that what he said to his students in his talks to them not only captured their attention but aroused their intelligence and cultivated their mentality. I know that I have been all my life since I was a student of his very deeply indebted to him, and the memory of him is ever vivid and precious to me . . .' Letter dated 10 September 1934, (unpublished)

clearness of exposition, and his fertility in illustration, often derived from prolonged periods of patient research, would have sufficed to make him an admirable teacher; but, since he likewise in a pre-eminent degree attached his students to himself he brought to his lecturing table, and his students took away with them from their benches, more than can be put into manuscripts and notebooks.[1]

Professor Sully, Professor of Chemistry at University College and one of Jevons's Hampstead friends, has also given a picture of the lesser-known side of Jevons's character, in the course of a personal tribute after his death.

A thoroughly retiring and homely man, he cared nothing for the noisy distractions of so-called 'society', but in his own house among his chosen friends he revealed a truly sociable and convivial nature. His conversation, ranging over a wide variety of topics – from factory legislation to Wagner's music – touched everything with sagacious insight and a quiet playful humour. His hearty and genial laugh, coming as a surprise after his slow and impressive speech, will not soon be forgotten by his friends.[2]

Jevons's later letters to his wife also show him moving easily and with apparent pleasure in the meetings, soirées and dinners which his membership of various learned bodies caused him to attend. H. S. Foxwell, a close friend of Jevons during his time in London, has written the following account of the direction which Jevons's work was taking before he died.

For some years, Mr Jevons had been concentrating himself with ever-increasing interest and intensity upon his economic studies. His book on the *State in Relation to Labour* was one indication of the new lines of inquiry on which he was entering, and was full of promise of the important service his eminently wise and healthy judgement might have rendered in the treatment of the difficult social problems which now press for solution. Another direction taken by his many-sided activity was historical research and bibliography. These various studies, however, were but subordinate to one principal enterprise, towards which his later work and thoughts had been steadily converging, and for which both the time and the man certainly seemed ripe. He had planned and partly written a great *Treatise on Economics*, which was, as he hoped, to be *the* achievement of his life, and in which he would have worked up the immense store

[1] Obituary notice in the *Manchester Guardian*.
[2] *The Pall Mall Gazette*, 17 August 1882; letter to the Editor, p. 2.

of classified materials which he had been accumulating for more than twenty years. He had unrivalled qualifications for the task he had set himself.[1]

Jevons had just made a fresh start on this book a few months before his death, for it was on 30 March 1882 that he wrote to his brother Tom '. . . I am now going to make a new start with the large book on Political Economy . . .'[2]

Among other work which Jevons left unfinished were the notes for a book on Mill's philosophy, and for a book on the relation between science and religion.

Jevons, with his belief in progress and in several other respects, was a 'typical' Victorian. His adult life spanned the golden age of Victorianism – that era of peace, material progress and scientific advance ushered in by the Great Exhibition of the Works of Industry of All Nations in 1851 – which Jevons, visiting it as a boy, called that 'place of all places,'[3] with the sense of wonder and pride in the greatness of Britain which all Englishmen then felt.

'Not merely as an economist but also as logician, philosopher, re- former, he stands out as one of the most remarkable men of the age in which he lived', Lord Robbins has written, 'he is one of the great Englishmen of the nineteenth century.'[4] Yet it is quite certain that he would have been equally in place in the twentieth century. 'If Jevons were alive today', wrote W. Mays and D. P. Henry in 1953, 'it is unlikely that he would be surprised by modern digital computers and the arithmetical marvels which they perform.'[5] On 11 July 1855, from Sydney, he wrote to Harry Roscoe:

> . . . Through the whole of science there is nothing I should like to follow up more, and spend my whole life in than the *atomic theory* and theoretical chemistry, but my road seems to lie another way. Lately however a sublime idea (as I think it) occurred to me for the founda- tion of an atomic system, which would altogether beat Williamson's ideas; it is to suppose that the ultimate atoms of bodies (small spheres perfectly elastic and *similar* whatever element they form) are

---

[1] *Investigations in Currency and Finance*, edited by H. S. Foxwell, 1884; p. xx. Frag- ments of Jevons's notes for this book were published in 1905 under the title of *Principles of Economics*, with a preface by H. Higgs. It is most doubtful, however, whether these frag- ments can convey any idea of the shape which the work would ultimately have taken in view of Jevons's fresh start so soon before his death and the other work he was engaged upon in those months.

[2] See Vol. III, Letter 723.

[3] See letter of 5 July 1851 to his father, LJ, p. 10.

[4] Robbins, 'The Place of Jevons in the History of Economic Thought', p. 1.

[5] 'Jevons & Logic', p. 1.

subject only to the force of *gravitation* which is thus made quite universal, etc.[1]

Jevons 'intended to show the perfect compatibility of the teachings of modern science with religion'.[2] Both the *Principles of Science* and the *Letters and Journal* end with the problem of God. Jevons believed there was a Creator, but he did not believe in the inspiration and authority of the Bible.[3] Writing in his Journal in December 1862, he says: 'Now when I look upon Christianity from a very exterior point of view – it is amusing to look back on times when I reverenced christy. like most others . . . etc.'[4]

It would appear that to Jevons God was manifest in the order of Creation and in some kind of evolutionary power. As early as 6 January 1857, when twenty-one, he wrote in his diary '. . . I am sure we are placed in this world to be more or less happy', and later in life he accepted 'without reluctance' Herbert Spencer's philosophy in the *Principles of Evolution*. 'According to Spencer, as I . . . interpret his theory, we are the latest manifestation of an all-pervading tendency towards the good – the happy. Creation is not yet concluded, and there is not one of us who may not become conscious in his heart that he is no Automaton, no mere lump of protoplasm, but the creature of the Creator.'[5]

Jevons never altered his Unitarian view in order to accept the orthodox faith that the ultimate revelation of God, that 'infallible criterion', is to be found only in the full Trinitarian doctrine of the Deity and Sacrifice of Christ. 'I examine Mind and Matter to found my conception of God',[6] he wrote as a young man. The same position is evident in the 'Few brief notes . . . showing the religious opinions of his mature life', where it is his own idea of piety which concerns him, not the biblical teaching, which he directly contradicts. 'It borders on impiety' to petition in prayer, he concludes; 'It is an impeachment of His goodness and Wisdom. It is as much as to say that God has ordered things in one way and we think they should be otherwise.'[7] Thus at the close of the *Letters and Journal* he was still speculating as to the nature of God and religion.

[1] See Vol. II, Letter 66.

[2] In his projected 'The Tenth Bridgewater Treatise'; LJ, p. 451.

[3] and [4] See Journal for 28 January 1857, p. 155 below. Cf. the final section of the *Theory of Political Economy*: 'The Noxious Influence of Authority', p. 276. '. . . in Science and philosophy nothing must be held sacred. Truth indeed is sacred; but, as Pilate said, "What is truth?" Show us the undoubted and infallible criterion of absolute truth, and we will hold it as a sacred and inviolable thing. But in the absence of that infallible criterion, we have all an equal right to grope in search of it, and no body and no school nor clique must be allowed to set up a standard of orthodoxy which shall bar the freedom of scientific inquiry.'

[5] Essay on *Utilitarianism* in *Pure Logic and Other Minor Works*, ed. by R. Adamson and H. A. Jevons (1890), p. 294.   [6] Journal, 28 January 1857, p. 155.   [7] LJ, p. 452.

THE JOURNAL OF
WILLIAM STANLEY JEVONS

This book I believe to have been a Law Common Place Book belonging to my Uncle Henry Roscoe.[1]

23 August 1852

I am again beginning a journal or diary for the second or third time, I suppose, but on a different plan & with perhaps rather a different object than before. My plan is, to write down at the end of every few days, the number of days being regulated by the number of occurences worth mentioning, a description of the manner in which I have been engaged & the projects that I am contemplating, beginning or finishing. It will thus afford a measure of my industry, & will prevent me beginning a number of designs only to be left & forgotten. I shall then mention any events domestic, political, scientific or respecting college,[2] that have occured, & this journal will thus become a record of many things that will be worth remembering & reading many years hence. But perhaps the most useful & important part of my entries will be my thoughts on any subject[,] as my own character & prospects, or on religion, for to be able [to][3] write these down, they must be definite and I may also say *sensible*, though[4] . . . pleasure in them. This journal will, I hope, extend long beyond these holydays for which however they are specially intended & will help to give me the habit of regularity. So much writing as I shall have in it, cannot but improve me in composition.

I have written a long enough introduction & will now begin the journal itself with a very short account of the last few months.

The College lectures ended on the 15th of June & the examinations[5] in

---

[1] The youngest brother of Jevons's mother. See p. 61 below.
[2] University College, London.
[3] This word is omitted in the text.
[4] The bottom part of this first page – about five or six lines – has been cut off here.
[5] The College held sessional examinations in which Certificates of Proficiency were awarded by the Professors. These certificates and prizes were distributed at the Annual Distribution of Prizes and Certificates of Honour.

Mathematics, Greek & Latin, for the Chemistry ended at Easter,[1] were finished on the next Monday. The Mathematical Exam. was 6 hours long, while the chemistry one had been 8, but nevertheless the mathematics tired me far more & before the end I got quite stupid, to which I must partly attribute my low place. Soon after was the Distribution, by the Earl of Carlisle.[2] Robarts got 1st in Higher Junior Mathematics & Junior Greek, Manning got 1st in Junior Latin & 2nd in Greek; Edmunds got Natural Philosophy, Hayward second in Mathematical Natural Philosophy. My certificates were, 4th in Latin, 5th in Greek, & 6th with Colvill in Mathems.[3]

The Matriculation[4] was to begin on the 6th of July, & till then of course I worked hard; I had got up all the Latin & Greek for the college exams. & so attended chiefly to English History & Grammar, Chemistry & Botany.[5] It was only a few months before that I had begun to think of going up in Botany & considering that I did not know any more than I had learned from reading a few small, 'Introductions' &c, & Henslowe's Botany,[6] with my botanizing at West Kirby[7] for 6 weeks, it was rather adventurous. But I went over the orders again & learnt Lindleys Elements[8] & wrote home for Henslowe's to read again. In the chemistry I learnt the Inorganic exclusively, as that only is required in the Pass.

[1] Chemistry was taken mainly by medical students and classes were arranged to fit in with those of the Medical Department, which ran from October to May. The end of session chemistry examinations were held at Easter. See Bellot, *University College, London, 1826–1926*, pp. 124–5; also entry for 12 October 1852, p. 64 below. Jevons gained a Silver Medal in these examinations. See entry for 24 September 1852, p. 61 below, also letter of 3 May 1852 to Jevons from his father, Vol. II, Letter 16.

[2] George William Frederick Howard, seventh Earl (1802–64); at this time he held, among other posts, those of Chancellor of the Duchy of Lancaster (1850–2) and President of the Royal Society of Literature (1851–6). He attended the opening ceremony at Queen's College, Liverpool, 5 November 1857. (For Jevons's Professorships there, see p. 198 below.)

[3] Classmates of Jevons, aged between fifteen and eighteen at this date. Only Frederick B. Edmonds and W. H. Colvill remained friends of Jevons in later life: see letters of Jevons to Edmonds, 26 January 1855, and Edmonds to Jevons, 22 December 1879, and 20 January, 13 and 22 June 1880, Vol. II, Letter 52, and Vol. III, Letters 635, 640, 649, 652.

[4] The University examination of matriculation was normally taken at the end of the first year at College, rather than on entry. Since examinations bulked so large in college life, so does the record of them in Jevons's journal.

[5] Students were free to choose their own course of study; Jevons had decided to try for honours in chemistry and botany.

[6] Henslow, *Principles of Descriptive and Physiological Botany*, Lardner's Cabinet Cyclopaedia (1836). John Stevens Henslow (1796–1861) was Professor of Botany in the University of Cambridge.

[7] A seaside town on the northern side of the Dee Estuary where the Jevons family often spent their holidays; now a dormitory of Liverpool.

[8] Lindley, *Elements of Botany* (1841). John Lindley (1799–1865) was Professor of Botany at University College, London, 1828–60. See entries for 24 September and 23 October 1852, pp. 61 and 66 below.

Sam Archer[1] now came to stop with us to pass the Matric. The examinations were from 10 to 1 & from 3 to 6 on the 6th, 7th, 8th & 9th of July. The first exam. in Mathematics I did only *pretty* well, & the History in the afternoon decidedly badly, so much so as to put me into rather bad spirits but all the rest were very easy & the Geometry & Grammar were the most pleasant of all. I had to try most of course at the chemistry on the second afternoon & was satisfied with what I did. The Natural Philosophy on the third afternoon I missed. In the two hours between, Sam & I went to a coffee house where we looked over a book or learned off our notes for the afternoon but the heat, everywhere indeed was most tremendous. On the Saturday after the exams. were finished Sam & I set off for an excursion to Epping Forest. We went by railway to Tottenham from which we walked, very slowly, to the River Lea. There we had a two-hours row on the canal which was rather a new thing to me. We found the walk to the forest rather longer than we expected & did not reach it till nearly seven, though we had set off at ten in the morning. The forest was a splendid place, & quite wild though the trees are very small, but we could not stay long from the lateness. We then walked to Chigwell which I wanted to see very much as it is part of the scene in Barnaby Rudge, my favourite novel, but we missed seeing the Maypole,[2] which I believe really exists & is called Queen Elizabeth's Lodge. We got to Chigwell at 8 o'clock (!) & considering we were 10 or 11 miles from home, without any prospect of getting an omnibus, & very much tired already, we were rather alarmed, but set off at once determined to walk it. We reached Bow after 10 but fortunately found an omnibus just starting by which we got to St Pauls from which we walked home, considerably tired. The country was very beautiful & in the naturalising way, I found several new flowers and a glow worm for the first time. On the Monday[3] I set to work seriously for the honours, having few doubts of passing in one of the divisions.[4] I worked chiefly at home for about 7 or 8 hours a day & finished nearly all I intended by the[5] 23rd the day of the examination. In the chemistry I really believed I should do very badly & in the examination I actually felt quite lazy & careless! but the Botany examination in the afternoon of the same day was

---

[1] Samuel Archer (d. 1902), a friend of Jevons (son of Francis Archer, a Liverpool surgeon and botanist, see entry for 16 January 1853, p. 79 below). He saw active service overseas, retired with the rank of Colonel in 1895 and died in Italy. In the course of his service in the Tropics, he gathered specimens for the natural history collections of his father. (The editor is indebted to the City Librarian, Liverpool, for this information.)

[2] Jevons's special affection for this novel is understandable, since he may have seen in the simple and lovable Barnaby reflections of his own brother, Roscoe. Several scenes in the book are set in an ancient hostelry, 'the Maypole', at Chigwell. [3] 12 July.

[4] The honours examinations were held after the result of the matriculation was known. Jevons learned on the following Monday, 19 July, that he had passed in the first division (unpublished letter of 18 July 1852 to Henrietta). [5] 'to' in the text.

far more interesting. The definitions I did *pretty* well & the descriptions of the four specimens which Henslowe, the examiner & [a][1] very kind, pleasant-looking gentleman, gave us & which were, the Solanum Dulcamara,[2] the Antirrhinum Majus,[3] the Iberia,[4] & the [*blank space*]. I wrote concisely & therefore I suppose well, though I made several mistakes. The question on the chemical products of 'assimilation' I did easily of course as I had learned it in the chemistry. Sam went in for Zoology with four others, while I had only one other named Turner,[5] who like me, went in for chemistry.

I got home with a bad head ache but managed to get to the 8¾ mail train, by which I got to Liverpool at 4 in the morning & after spending the day at Chatham St.[6] I went over to West Kirby with Papa in the afternoon.

I found them all quite well at home & apparently enjoying the country as much as possible for they were all, especially Henny[7] quite brown. They had rather too many visitors with them however to please me, namely Mary Catherine[8] & some Thornelys,[9] but I set to to enjoy myself as much as possible in one week for I found that they were going to stop only one week more & not ten or fourteen days. I had expected to be able to press nearly ten plants a day, having brought proper paper with me but I believe I did not do more than one a day fit to keep, which is not surprizing when I did not know how to set about it. The country was very pleasant certainly, & the weather pretty fine except on the Monday & I enjoyed 3 or 4 bathes with Tommy[10] very much in spite of the bad shore. One day we went an expedition to Hilbre Island,[11] where Tommy, Henny & myself spent most of the time *catching crabs* but I also got six new kinds of sea-weeds & several plants including the fern Asplenium Marinum.[12] The rest of the time I spent pleasantly, sometimes lazily, in walking about the hill, sand-hills, &c, but I was not in the best spirits.

On again reaching Chatham Street, the next Saturday, I felt completely at a loss, what to do first of the many things I intended to do. I began however on Monday by cleaning[13] out my workbench, which with

---

[1] Omitted in the text.   [2] Bittersweet, or Nightshade.
[3] Great Snapdragon.   [4] Possibly a reference to Iberis (Candytuft).
[5] Frederick H. Turner, a middle-aged student, who attended classes in practical chemistry in the Medical Faculty in the session 1851–2. One-year students were not uncommon in this Faculty. Bellot, op. cit., p. 146.   [6] The Jevons family home in Liverpool.
[7] Jevons's younger sister, Henrietta, aged thirteen at this time.
[8] Mary Catherine Jevons (1827–1908), a first cousin, eldest daughter of Timothy Jevons.
[9] A large and well-known Liverpool family, members of which intermarried with both the Jevons's and the Roscoes. Both Henry Jevons and George Jevons, who carried on the family business after the bankruptcy of 1848, married Thornelys.
[10] Jevons's youngest brother, then aged eleven.   [11] At the mouth of the Dee Estuary.
[12] Sea Spleenwort.   [13] 'clearing' has been substituted here in LJ, p. 18.

the bottles, cupboard, &c I found in a very dirty state. It was a long & unpleasant job, but I made it very nice in a little time, putting all the glass apparatus in a box by themselves, so as to be out of the way. The only thing I did in chemistry was to put some salts to crystallize on the kitchen chimney-piece, but they have not succeeded at all, & to make some acetic acid from old sour beer. This I first tried to do by letting it run drop by drop over cinders in a tall glass jar, in imitation of the process on the continent but it did not succeed at all, as I might have expected; I then kept it warm for two or three days at about 88° in a flat dish over the gas, which turned it very acid, so as to effervesce with $NaO.Co_2$,[1] with which I neutralized it, & at the same time concentrated it into a thick black syrupy liquid, which after straining & further concentrating I shall purify & decompose with SO_3[2] to obtain pure acetic acid. I do not see why such a process as this performed with sour beer! should not teach me as much as if I went & spent pounds in making a pure acid by a similar process from some expensive substance, though I should be laughed at by Harry[3] for it, I at last began my herbarium by buying 3 quires of foolscap paper to put the specimens on, cheating myself as usual by buying it at 1s a quire when much cheaper paper would have done equally well, I soon after bought 6 feet of $\frac{1}{2}$ inch-board, 14 inches wide to make the shelves, in which & other things I was chiefly occupied till within the last few days.

Thursday, 26 August

My chief, almost exclusive occupation lately has been Botany. The herbarium is now nearly finished for I have put shelves in one compartment, as much as I am going to do these holidays, made the covers & labels for all the orders I require now, & mounted most of the specimens I have yet got, in number between 50 & 60. I have also pressed a good many, chiefly out of the Parliament Fields, where there are yet enough to last me some time. I got several also by an expedition to Upton & Moreton[4] with Sam Archer, & I got several garden plants too. I have not altogether omitted the less agreable[5] part of Botany, the learning of the orders.

[1] Probably sodium carbonate (washing soda).

[2] Sulphur trioxide, which would not have been available to Jevons: he is almost certainly referring to sulphuric acid, which would have had the same effect in this experiment.

[3] His cousin, Henry (later Sir Henry) Enfield Roscoe (1833–1915), at whose home Jevons was living in London. Harry Roscoe had entered University College in 1848 and was at this time private assistant to A. W. Williamson, then Professor of Practical Chemistry. See p. 69 below.

[4] Two villages in the Wirral, between West Kirby and Birkenhead, now part of the latter.

[5] Jevons habitually spelled 'agreeable' and 'disagreeable' with one 'e'.

I did not mention I believe last time that on Saturday night I heard for the first time that I had got the prize in Botany at the Matriculation. Turner is the name of the other one who went with me & he has passed too & also has got the prize in chemistry, in which I am second with another person. Robarts is fourth in both chemistry & classics.

I have often thought much about what is called cleverness & genius. The oftener an[1] action is repeated, the more easy is it to perform it again, & the more perfectly will it be performed. It is by long repetition that workmen or jugglers acquire such perfection, & the only credit given to them, is for their diligence. But I think that it is exactly the same case with students, for if they have been accustomed for a long time to study diligently, but particularly, *in a good way*, they get *practised or clever* in acquiring knowledge while those who have been lazy or have studied in a careless manner cannot expect to become expert in it. I know that at least since I went to Mr Beckwiths[2] I have worked pretty hard, & I am very sure that if I had not I should never have got the prizes I have. By this time, perhaps, I have become more practised in acquiring knowledge than some others who have not attended to study, & this it is that constitutes all the cleverness I may have.

Friday, 3 September

It is some time since I wrote last, but not because I have had nothing to say. I have several times lately been in rather low spirits from some cause & last Sunday in chapel I wrote a long account of it, on an old envelope, as I said, 'to ascertain to the cause',[3] instead of listening to a dull sermon from Mr C. Rolberd[4] who is to preach for some weeks instead of Mr Thom,[5] but on second thoughts, while I am

---

[1] 'a' in the text.

[2] The private school in Liverpool which Jevons attended from 1847 to 1850.

[3] Jevons seems to have had in mind the example of his father. Cf. the following written in a letter to Jevons by his father, dated 7 July 1849, '. . . When I have been sometimes in a low mood I have turned my thoughts to find out what has caused it, and on tracing my feelings from one cause to another I have almost invariably found the lowness of spirits to have no good cause and then immediately succeeds a cheerful self-satisfied temper and feeling . . .' (see Vol. II, Letter 1).

[4] The preacher referred to would seem likely to have been Charles William Robberds, minister of Lord Street Chapel, Oldham, from 1853–69, eldest son of Rev. John Gooch Robberds (1789–1854).

[5] The Rev. John Hamilton Thom (1808–88), the well-known Unitarian preacher, minister of Renshaw Street Chapel, Liverpool, 1831–54 and 1857–66. He was a man of unusual spiritual authority whose influence extended far beyond his congregation through his printed sermons. Both the Jevons and Roscoe families attended the Unitarian chapel in Renshaw Street (now the site of the Central Hall) for many years and William Roscoe was buried there, the funeral sermon being preached by Mr Thom. See A. M. Holt, *Walking Together: A Study in Liverpool Nonconformity 1688–1938* (1938).

now 'up' again, I will not write it out in this book again. It is little consequence I think & appears to go away by being a little cheerful or by going out somewhere. I think I shall be glad also when all visitors are gone, & I can see more of Lucy[1] & Papa.

I have not however been at all inactive as will be seen. Last Saturday, Lucy agreed to go with me to the South Shore as a walk; we went by the omnibus to the Iron Church[2] & then walked as Lucy wished to the shore below the Dingle.[3] There she made two small sketches, while I collected plants, in which however I was not so successful as I expected. I got the Plantago Maritima, Aster Tripolium[4] & others. Sunday passed quietly, but on Monday I went a second walk with Lucy to see Cousin Daulbies,[5] & saw also some of their dried plants, which were well done though they did not, I think make me wish to change any of my own arrangements. They were kept in portfolios, each specimen having a full sheet, the orders being put in blue paper covers & each class, of the Linnaean system, in one portfolio. I enjoyed both walks very much & resolved to take more. On Tuesday I went with Sam Archer to get some shells from the bottom of ships in the graving docks. I got three kinds & a sea-weed. Wednesday was my birthday, when I became seventeen, but I began the day in an unusually bad humour. I began a letter to Aunt Jane[6] of which however I could finish only a few sentences, & had hard work in keeping my agreement with Sam Archer to go to Crosby.[7] We set off all right however, & at the Railway I met a man named Sansom[8] who is a very good botanist, though a

[1] Jevons's elder sister, aged twenty-two at this date.

[2] St Michael's Church, St Michael's Hamlet, Toxteth Park. The use of iron as a structural material was pioneered in Liverpool, and between 1813 and 1816 three churches almost entirely of iron were built in the city. See R. Dickinson, 'James Nasmyth and the Liverpool Iron Trade', *Transactions of the Historic Society of Lancashire and Cheshire* (1956), 108, 88–9.

[3] A beauty spot near Jevons's former home at Toxteth Park. William Roscoe lived in a house there, 1790–93, writing his poem *The Dingle* in 1790, the principal attraction of this residence being 'the immediate vicinity of a small but beautiful dingle, leading to the shores of the Mersey, and presenting many delightful prospects of this river, and the country beyond' (Henry Roscoe, *Life of William Roscoe* (1833) p. 139). See p. 61 below.

[4] Plantago Maritima: Sea Plantain; Aster Tripolium: Sea Aster.

[5] First cousins of Jevons's mother. William Roscoe's sister married Daniel Daulby, friend of Roscoe, art collector and art historian (author of *A Descriptive Catalogue of Rembrandt*, 1796) and one of the eight Liverpool subscribers to the London Committee for the Abolition of the Slave Trade. See Chandler, *William Roscoe of Liverpool*, p. 65. The five daughters and two sons, all of whom remained unmarried, had been the constant companions of Mrs Jevons in her youth at Allerton Hall. The two male 'cousin Daulbies' were experts on Iceland, and in 1860 the Daulby–Roscoe Icelandic Collection of books was presented to the Library of University College, London. Bellot, op. cit., p. 424.

[6] His mother's younger sister, Jane Roscoe (1797–1853).

[7] Crosby, now a dormitory town, lies on the coast north of Liverpool.

[8] A Thomas Sansom contributed papers on botany to the Literary and Philosophical Society and the Historic Society of Lancashire and Cheshire in Liverpool at the period. (The editor is indebted to the City Librarian, Liverpool, for this information.) His name is given as Sanson in L J, p. 19.

custom-house clerk, & I should like to know him. We wandered about the Crosby sand hills for several hours, & I got a good many rather nice specimens, as, Triglochin Palustre, Gentiana Amarella, Parnassia Palustre, Anagallis Tenella, Echium Vulgare, Polygonum Paralias, Euphrasia vulgaris, Spergula Nodosa &c,[1] & Sam found some willows with numbers of pretty good caterpillars, & Hawks, Pusses; I got home at 6, got my tea, pressed several plants, & had to get ready immediately for the Philharmonic concert, but as I had to sit by myself & was moreover in a bad humour & tired, I enjoyed it but little, as I expected. It took all Thursday morning to examine & press my plants, in which however I succeeded better perhaps than I have ever done before, & in the afternoon I again went out with Lucy, to the Botanic gardens;[2] it chiefly consisted in looking on at the grand dresses, & I actually put my gloves on to go. The show was not as good as I expected to see it, but I have never been to one before. Last night I spent chiefly in sorting what few shells I have. This morning I screwed myself up to getting a little business done in town for I went first to get my teeth stopped by Mr Higginson[3] which however he put off till tomorrow, & my hair cut, with some other things. I also walked along the docks a little & was fortunate[4] in finding some large foreign snail shells on some dye wood. I am going to set to work to day at arranging the minerals & have got the card-board for the boxes.

24 September

I have let a long time pass over without any entry, & had once indeed resolved to give up my journal. But I dare say I shall find it easy to write regularly when I am working hard at London for my energy is like that of others I have heard of, never excited but by pressure & difficulties. For instance during the whole of these holydays I might easily have done 2 or 3 hours work a day at[5] lessons, & got a great deal

[1] Triglochin palustre (arrow grass); Gentiana amarella (autumn gentian); Parnassia palustre (i.e. palustris) (grass of Parnassus); Anagallis tenella (bog pimpernel); Echium vulgare (Viper's Bugloss); Polygonum paralias (Euphorbia paralias); Euphrasia vulgaris (Euphrasia officinalis – common eyebright), Spergula nodosa.
[2] The Liverpool Botanic Garden was instituted in 1802 by William Roscoe, Dr John Rutter and Dr John Bostock, the opening address being delivered by Roscoe. It provided the pattern for others, including the Botanical Gardens in Philadelphia and Calcutta. See Chandler, *Liverpool*, Introd. p. xvii.
[3] The family doctor, probably Alfred Higginson, the Liverpool surgeon who in 1844 married Ellen, younger sister of James and Harriet Martineau. The Liverpool Directory for 1853 includes a reference to a Doctor Alfred Higginson. He attended Jevons's brother Tom, see letter of Thomas Jevons of 3 May 1855, Vol. II, Letter 59. Alfred Higginson's sister Helen (1804–77) had married James Martineau in 1828.
[4] Jevons wrote 'fortunately' here in the text.   [5] 'a' in the text.

done but I have not done so for more than a week altogether. I am indeed very much vexed at having done so little these holydays, for during 2 months I have only collected about 50 or 60 plants, arranged them as an herbarium, arranged my minerals, gone a few excursions & walks with Sam Archer, read Grandpapa's life,[1] & done some few other things hardly worth mentioning. During the same time at College, I have no doubt I could have done as much while attending regularly to all my classes. I think this will be the last opportunity I shall have of wasting my time for till next July I shall be at College almost continually & then (after a short tour in the country I hope) I shall go at once to business & need not hope for any more holydays for some time.

That I shall go into some ordinary business as I wanted is now pretty sure I think. Papa had always imagined that I wanted to be a chemist[2] or something like that & was rather surprised that [I][3] wanted to spend so much time at College, which would only he thought unfit me for business. But I feel sure that after I have looked forward to it so long & have chosen it myself after such long consideration, I shall be quite able to give my attention to it & to make study a secondary object as long as necessary. To become a manufacturing chemist as Papa was intending, I should have to work at the laboratory for two sessions & then spend a good many years in some manufactory, away from home, & should have far less leisure for other pursuits, which I like quite as well or better than chemistry such as Botany, Nat. Phil.[4] & Latin, Greek, Mathematics, History, which, if I am not so forward in & fond of, are of much greater importance & good & are the best means of preparing me for my object. I rather think too that I should not necessarily take any interest in the practical part of chemistry because I like the theoretical part & have got a few prizes through it.[5]

---

[1] William Roscoe's biographer was his youngest child Henry (1799–1836), a barrister and noted legal writer, the father of Sir Henry Enfield Roscoe.

[2] A manufacturing chemist. A career in theoretical chemistry at that time would have been restricted in scope and very uncertain; it would also have been unusual. 'I soon made up my mind to follow chemistry as a profession,' wrote Sir Henry Roscoe, 'much to the astonishment and even dismay of some of my friends and relations, who asked me if I intended to open a shop with red and blue glass bottles in the window. And this was not an extraordinary question, for in the early fifties the position of science in public estimation was very different from that which it now holds in England . . .' (*Life and Experiences*, p. 33).

[3] Omitted in the text.

[4] 'The Department of Natural Philosophy embraced physics and what would now be called applied mathematics. "The principal work of the department appears to have had relation to Mechanics, Dynamics, and Hydrostatics, but lectures were also given on Astronomy, Optics, and Heat." ' (A. W. Porter, quoted in Bellot, op. cit., p. 130.)

[5] At Easter 1852 Jevons had been awarded the Silver Medal in chemistry at University College, London. There is no record of chemistry prizes at U.C. School though apparently Jevons must have received one.

The idea that I have formed of the manner of spending the few next years, though of course I cannot expect that it should turn out, half as I like, is, to devote this next session at College to learning as much science as possible, expecially Natural Philosophy, Mathematics, Botany, & chemistry, the last perhaps less than the others because I am more advanced in it. I shall spend some time also in walking over London, especially the remote & low parts &, during the season, taking walks & excursions into the country to collect plants for my herbarium. After a short tour most likely among the lakes, on which I shall collect plants, I suppose I must begin some business directly, the nature of which does not matter so much, but as far as I know at present, I should like that of a general broker, since there is more variety. The office, meals &c. will occupy me from about 8 in the morning till 7 in the evening (though no doubt I could devote at least an hour of *that* to reading, particularly if it is light reading), and there will be left for real study at least two hours in the evening & one in the morning. I shall thus work for about 11 hours a day, but the 8 of them spent at the office will not be nearly so fatiguing as the 7 or 8 at college while the study in the evening will become I expect more a pleasure than a trouble. Of this study only a little will be given to science, & the rest to Latin, Greek, History, French or German, &c. &c. This appears a grand but practicable scheme, but I must be prepared to see it frustrated any time, & to find it a far less easy job than I had expected to accustom myself to going to business in the middle of the noisy town for nothing but to write out dry letters, invoices, &c, run errands, & the like. But it has been done before under harder circumstances.

I have done very little during the last few weeks worth mentioning. My minerals are most of them in neat boxes, & some of them with names. I have added about 20 new specimens to it,[1] many of them pretty good as, Iserine, several iron ores, two carbonates of copper, obsidian, &c. but I hope to get many more in London. I think I shall take a vow to spend the whole of the christmas holydays in learning mineralogy & crystallography & finishing the arrangement of my collection by putting a paper to each specimen telling its names, composition, form, & a little of its history.[2] I shall buy the minerals chiefly which are mentioned in the chemistry, & study these chiefly, & thus I shall be gaining something useful for the examination at Easter.

I have collected very few plants lately but Sam Archer has given me

---

[1] 'them' has been substituted here in LJ, p. 21.

[2] Jevons's grasp of these subjects has been recorded by Harry Roscoe: 'Stanley had been at University College School, but soon afterwards attended the classes at the College. I was not long in finding that in him I had to do with a remarkable mind. The first instance of his power was shown by his examining a number of crystallised minerals which I possessed, and giving the crystallographic nomenclature to their faces . . .' (*Life and Experiences*, p. 31).

several rare ones as, the Drosera Anglica,[1] Andromeda, Oxycoccus, Polystichum Aculeatum[2] var. &c; I shall get specimens of them myself as soon as possible for I never like other people's speci- as well as my own. I shall take a few of my own specimens to London for Colvill, & I have promised Sam to get him duplicates of some of the best I find in London.

One or two days I spent in making some stray sheets & plates of 'Roscoes Monandrian Plants',[3] into four copies, as complete as possible. The first the most perfect that can be made has all the printing but wants 19 plates, some of which Lucy will copy for it. I have of course looked well through the book in doing this, but though it is very spendidly executed I should think it was not of much use as a botanical work, since Grandpapas arrangement is not mentioned in the Penny Cyclopaedia[4] (Art. Scitaminea) He has made also a great mistake in defending the Linnaean against the Natural system.[5] The former is no better an arrangement of plants than that would be of animals which made the classes depend on colour, as the 'white class', red class, brown class, &c. It might often happen that all of one natural class were of one colour & were in one class of this system as sometimes happens in that of Linnaeus, while the variations in colour of single animals scarcely exceeds those of plants in the number of stamens & pistils. Linnaeus has acknowledged the imperfection of his system by making the classes Didynamia & Tetradynamia which are nothing more than Natural classes.

12 October

I am again in London & writing quietly in my bedroom for a short time before going to bed. I have been here rather more than a week but on my way up from Liverpool, I stayed almost a week at Nantwich. Papa as I expected made no objection to my going to College, & I think that he never seriously thought of it at all, though he spoke rather as if he did, once. Aunt Jane was as glad to see me on Tuesday 28th as ever and

[1] English sundew.
[2] Hard shield fern.
[3] William Roscoe, *Monandrian Plants of the Order Scitamineae, chiefly drawn from living specimens in the Botanic Garden at Liverpool* (issued in 15 parts, 1824–8). Only 150 copies were issued and the printing and production of the book were so splendid that it 'still fetches high prices as a collector's piece . . .' (Chandler, *William Roscoe of Liverpool*, p. 132). Some of the plates were by William Roscoe himself.
[4] *The Penny Cyclopaedia of the Society for the Diffusion of Useful Knowledge*, edited by G. Long, 30 vols. (1833–58). See note to entry for 4 November 1855, p. 113 below.
[5] John Lindley was a constant advocate of the natural, as opposed to the Linnaean, system of classification.

I was as pleased as ever to see her & Uncle H[1] again & spend a few days with them in Stanley Cottage as ever. The weather however showed itself adverse even the first afternoon, for it rained. My time was spent generally in a walk in the morning, even in spite of rain, to get a few plants which I examined & pressed in the afternoon or evening, but sometimes I went two walks in the day. In the evening, I read a chapter of the New Testament with Aunt Jane, played 3 to 6 games of cribbage & read a little of Buff's Physics[2] or other books. What most disturbed me was that I felt I was continually eating too much, with the usual large dinners, breakfasts & suppers, & a continual supply of apples, cakes, &c &c, at frequent intervals between.

The chief plants[3] I got were, Drosera Rotundifolia from Beam Heath[4] (for I made one good search there & found also, Alisma Ranunculoides, Epilobium Limosum &c.) Senecio Tenuifolia, Œnanthe Fistulosa.

I came up to London by the night mail on Sunday night, $10\frac{3}{4}$ from Crewe. I had to have a gig to myself to Crewe, & this with the increase of the railway fare made me rather sorry that I had not gone by the ordinary train on Sunday.

I got here at about five in the morning very much tired, for I had not slept all night & had had two exceedingly disagreable smokers & drinkers in my carriage all way. I found I was in time for the introductory lecture,[5] but though I took long notes it was rather a stupid one, & nothing but a very brief outline.

23 October

I am now fairly at work again for my last session, and shall try to get through a good deal of work, but rather with the intention of enabling myself to go on easily afterwards, than of finishing up. During the first week and a half I had only chemistry, but though this took very little time I got through little else, except reading the first three chapters of De Morgans Trigonometry.[6] and a few other things. In chemistry I began by reading the subject of the lecture up in a number of books,

[1] Rev. Francis Hornblower (1812–53), husband of Jevons's aunt, Jane Roscoe. See entry for 17 February 1853, p. 88 below.

[2] Heinrich Buff (*Zur Physik der Erde*) *Familiar Letters on the Physics of the Earth*, edited by A. W. Hoffman (1851). See entries for 31 October 1852 and 4 November 1855, pp. 67 and 114 below.

[3] Drosera Rotundifolia: common sundew. Alisma Ranunculoides: lesser alisma. Senecio Tenuifolia: narrow leaved senecio. Oenanthe Fistulosa: water dropwort.

[4] Beam Heath, near Nantwich; at that time open ground north-east of the town centre.

[5] In chemistry. The Inaugural Lecture was given before the start of the term for arts and other sciences – causing Jevons to return earlier to College. Bellot, op. cit., p. 125.

[6] Augustus De Morgan, *Trigonometry and Double Algebra* (1849).

as Grahams chemistry,[1] Heat in Encyclopaedia Metrop,[2] Library of Useful Knowledge,[3] &c, but I found that while I got but little new from so many it confused me very much, and I have left it off.

In reading difficult mathematical things, I found that the best way to make them out, was to go over them very carefully for two or three days together, instead of puzzling yourself for several hours to understand one sentence or one mathematical transformation. On the 15th, Thursday, was the Introductory lecture of the Arts end by Prof Clough[4] on the literature of England, but I did not make much out of it. The next morning I attended De Morgans Higher Junior and had the usual lecture on our necessary notions of ratio, with which he always begins.

Prof. Potter[5] in the afternoon gave us an Introductory lecture on Force, as the universal agent, as in Motion, Heat, Electricity, Chemical Action &c &c. I also began the long job of copying out De Morgans tracts,[6] with those on Ratio. I intended to do them all as they come out in my classes, because I think that whenever I work at any of the subjects again, I shall miss them very much; I also intend to have all De Morgans books. A few days after I got here I went to the University

[1] Thomas Graham, *Elements of Chemistry* (1842), see p. 70 below. Graham (1805–69) was Professor of Chemistry at University College, London, 1837–54 and Master of the Royal Mint, 1854–69. See p. 97 below.

[2] E. Smedley, Hugh V. Rose and Henry J. Rose, *Encyclopaedia Metropolitana* (1845) 25 vols. The article 'Heat', by Rev. Francis Lunn, F.R.S., appeared in Vol. IV, pp. 225–40.

[3] The article 'Chemistry' appeared in Volume IV of the series *Natural Philosophy* published in the 'Library of Useful Knowledge' between 1829 and 1834. The author was J. F. Daniell, F.R.S. (1790–1845), Professor of Chemistry at King's College, London.

[4] Arthur Hugh Clough (1819–61), poet and writer; Professor of English Language and Literature at University College, 1850–2. (He succeeded Professor Scott, who became first Principal of Owens College, Manchester.) This was Clough's last Introductory Lecture for he resigned soon afterwards in anticipation of being appointed the first Principal of Sydney University. He did not obtain the post. Clough had a great literary reputation and he was a potent intellectual influence on Walter Bagehot and many other young men, including Jevons's elder brother, Herbert. Bellot, op. cit., pp. 261–2; Mrs Russell Barrington, *The Life of Walter Bagehot* (1914) p. 183.

[5] Richard Potter (1799–1886), Professor of Natural Philosophy and Astronomy in University College, London, 1841–3 and 1844–65. In 1843–4 he served as Professor of Philosophy and Astronomy in King's College, Toronto. On leaving Manchester Grammar School in 1815, Potter spent several years in business before taking up the study of optics under Dalton. He became a Scholar of Queen's College, Cambridge, in 1834 and was sixth wrangler in 1838. He also qualified as a physician in 1841 but never practised.

[6] These were unpublished mathematical tracts, prepared by De Morgan for the use of students.

The notebook into which Jevons copied these tracts is now in the Library of the University of Glasgow, together with two other notebooks, one containing notes made by Jevons on De Morgan's 'Higher Junior' and 'Lower Senior' lectures of 1852–3, the other 'Notes and Extracts, concerning Lectures on the Pure Mathematics, delivered in University College, London, by Augustus De Morgan, Professor, etc., Session 1860–61'. The three notebooks were bequeathed to Glasgow University by G. A. Gibson, Professor of Mathematics there from 1909 to 1927; there is no evidence as to how they came into his possession. For further details, see R. D. Collison Black, 'Jevons, Bentham and De Morgan', *Economica*, 39 (May 1972) pp. 119–34.

at Somerset House[1] and got my three certificates for the matriculation and an order to the bookseller for my prize books. I had to go
several times to the booksellers, Richard Taylor, but at last fixed upon
Regnaults, 'Cour de Chimie' 4 vols. 21's Schleidens Scientific botany,
21's and Lindleys Vegetable Kingdom[2] with *glossary of Botanical Terms*,
about 35s, the rest of the £5 being taken in the binding.

I have had several rather learned discussions with Harry about
Moral Philosophy, from which it appears that I am[3] decidedly a 'Depen-
dant Moralist', not believing that we have any 'Moral Sense' altogether
separate and of a different kind from our animal feelings. I have also
had a talk about the *Origin of species*, or the manner in which the innumerable races of animals have been produced. I, as far as I can
understand at present, firmly believe that all animals have been trans-
formed out of one primitive form, by the continued influence for thousands and perhaps millions of years of climate, geography, &c, &c.
Lyell makes great fun of Lamarck's that is of this theory but appears to
me not to give any good reason against it.[4]

31 October

I have been working steadily all this week at College. I was invited last
Sunday to go and spend a night at Englefield Green[5] but made one of
my usual messes of it by making a pretence of the weather. I tried to
sell my Iserine the Saturday before but was told it was worth 03.6
instead of 10's a pound. Lucy has been at Nantwich this week and I
have had one letter from her, but none from home for two weeks at
least; I suppose Papa must be very much engaged with business as I
believe he is moving into a new office. I have worked full 9 hours a day,

[1] The offices of the Board of the University of London occupied a portion of Somerset
House, and the matriculation examinations were also held there.
[2] H. V. Regnault, *Cours élémentaire de Chimie* (1849–50); M. J. Schleiden, *Principles of
Scientific Botany*, translated by E. Lankester (1849); John Lindley, *The Vegetable Kingdom;
or, the structure, classification, and uses of plants, illustrated upon the Natural System* (1846).
[3] In the text it reads 'ap = than I am . . .'
[4] Darwin's *Origin of Species* was published in 1859, seven years after this entry. Both
Lamarck and Lyell prepared the way for this work. Lamarck (1744–1829), the French
naturalist and evolutionist, published his famous *Philosophie Zoologique* in 1809 and his
Histoire des Animaux sans Vertebres, 1815–22. Sir Charles Lyell (1797–1875), published *Principles of Geology* (1830–3) which revolutionised ideas of geological changes by propounding
an evolutionary as opposed to a catastrophic theory. For a further reference to Lyell, see
p. 82 below.
[5] At Englefield Green, near Windsor, lived the widow and large family of Jevons's uncle,
Robert Roscoe (1789–1850). Robert Roscoe had been a solicitor and founded the firm of
Field, Roscoe and Co., now Field Fisher and Co. It was for Robert, his fourth son, that
William Roscoe wrote the classic children's poem 'The Butterfly's Ball and the Grass-
hopper's Feast'. Robert was himself author of the poem 'Chevy Chase'.

chiefly at mathematics, which I get to like more as I attend to it better. We have just finished what we are to do at present of Double Algebra, and series which I think rather interesting though hard. In the Higher Junior class we have been at Ratio and Fractions. I have finished copying out the 4 tracts on Ratio and the one on Series.

The chemistry has been going on very slowly and stupidly for we are only as far as 'Gases', although we have gone over the last few subjects very quickly. The best way to do well in the examination will be, I think, to work up the whole of Graham, and some out of Regnault &c well a week or two before.

In natural Philosophy we have got to levers but I do not like either the class nor the present subject much. I have gone through the subjects in Potters book.

By myself, I have given most of my time by far to mathematics, and have done nearly all the exercises for both classes. I have nearly finished reading Buff's Physics of the Earth, and have also been reading the Introduction to Regnaults Chimie on Crystallography, which I intend to study in the Christmas holydays. I think I shall try to make wooden models of the crystalline forms and a Wollaston's Goniometer.[1] I have bought a few minerals since I came but I have chosen them badly I shall spend about 5s more on them before christmas and get chiefly those which are mentioned in the chemistry.

I have long had a curiosity about the dark passages and arches between the Strand and the river; so having read 'the Strand' in Knights London[2] I went on Friday. The first thing I saw worth mentioning was the 'dark arches' under the Adelphi but the first time I only looked in and was afraid of going further. Then after having a look at the Savoy Chapel, the only remains of the old Savoy Palace, I got down to the river below the arches by one of those extraordinary passages to the boats, and took courage to walk up through the arches. There were some women in them then, and I read a little time ago in the newspaper of some women who were found almost starved in them.

Yesterday, I made one of my excursions to Spitalfields. I walked to Kings Cross from there by the New Road and City Road to Finsbury Square, through Crown Street[3] to Bishopsgate Street, and from there into Spital Square.[4] The appearance of the houses from the first was

---

[1] In 1809, William Hyde Wollaston (1766–1828) invented the reflecting goniometer, an instrument for measuring solid angles, which first made possible the exact measurement of crystals, and the determination of minerals. See entry for 16 January 1853, p. 79 below.

[2] *London*: edited by Charles Knight (1842) Vol. II; chapters 35 and 36 are on 'The Strand'.

[3] Cannon Street has been substituted here in LJ (p. 24); however, at the time of Jevons's visit, Crown Street was situated between Finsbury Square and Bishopsgate Street. See S. Lewis, *Atlas to the Topographical Dictionaries of England and Wales* (1844).

[4] A small street leading from Bishopsgate to what is now Spitalfields Market. At this time it was still a residential area inhabited by silk manufacturers and master weavers,

rather peculiar, and the greater proportion of the houses have the large weavers windows running the whole width of the house, for the top storey at least. It was some time however before I found any of the wretched places I have heard so much of. One narrow lane, was the worst I think, that I ever saw; almost every house had a dirty piece of paper in the patched and dirty window, with, 'Lodging for single men'[1] at 2d or 3d a night. The chief rooms of the houses opening of course to the street were very small and exceedingly dirty, and by the light of the fires, for it was getting dark, I could see that there was[2] nothing but a narrow bench or two inside. Nothing looks more unwholesome also than the crooked little back doors leading into a few filthy square feet of yard behind each house. There were a few of the bird traps on the tops of the houses so characteristic of the Spitalfields weavers.

But I was most astonished, *at the great many improvements that are going on there.* One wide road appeared to have been lately cut right through the worst part, and on either side, I had an opportunity of seeing the backs of the houses over the empty spaces where other houses had been removed. In almost every street there seemed to be some building, and south of Spicer Street,[3] I came upon a whole batch of Model Lodging Houses called 'Metropolitan Chambers',[4] with churches schools &c around them. In another street I saw a very clean, new and handsome, though small swimming baths. The people often looked exceedingly wretched and destitute but quiet and peaceful and not the blackguardly set that you generally see. I shall go again soon.

This afternoon I took a walk all over Westminster beginning at Charing cross, down Whitehall, past the Houses of Parliament, and as far as the Mill-bank Penitentiary, where I turned up, through the poorer parts. There were several rather dirty narrow places, but great improvements are going on there also, such as the making of a grand new road, the Victoria Road, through the worst parts.

---

many of whom had workshops on the top floor of their houses, with the large windows described by Jevons. The poorer operatives generally lived farther east. See *Survey of London* (ed. F. H. W. Sheppard, 1957) xxvii, 56.

[1] Common lodging-houses such as those noticed by Jevons had achieved public notoriety since the cholera epidemic of 1849, in which more than 53,000 people died in England. Cf. *Seventeenth Annual Report of the Registrar General of Births, Deaths & Marriages in England,* Abstracts of 1854 (1856) p. 75.

[2] Jevons wrote 'were' in the original text.

[3] Spicer Street, now part of Buxton Street, was the site of a Domestic Mission founded by the Unitarians in a weaver's shed in 1832. The 'wide road' referred to by Jevons was presumably Commercial Street, newly opened at this period.

[4] South of Spicer Street was Deal Street, the site of the Deal Street Metropolitan Association Estate, established in 1849 by the Metropolitan Association for Improving the Dwellings of the Industrious Classes. It comprised a lodging house with accommodation for 234 persons, and a block of family dwellings. The nearby churches (St Anne's, Underwood Road and All Saints, Spicer Street) were not a part of the estate. Cf. *Survey of London*, xxvii, 273-5.

I have written a very poor letter home today, sometimes I cannot think of anything at all to say, however much I try.

Sunday, 7 November 1852

I have little to put down this week, for I have done little but work quietly at College. Mathematics, chiefly, and we have been doing, series, the binomial theorem and logarithmic series. In the Higher Junior we have just finished the fifth book of Euclid. I never feel satisfied with my knowledge of anything without I have gone over it connectedly and systematically and so I am writing out the fifth book, shortly but distinctly with De Morgans proofs. In the chemistry we have had three or four lectures from Dr Williamson,[1] instead of Graham. He lectures very well indeed, but is very fond of giving general opinions and propositions. He examined very well also on Friday. The subjects have been oxygen, and hydrogen, and I have read them up in Regnault as well for the chemistry as the French reading. He said a little about *ozone*, and seemed to think that it was an allatropic[2] form of oxygen. He said also that allatropy was most likely caused[by][3] a difference in the quantity of combined heat, the most active as a general rule retaining most, in a state of combination. This is undoubtedly the cause of dimorphism, and hence it is probable that allatropy is caused by a difference in the arrangement of atoms in the crystalline molecules, which may exist though they cannot arrange themselves into symmetrical crystals. But in gases, it is hard to see how heat can effect any change in the position of atoms since they seem to move perfectly freely among each other, and therefore gases ought not to be capable of assuming different allatropic forms.

In Natural Philosophy, we are near the end of the mechanical powers: it is very necessary to know all this mechanics, of course, but there is very little interest compared with what there is in any of the parts of chemistry.

The history class, by Prof. Creasy,[4] began this week and we have had three lectures from him already, from $8\frac{1}{2}$ to $9\frac{1}{2}$ in the morning. It has been chiefly about Grecian history, and will be for several more days,

---

[1] Alexander William Williamson (1824–1904), Professor of Practical Chemistry in University College London, 1849–93.

[2] i.e. allotropic.

[3] This word is omitted in the text.

[4] Professor (later Sir) Edward Creasy (1812–78), held the History Chair at University College London, 1840–60. A distinguished scholar and a lawyer by profession, 'he was interested rather in the use of history as an instrument for the training of citizens and public servants than in its development as a science. . . . He was accustomed to deliver three courses a year, one each on Greek, Roman, and English history.' (Bellot, op. cit., p. 253.)

I expect. I think I shall be interested in it and though I shall read pretty much, I cannot expect to do well in the examination. I shall read a good deal of history after leaving college.

I had a fierce discussion last night with Harry for several hours, about *Solution*. I believe that there is a general and *ultimate* property of matter to mix with other matter of similar nature. The diffusion of gases is the most perfect exhibition of this, the law of which has been settled beyond question by Graham.[1] But all gases, more or less, are the vapours of very volatile liquids, and as most liquids have the power of diffusing into each other, so the tendency of a gas to diffuse through another liquid as a liquid is sufficient to reduce a part of the gas to the liquid state. The tendency of solids to diffuse through any liquid, as water, is in the same way able to liquefy a certain portion of the solid, the quantity liquefied being proportional to the diffusive power and inversely proportional to the force of cohesion of the solid.

Monday, 15 November[2]

A very eventful week has occurred and I have much that I think worth remembering.

Monday, Tuesday, and Wednesday last were passed quietly at work spending the whole day from 9 till 5 at College. In Mathematics we have been upon logarithms, logometers, or logarithms in the extended system of mathematics, and the introduction of the unexplained symbol $\sqrt{-1}$; I have at times got rather discouraged about it but have kept up pretty well on the whole. The three lectures in History have been upon Greek history which I think very interesting though I cannot give much time to reading at present. We have finished Statics, and had an examination to day at which I answered about 4 questions; I only wish we were over the whole of mechanics.

On Thursday afternoon, partly for a walk and partly for pleasure, I went in the rain to see the Queen go to open Parliament. I took my stand nearly opposite the Horse-Guards, in Whitehall and as it was

[1] Thomas Graham started to investigate the diffusion of gases in 1831, '. . . and this led him later to the diffusion of liquids and of solids dissolved in liquids. At first sight these experiments do not appear to be of great importance, but the laws which Graham discovered, deduced from his experiments, lie at the bottom of chemistry; they are fundamental.' Collie, *A Century of Chemistry*, quoted Bellot, op. cit., p. 127.

[2] This entry, though begun on 15 November, was continued some days later. The funeral of the Duke of Wellington, described on pp. 73-5 below, took place on 18 November. The sequence is, in fact, somewhat puzzling, for the letter Jevons mentions from his father about the Liverpool earthquake was not written until 17 November. Yet the visit to Clerkenwell, described as having taken place 'yesterday' was made on 14 November (see list of events, p. 83 below).

raining had no difficulty in getting and keeping the front place. The procession came exactly at 2 oclock but it was a poor one, consisting of about five carriages, with the attendants, but with splendid horses and trappings and then the state carriage itself drawn by 8 splendid bays and containing the Queen, Prince Albert, the Duchess of Athol and the Master of the Horse.

Last [*blank space*][1] a very unusual event occurred at and surrounding Liverpool, and that is an earthquake. It happened at 4 o'clock in the morning and numbers of people were awoke by it, who describe the vibration and movement of the earth as very alarming and something like the vibration caused by a heavy waggon gappoling[2] over a paved street before the house. It was felt also in Cheshire, North Wales, West & north of Ireland, and at other places in Lancashire, and it [is][3] amusing to read the different accounts given by different persons of whom none agree in the time at which it happened. Many jumped out of bed thinking there were robbers in the house and Papa says that at Birkenhead some people ran into the street with fright. He thought the feeling was something like floating on a quickly moving sea, and he heard a noise which he is persuaded was the jingling of the jugs on his washhand stand.[4]

Yesterday I explored Clerkenwell. I walked to Kings Cross, and by the New Road, Hamilton Row, Bagnigge Wells, Guilford Place, and Coppice Row, to Little Saffron Hill. This I went down till near Holborn, when rather frightened by the appearance of the inhabitants of pickpockets I dashed to the left and got[5] to the site of Hicks Hall in St. Johns Road.[6] From there by St Johns Lane up to Clerkenwell square, Jerusalem Passage and Clerkenwell Green, where the Session House is. After examining this as well as, the Close, Red Lion Street, and the surrounding neighbourhood pretty well, I struck out North, and having got as far as the neighbourhood of Northampton Square which is I believe, a good specimen of Clerkenwell, I returned by much the same way as I came. Clerkenwell seems to be the seat of a great many little manufactures besides watchmaking such as, work boxes, jewellaries, jems, musical boxes, &c &c. The genuine Clerkenwell has a quiet respectability and industrious appearance, and must be carefully distinguished from the

[1] Tuesday, 9 November 1852.

[2] Jevons presumably intended to write 'galloping' here.

[3] This word is omitted in the text.

[4] See letter from Thomas Jevons of 17 November 1852, Vol. II, Letter 20; also Journal entry for 17 February 1856, p. 117 below. *The Times* carried extensive reports of the event in its editions for 9, 10, 11, 12, 13 and 15 November 1852.

[5] 'go' in the text.

[6] A district at that time notorious for pickpockets, featured by Dickens in his novel *Oliver Twist* (1838). Jevons mentions an earlier visit to the area in an unpublished letter of 23 May 1852 to Henrietta.

neighbouring rascally parts, which are the headquarters of the pickpockets and thieves of London.

This morning[1] I saw a sight which I have no doubt I shall remember and value all through life, viz, the splendid Lying in State of the Great Duke of Wellington. His death took place suddenly and of epileptic fits in the afternoon of [*blank space*][2] at Walmer Castle where he lived, I believe, as Warden of the Cinque Ports. The Queen immediately ordered that he should have a public funeral, which however should be put off till the Parliament should meet and vote the necessary supplies. His body was embalmed, and lay at Walmer Castle, guarded by soldiers and in the greatest privacy till a few days ago.[3] At the time of his death I was in Liverpool and there numberless flags were immediately hoisted half mast high. All the Papers were immediately filled with lives of him and there was of course much talking about him.

Before Parliament met, it was decided that the funeral and lying in State should be more magnificent than anything of the sort that had ever been seen in this country. Parliament was opened by commission about two weeks ago, but the speech was not given till the 11th. The same day the Queen, Prince Albert, with some of the children[4] & the rest went to see the lying in State at Chelsea hospital and the next day it was open to those who had tickets from the Lord Chamberlain.[5] Harry and Harriet[6] had tickets and saw it very well soon after it opened. I had not one and I therefore determined to go in with the crowd, but not on Saturday afternoon with most others, and when I had most time to spare, because I thought the crowds would be terrible. It turned out so, indeed; the crowd was most enormous, in spite of the rain, and as the police regulations were very defective, the people could not be kept in any order. Two women were killed, and numbers of others more or less hurt. MacAndrew[7] went that afternoon but like several others that I know, came back before getting into the crowd too far to get out again.

I went early on Monday morning, when I found very little of a crowd, and got in very easily. The Lying in State was a very splendid sight, the dazzling effect of the light being increased by passing through a long dark passage first. By this passage you entered the vestible, a round

---

[1] Monday, 15 November.

[2] 14 September 1852.

[3] On the night of 10 November, the body was brought to Chelsea, where it remained for the lying-in-state until its removal on 17th to the Horse Guards, for the funeral procession the following day.

[4] The Prince of Wales and the Princess Royal.

[5] Brownlow Cecil, second Marquess of Exeter (1795–1867).

[6] Harriet Roscoe, sister of Harry Roscoe.

[7] Robert MacAndrew. See also Jevons's letter of 25 June 1854 to H. E. Roscoe, Vol. II, Letter 41.

room entirely hung with black and lined with Horse Guards; opposite the door were displayed all the banners, belonging to the Dukes Victories. On either side of this vestibule were the chapel and the hall; to the latter, you went up steps to the right, and immediately saw before you the coffin, covered with splendid velvet, and surrounded with all his trophies, &c and covered with a magnificent canopy, the whole perfectly dazzling from the bright light thrown upon it from candles and concealed gas lights.

The people entered at the opposite end of the hall and went up a passage on the left hand side till near the coffin, when they passed close before it, and out of the hall a little way down the right hand side.

The hall, about 100 feet long & 30 broad was hung completely with black variegated by white chords and tassels, and lighted by four rows of immense wax candles in large silvered candelabra. On a raised step round the walls stood grenadier guards, perfectly still and silent, and with reversed arms.

The coffin rested upon a bier covered with a most costly and magnificent gold cloth, the inside of the canopy being silver cloth, and the outside velvet. At the top was the coronet, at the foot an extraordinary group of the Duke's orders, and on supports around his Marshall batons about 8 in number.

On each side were two officers as mourners and yeomen of the guard stood round. There were also candles around and in front 4 large black pillars formed of velvet around spears with black plumes at the top. Within these pillars, which had only one side were the gas lights, concentrated by reflectors. The effect of the whole was most dazzling, so that I could not at first distinguish the parts. It was open on the two next days but though enormous numbers went, no accident of any importance happened.

On Thursday Nov. 18th 1852, was the magnificent funeral of the Duke of Wellington. For a week or two before the excitement about it had been gradually increasing, and for the few days before, indeed, it had been almost exclusively the subject of conversation. Conjectures were continually being made as to the number of soldiers to be present, the shape of the car, the order of the procession and so on, and the most frequent of questions was, 'how are you going to see the procession?' Fears often were expressed that the day would be wet and the poor soldiers get drenched; the weather however turned out far different. Out of our house, Harriet went with M^r & Mrs Osler[1] to the Reform club, where the procession was seen splendidly, Aunt

[1] Jevons's first cousin Henrietta (1821–69), daughter of Robert Roscoe, had recently married Timothy Osler, a barrister and University College friend of Walter Bagehot, Richard Hutton and William Caldwell Roscoe.

Henry[1] stayed at home, Henry[2] went into Cockspur Street with the crowd, and Harry and I set off to get places in the Strand, on the top of a roof if possible. I, with most other people I think, expected the crowd about the Strand to be immense, and getting places in such a state of things impossible. As every street leading there also was full of people all going in the same direction, I got rather frightened and persuaded Harry to go in the direction of Hyde Park Corner. There we arrived about $7\frac{1}{2}$ for it is to be remembered that every body had to get up at 5 or 6 as the procession was to start punctually at 8. The crowd at Hyde Park Corner turned out to be less than we had expected and we very easily got standing places on a stand between the columns of the gate into Hyde Park for half a crown each.

The Procession was formed in the area opposite the Horse Guards in St. James' Park, and the first appearance of [it][3] at the Duke of Wellington Statue immediately opposite us was at about $8\frac{1}{2}$. Horse Guards came first, and then battalions of different foot soldiers, as Rifles, Foot Guards, marching slowly and with reversed arms. Then a number of Cavalry and Artillery. I got a very bad idea of the soldiers, as my place was not at all a good one & I missed many things which other people saw.

After some Pensioners, Conductors, &c, not however the Old Chelsea Pensioners, came a great number of carriages some mourning, others private, and the Speaker[4] in his curious old state carriage. At last came the coffin on the top of a most splendid car, which I must now describe. The coffin rested at a great height from the ground on a large bier, perhaps 15 feet long covered by a magnificent pall with a fringe of silver a foot or two in depth. The coffin was covered with red velvet and upon it were his hat and sword. The base of the car was very large and all of bronze. It was supported on 6 wheels and splendidly ornamented with arms, flags, &c. Over the coffin was suspended on the ends of four halberts, a magnificent gold cloth as a canopy. The car was drawn by 12 dray horses covered with velvet.

After the coffin had passed, (it halted for a little time under the arch) the rest was soon over, consisting of some carriages and a few more troops. The whole of the soldiers in the procession were between 6000 and 7000 but there were many more also to keep the road. Opposite us for instance were light dragoons. Many of the soldiers, as the Highlanders, Hussars, I admired very much but the Horse Guards after all are

---

[1] Maria Roscoe, formerly Fletcher (1798–1885), mother of Harry and Harriet, widow of Henry Roscoe.

[2] Jevons's first cousin, Henry Roscoe (1830–99), eldest son of Robert Roscoe and brother of Mrs Osler. He was at this time living, like Jevons, at Harry Roscoe's home.

[3] This word is omitted in the text.

[4] Charles Shaw-Lefevre (1794–1888), later Viscount Eversley.

the finest. We saw the procession coming under the arch and turning into Piccadilly but had not any extended view, so that on the whole I may say[1] that we did not see it well. From us the procession went along Piccadilly, down St. James Street, and along Pall Mall, the Strand &c to St Pauls where it arrived about three.

The service is said to have been very fine, and St Pauls looked beautiful, filled with people, hung with black cloth and brightly lighted by gas. The Bands during the procession played the Dead March out of Saul, & another, very beautifully. I got home about one to dinner but found myself very little fitted for work during the rest of the day. MacAndrew saw the soldiers *returning* rather better than we saw them.

Thus the grand affair went off; I was very glad indeed to have seen such a sight, to be able to remember it, but it was a relief next day to have got it over. Though it rained the day after and the day before, it was very fine on *the* day, and the sun appeared just as the car got opposite Apsley House, i.e. opposite us.

Monday, 22 November

I went yesterday with Harry to Richmond in the rain but had a pleasant day at Uncle Richards.[2] The Thames was very much flooded and running with a very strong current, from the great rains there have been lately. The rails in the railway station also were a foot or two under water and the engine came splashing through it.

For the last month or two there has been rain almost every day, sometimes very heavy; from July to the end of October, 22 inches of rain fell, the average of the whole year being about 24 in. only, but in the spring there was almost a proportionate length of very dry weather.

Monday, 28 November[3]

Yesterday morning I had a change from the tiring music of the Unitarian Chapels here to the splendid organ and singers of the Temple. The Church is certainly the most beautiful and interesting I have seen. 'Comfort ye' was played and sang most beautifully.

[1] 'saw' in the text.
[2] Dr Richard Roscoe (1793–1864), medical doctor, sixth son of William Roscoe; a favourite uncle and helper of the Jevons family. Jevons's mother had died at his house at Richmond.
[3] 28 November 1852 fell on a Sunday: the correct date of this entry is therefore presumably Monday 29 November.

Sunday, 12 December 1852

Towards the end of last month, I began to think rather seriously of Herberts[1] arrival from Madras, as his ship had been due some time. I wished very much to see him before he went to Liverpool, as his ship was to come to London, but did not expect to catch him. On Wednesday 1st, I began to look in the papers each day for his arrival, and that very day I saw it, at about $12\frac{1}{2}$. I immediately set off straight for the custom house. I went there with a vague idea I should get to know where the ship was; I was directed to the Ships Report Office where in a large parchment book was the Devonian put down as in St Katherines Dock. There I found her, after searching for an hour or two but the captain told me my father had come to London for him, and they had gone to look for me. I got home a short time after they and there I found them in the drawing room. Herbert looked strangely altered, but in the best health. His face was of a dark reddish colour and his voice seemed rather changed; he was rigged out in a complete new suit from F. Moses & Son, as his own clothes were quite worn out, and altogether I should hardly have known him if I had met him accidentally in the street.

We talked about his journey till tea, after which I went with them to Albert Smiths Ascent of Mont Blanc.[2] This was very excellent; he described his journey to Switzerland and then the ascent, illustrated by pictures, which altogether with his jokes were capital.

Next morning I went to breakfast with them at their Hotel, and after going with Papa to the docks about Herberts luggage which had to be searched, I went with Herbert to see Uncle Richard at Richmond. We saw him & Aunt Richard and were back at the Hotel in Aldersgate Street just in time for dinner and to see Papa off by the five oclock express train for Liverpool. Herbert went home to tea with me and I

---

[1] Stanley's brother, Herbert, had been on a journey to the East on account of his health, during which he had visited a cousin James Jevons, who had settled in Natal. His ship had left Natal on 17 March. See letters of Thomas Jevons to Jevons of 8 June 1852, and of 26 August 1855, Vol. II, Letters 18 and 70.

[2] Albert Smith (1816–60), author and lecturer, was known as 'the man of Mont Blanc'. He had climbed the mountain 37 times by 1851 and his stage entertainment 'The Ascent of Mont Blanc' ran for more than six years after its first night in 1852. It was '. . . a quasi-mountaineering entertainment at the Egyptian Hall in London . . . peopled by real Swiss girls and genuine St. Bernard dogs; it . . . displayed panoramas and transformations of Drury Lane splendour which opened out as Smith conducted his audience from Chamonix to the Grands Mulets . . . and finally to the summit of Mont Blanc itself. It was naïve, slightly vulgar. . . . Yet Smith's performance typified, just as he himself typified, the age of wide-eyed wonder with the mountain scene that formed the first chapter in the Victorian conquest of the Alps. . . .' ('The Mountain World of 1860', article by Ronald W. Clark in *The Guardian* of 27 May 1960).

finished the day by seeing him off by the $\frac{1}{4}$ to 9 night mail, by which he went to save 13s.

Herbert seemed very well but very little altered in his opinions. I had not of course very much talk with him, but I shall see him again for a little time in the Christmas holydays which are very near now.

Sunday, 29 December[1]

The last sunday before Christmas has now come and I must conclude my account of this term before turning my thoughts to the Christmas holydays, and to home, which last however I hope they seldom leave.

I have no walk worth describing this time, partly because the dark comes on so soon on an afternoon now and partly because I have been pretty busy at home. I made an attempt at a walk through Bermondsey, the Sunday before last, going to Fenchurch street by Railway, and walking across London Bridge, but it was nearly dark when I got there. The narrow dirty streets looked so lonely that I was frightened and made my way as quickly as possible to Westminster Bridge & so home.

On Wednesday I went for my Botany prize books from the University and was very much pleased by their handsome appearance. Regnaults Chimie, I have been reading a good deal lately, and I have nearly been through the first volume; but I hardly like it as much as I expected, as it is chiefly on the practical not the theoretical part.

1853

Sunday, 16 January 1853.

Christmas and the Christmas holydays have passed since my last date, and I am again settled down for three months, perhaps six or seven months hard work.

The last lectures at College were on Thursday Dec 23rd, and on Friday morning at half past six, I left for home with Harry who was going to stay a week or two with the Booths.[2] I got home to dinner, and found

---

[1] i.e. Sunday, 19 December 1852.

[2] The Charles Booths of Liverpool. Charles Booth was Harry Roscoe's uncle by marriage and was the father of the Rt. Hon. Charles Booth (1840–1910), one of the founders of the Booth Line of steamships who was also a statistician and author of *The Life and Labour of the People of London* (completed 1903). See *A Liverpool Merchant House, being a History of Alfred Booth and Company 1863–1938* (1959.) Thomas Booth, brother of the statistician, had been one of Jevons's schoolfellows at Mr Beckwith's in Liverpool (Family Book, note by W. S. J.).

everything as usual, except that there was Herbert in addition, making the whole of our family – one. Lately, I have found myself thinking more and more of home, and now it is settled that this is to be my last half-year in London, I think more of it than ever, and feel a kind of anxiety that the time may pass as quickly as possible, and that there may be no alterations of any kind in that home. My wish to be at or near home has been one of my reasons for choosing a common business in preference to any profession or other occupation, and I have felt as if it savoured of selfishness to leave home altogether and go and take care of your own interests at some place a long way off.

It is now however settled *finally*, I hope, in my own mind as well as in Papa's and Lucys, that I am to go into some office at Liverpool. I have had doubts whether it will not be exceedingly difficult for me to acquire ready, business habits, but I think that after setting my mind upon it for a year before, I shall have sufficient determination to do it. In every other respect, I believe that my two [years']¹ colleging in London will be a great advantage even in business. One necessary will be that I should not think of my business in the day time and my work at night as on an equality, but the latter as altogether subordinate at least for a long time; not that I think it actually of less importance to success.

My plan of work as far as I have thought of it as yet will be this; for the rest of this session I will give almost all my attention to the following, and in the order in which they are mentioned; – Mathematics $\begin{cases} \text{Natural Philosophy} \\ \text{Chemistry} \end{cases}$ Botany, Crystallography or Mineralogy. For several of the first years that I shall be at home, I shall also give most of my leisure time to science, because I know that to do a thing well the mind should be engaged with it as singly as possible. That is to say, when you are thinking much about such things as the Theory of equations, Diffusion, the Atomic Theory, relation of the forces &c, &c, the mind cannot take such interest in, and therefore cannot so well learn, history, or Latin and Greek. The case is quite different I believe when you are working for prizes or a degree and not for the sake of the knowledge.

I shall however as soon as I am home, begin to work a little at French or German, and I shall of course read more novels and common books than I do now. I shall also *amuse* myself, down in the cellar, with chemical experiments, making instruments which however I think are not altogether useless amusements.

After those years are past, and when I shall be a man at 22 or 23, I shall make a gradual transition to Literary studies, and especially history, though always keeping up my scientific knowledge, a little. I

¹ This word is omitted in the text.

dont know how far I shall be able to learn any mathematics by myself.

So much for all my grand schemes and anticipations, which will all be upset most likely some fine day. I passed the Christmas holydays better perhaps than most of my holydays on former occasions but perhaps because there was not time to get into my usual lazy way. The same day I got home I actually went out with them to an evening party at St James Road[1] to hear the celebrated Budget[2] read; I thought it remarkably good. The next day being Christmas day, we had the usual Christmas dinner at our house. During the next week I set my bench in order and began my 'Reflective Goniometer' which I had had in my head for some time. I made it entirely of soft mahogany, zinc plate and a few brass screws, but it has succeeded and is correct I believe to the tenth of a degree. I had nearly knocked under to making and graduating the dial, and I did not finish it till the last day of the holydays.

I played the organ[3] a good deal, especially out of the Messiah. The New Years Day Dinner at St James Road was decidedly pleasant and well finished up by a good game at blind mans buff. Almost every party I go to makes me like dancing parties worse but other ones rather better, so I think I shall *never* be a dancer.

I spent a part of two evenings in looking over half of M[r] Archers[4] collection, and I saw Phillips's[5] the great mineralogist at the Medical Institution. I also bought 3s 6d worth of minerals from Wright, chiefly forms of carbonate of lime.

[1] The home of his uncle, Timothy Jevons.

[2] The Budget was introduced on 3 December 1852 by Disraeli and bitterly opposed by Gladstone – at that time a Conservative, but a 'Peelite'. The subsequent Parliamentary Debates caused great excitement in the House of Commons and culminated, on the night of 16/17 December, in a passionate oratorical duel between Disraeli and Gladstone, in which the latter was victorious. The Budget was rejected by 305 votes to 286. This was Gladstone's first great triumph – a matter of no small local interest, since he came of an influential Liverpool family – and he became Chancellor of the Exchequer for the first time in the next Government. (See Journal entry for 23 January 1853, p. 187 below.)

[3] The organ had belonged to Jevons's grandfather, who had lived with the family from 1846 until his death in January 1852. (LJ, pp. 8, 15.) Thomas Jevons was a connoisseur of organs, as his letters show, but only Jevons was able actually to play the instrument. It was a lifelong passion. He bought a harmonium in Australia in 1855, and took lessons on the organ in London in 1862 and 1864, availing himself of every opportunity to play. In 1871 at Manchester he bought an organ of his own for £133 (LJ, p. 252) and took it with him when he later moved to Hampstead (LJ, p. 365).

[4] The natural history collection of Francis Archer, surgeon to the Liverpool dispensary and from 1840 surgeon to the Borough Gaol for thirty years. He was the father of Sam Archer (see Journal entry for 23 August 1852, p. 55 above), who added tropical plants to the collection. Medical men were professionally concerned with botany, since, in the words of Lindley, they depended 'so much upon the vegetable kingdom for their remedial agents' (*Veg. Kingdom*, viii). Thus Lindley's botany lectures like the chemistry lectures, were mainly for medical students. (The editor is indebted to the City Librarian, Liverpool, for this information.)

[5] John Arthur Phillips (1822–87), the geologist, one of the first to devote himself to the study of the microscopic structure of minerals and rocks.

A day or two after I got to Liverpool, a great storm occurred, early on the monday morning in Christmas week. It was said to be the greatest and most destructive since 1839, and some say that it was even worse than the one in that year. I appear to have slept through it but I had sufficient evidence of it in the scene of the river from the landing stage next morning and in the number of chimnies, walls, boarding, slates &c, blown down; the river was magnificent, for it is a 16 foot tide, just about 12 oclock, increased to 24 feet by the wind. The water was almost on a level with the pier and the waves were dashing over. The river was entirely covered with spray.

The storm was also felt all over England and at sea, and a great many ships were wrecked and lives lost. Several people were killed in London by falling chimnies.

Sunday, 23 January

A few days ago news was received that Mrs Richard Hutton (Mary Roscoe)[1] had died of *yellow fever* at Barbadoes early in the morning of Dec 20th last. She was married to Richard Hutton last summer but one, and lived partly at Manchester and partly at University Hall[2] of which Richard was principal, till he was taken very ill, with the loss of one of his lungs. They went out to Barbadoes a little before the end of last October, for his health. He had had the yellow fever slightly but had recovered, when Mary was seized.[3]

Since I came to London at the beginning of this term I have chiefly kept to my work, and have therefore little worth putting down. I have been twice to the British Museum and find I can take as much interest in the Sculptures and other antiquities as the minerals &c. I have been wanting very much to get Mayhew's[4] 'London Labour and London

[1] Mary Ann Roscoe (b. 1821), Jevons's first cousin, was the daughter of William Stanley Roscoe (1782–1843), the eldest son of William Roscoe. She was a close friend of the Jevons family. Her marriage to Richard Hutton on 26 June 1851, is described in Thomas Jevons's letter of 28 June 1851, Vol. II, Letter 12.

[2] University Hall, Gordon Square, London, W.C.1. (now Dr Williams' Library) was established in 1848 as a hall of residence for University College and a place where students might receive good theological instruction.

[3] Richard Hutton later married another first cousin of Jevons, Eliza Roscoe (1823–91), daughter of Robert Roscoe of Englefield Green, as his second wife. Professor J. H. Hutton has given the following information about the Hutton and Roscoe families: 'The friendship between the Hutton family and the Roscoes certainly goes back a generation earlier (than W. Stanley Jevons) for my grandfather (Joseph Hutton I, 1765–1856) preached the sermon at the ordination, in 1828, of James Martineau, who went from Dublin to Liverpool thence to Manchester and was probably the link between the Hutton and Roscoe families in the first instance.' It is interesting to note that Jevons's sister Lucy was at one time engaged to marry Russell Martineau, son of James Martineau.

[4] Henry Mayhew, *London Labour and London Poor*. Published in 1851, the complete work comprised four volumes.

Poor', as that is the only book I know of to learn a little about the real condition of the poor in London. I managed to root out a dozen of the numbers in rather a dirty condition at a shop in Holywell St., & yesterday I bought them at a penny a piece. They will lead I expect to a few walks this term.

Last Friday I had a great treat in attending one of Faraday's Friday evening lectures, at the Royal Institution.[1] Harry got the ticket from Mr Brodie[2] for Aunt Henry, who could not use it from the death of Mrs Hutton. The lecture was chiefly on some experiments he had been making on the magnetic and diamagnetic properties of a number of substances in air water spirits of wine, and other media. His method of measuring the amount that such substances as bismuth, water oils, salts, &c are attracted or repelled by a very large and splendid permanent magnet, is to suspend equal bulks sealed up in small glass tubes before the poles of the magnet at the end of an exceedingly delicate torsion balance. This consisted of a glass beam suspended by a long fine wire, which is turned at the top by a nob with an index and dial. After the glass tube has been suspended from one end of the beam amd counterpoised by leaden weights at the other end, the experimenter who sits at a distance of 3 or 4 yards turns the index by a long rod till the end of the beam is seen, through a telescope and by a mirror behind the beam, to be opposite zero in a scale placed about a foot above the telescope. The motion of the beam can thus be measured as accurately as to 1/1000th of an inch, the distance of the scale being equivalent to a very long index and dial. The intensity of the attraction or repulsion is measured by the angle through which the index at the top of the wire had to be turned to bring back the beam to zero.

He found that when a body is suspended in a liquid it is actually more magnetic or diamagnetic sometimes when further off than when nearer. From this he concludes that magnetic force does not follow the same simple law as gravity, but this I have heard does not necessarily follow.

He showed us a very beautiful experiment in which coloured sulphuret of carbon is poured into dilute sulphuric acid of exactly the

[1] By 1853, Michael Faraday (1791–1867) was nearing the end of his life's work in the laboratory and lecture theatre of the Royal Institution of Great Britain, established in 1799 for 'the Promotion, Extension and Diffusion of Science and Useful Knowledge'. He had been made Director of the Laboratory in 1827 and Fullerian Professor of Chemistry in 1833. His great electrical discoveries of 1831 and the electrical researches of the following decade were, after an interval, followed by a new period of discovery, starting in 1845, in the fields of magnetic action on light and of diamagnetism. See Thomas Martin: *The Royal Institution* (3rd edition, 1961) pp. 32–47.

[2] (Sir) Benjamin Brodie (1817–80), Professor of Chemistry at Oxford from 1865; the discoverer of graphitic acid. At this period he was engaged upon difficult research on chemical elements and allotropy. Harry (Sir H. E.) Roscoe records having met him in 1850 and he became a friend (*Life and Experiences*, p. 41).

same density. It is thus divested of all gravitation, and remains in any part of the acid in large beautiful globules. He mentioned that a recurrence of the spots on the suns disk had been observed every[1] with a period of ten years, which has also been found to be the period in which the variations of the compass recur.

My chief pleasure in going was not so much to hear the lecture as to see Faraday as well as all the other learned men. Sir John Herschel,[2] I saw, a venerable learned looking man with a quantity of grey hair, and a fine face. I also saw Milman[3] the Dean of St Pauls and Murchison.[4] Sir Charles Fellowes,[5] Lyell and numbers of others were there, with De Morgan, Sharpey,[6] and Malden[7] from our college. Faradays lectures are exceedingly popular and there is quite a crush getting in and to good places. The lecture room was quite full nearly 1/3 being ladies in full dress, but what interest they can take in the lecture I cannot understand.[8]

Yesterday afternoon D[r] Williamson gave the first of a course of 9 lectures on Chemical Philosophy at the Royal Institution; it was not so good as Harry expected but the others will most likely be better.

As to College affairs, I am going on steadily, and just as usual. In Mathematics, we are just beginning the Theory of equations, and during the last week have got through Descartes, Fouriers & Sturms theorems of the limits of the roots of equations. They are the most truly difficult things we have come to, and I do not thoroughly understand them yet.

It is only about two months to the chemistry examination, and I am beginning to think seriously of it. The best way to learn the metals

---

[1] Some words appear to be omitted here in the text.

[2] Sir John Frederick Herschel (1792–1871), the astronomer, and Master of the Royal Mint, 1850–5. See Journal entry for 14 December 1865, p. 200 below; also Vols. II and III.

[3] Sir Henry Hart Milman (1791–1868), Dean of St Paul's, poet and historian.

[4] Sir Roderick Impey Murchison (1792–1871), the geologist.

[5] Sir Charles Fellows (1799–1860), the archaeologist, discoverer of ancient cities in Lycia, knighted in 1845 in recognition of his services in the removal of Xanthian antiquities to Great Britain.

[6] William Sharpey (1802–80), Professor of Anatomy and Physiology at University College, 1836–74, 'the father of modern physiology in this country' (Bellot, op. cit., p. 166), and in Jevons's words 'one of the best physiologists alive' (LJ, p. 15).

[7] Henry Malden (1800–76), Professor of Greek at University College, London, 1831–76, and joint Headmaster of University College School, 1833–42. Author of *On the Origin of Universities and Academical Degrees* (1835), written in connection with the application of the University of London for a charter.

[8] Under Faraday's presiding genius, the Friday Evening Discourses to Members of the Royal Institution had become celebrated 'occasions'. The lectures always included practical demonstrations and through them members of the public, whether professionally interested in science or not, were given an opportunity of obtaining some first-hand knowledge of the progress of research and discovery at a time when there was little or no organised teaching of experimental science in England. Faraday was a master of scientific exposition and his lectures were crowded to capacity (Martin, op. cit.).

thoroughly, I think to be, to make a large table, containing the composition preparation, crystalline form &c of each metallic compound. I began the table last night. (It turned out a failure) I have been reading a good deal of Regnaults chimie, and a little of Daniells Introduction to Chemical Philosophy[1] which however I think a poor book. In the Chemistry class we have only just begun the metals, as we are very late; we are to do the metals and the organic together which I do not think a good way. Before the examination, I shall read most of Graham, some of Liebigs[2] letters, work at parts in Gmelin's Handbook,[3] read a good deal of Regnault, &c &c.

In Potters class of Natural Philosophy, we have been engaged since the beginning of the term, with electricity. He does the experiments magnificently, but gives us a minimum of all theory, which consequently I have to read for myself. I must read and work an awful deal for this class after Easter.

I now and then read a little of Schmitz's Greece[4] but I get on very slowly and shall not go into the examination.

[*1852*][5]

Oct.	29	Strand
	30th	Spitalfields.
	31st	Westminster
Nov.	6	London Wall, City.
	5	British Museum
		Greek Antiquities
		Minerals
	11	Opening of parliament.
	14	Clerkenwell
	15	Lying in State of the
		Duke of Wellington

---

[1] John Frederic Daniell, *Introduction to Chemical Philosophy* (1839).

[2] The *Chemische Briefe* of Justus Freiherr von Liebig (1803–73) had been published in 1844. German chemistry was supreme at this time. Its laboratories, of which Liebig's was almost the first, attracted students from England, including Harry Roscoe, who studied under Bunsen and visited Liebig's laboratories at Munich several times (*Life and Experiences*, p. 67).

[3] Leopold Gmelin (1788–1853), Professor of Medicine and Chemistry at Heidelberg before Bunsen. His great textbook on inorganic chemistry 'was for many years what may be called the Chemist's Bible', in the words of Harry Roscoe. It had been translated into English in 1849 (*Life and Experiences*, p. 47).

[4] Leonhard Schmitz (1807–90), a naturalised German scholar, teacher and historical writer, published his *History of Greece* in 1850.

[5] This date is omitted in the text. This list of activities is found two pages further on in the Journal from the end of the previous entry, occurring in the middle of Jevons's account of political events. It would appear that he reserved two pages of the Journal for the purpose but did not continue after April 1853, so most of the second page has been left blank. Here for reasons of simplicity the editor has placed the list between the two entries.

	18	Funeral Procession of F. M. Arthur, Duke of Wellington KG, &c &c.
	21	Richmond. Uncle Rich.
	28	Temple church
	30	St Katherines docks
	—	Albert Smiths M. Blanc.
	31	Richmond. Un. Rich.
Dec	5th	Bermondsey; a failure
	10	British Museum. Minerals. Trinity church
	24th	Budget Party at St James Rd.
	1 10	Christmas Holydays
	25th	Christmas day.

1853

	1st	New Years day party.
	2nd	Dinner at Uncle Williams.
	12th	Eaton Sq. Belgrave Square.
	17th	Royal Exchange St Pauls.
	14th	Brit. Mus. Greek Antiquities
Jan	21st	Brit. Mus. Small Antiquities
	—	Faradays Lecture.
	22nd	St Pauls &c.
	28	Dr Williamsons lecture
Febr	5th	Bermondsey, Jacobs Island.
	6th	Westminster Abbey.
	11th	Brit. Mus. Minerals.
	12th	Lambeth, Chelsea.
	13th	Holloway, Caledonian Rd.
	14th	Snow balling.
	18th	Lucifer Match factory.
	19th	Skating Regents pk. Serpentine.
	20th	Skating at Barnes.
	21st	Lecture. Spicer Street.
	25th	Brit Mus. Quartz.
	26th	Commercial Rd. Bow.
March	5th	Shadwell. Isle of Dogs
	12th	Bermondsey. Thames Tun.
	13th	Richmond

10th   Warington's lecture on Clays[1]
17th   Playfairs lecture on Pottery[2]
19th   Williamson lec. at Brit. In.
24th   To Liverpool.
25th   Birkenhead.
28th   Soap manufactory
29th   Iron Ship-building yard
30   Chester, Prestatyn, Steeles Soda-works, Birmingham
          to London.
April   1st   National Gallery.
12th   Chemical Examination
16th   Houses of Parliament
12th   Kinkels first lecture[3]
17th   Hampstead &c.
19th   Kinkels Second lecture.
22nd   D Conolly lec. on Lunatics.[4]
23rd   Hampstead.

There has been a great deal happening[5] in the political world lately and I have not put down anything on that subject yet. I do not give much of my thoughts to Politics yet but cannot help understanding a little.

During the session of Parliament last spring, the old Russel Ministry, containing Lord J Russel, Earl Granville Foreign Sec. (Lord Palmerston at first) Sir C Wood, Chan. Excheq. &c, was defeated on some measures, the Militia bill, or a Reform bill, if I recollect rightly. It went out after having lasted for a good many years, and was succeeded by the Derby Ministry. This contained, the Early of Derby, Prime Minister, Mr Disraeli Chan. Excheq. Earl of Malmesbury, Sec for Foreign Affairs, Sir J Pakington Colonial Office, Mr Walpole, home office &c. It was rather laughed at then and was supported by the Protectionists for it began as a Protectionist government.[6]

The Parliament remained sitting for some time that questions and

---

[1] Robert Warington (1807–67), Chemist to the London Apothecaries' Society.

[2] It would seem most likely that this refers to Sir Lyon Playfair (1818–98) the chemist, who in 1853 had been appointed Secretary for science in the newly established Department of Science and Art. He had been one of the principal administrators of the Great Exhibition of 1851.

[3] Gottfried Kinkel (1815–82) émigré German poet and art historian. In 1853 he gave 'a course of lectures at University College on the History of Modern Painting and Sculpture' (Bellot, op. cit. p. 345).

[4] Dr John Conolly (1794–1866) whose pioneer work in the humane treatment of the insane had a world-wide influence (Bellot, op. cit. pp. 156–8).

[5] This entry is undated, but it may have been written either on 23 January 1853, or between that date and 30 January, the date of the subsequent entry.

[6] See E. L. Woodward, *The Age of Reform, 1815–1870* (1938), p. 158.

bills of less importance than Free Trade or Protection might be dispatched. The Militia bill was passed,[1] though it was rather disliked in general; it has been raised since then, wholly by Volunteers, and having gone through the three weeks drill for the year, has disappeared again. Parliament was then dissolved, and a general election took place, in order that the question of Free Trade might be fairly and finally decided. Great bribing took place all over the country on the Government side, and more than 100 petitions have been sent up against the members elected.

In Liverpool the bribery was as bad as or worse than anywhere else, for Mackenzie and Turner,[2] two protectionists were got in by the 'Protestant dodge' chiefly I believe, instead of Cardwell[3] and Ewart.[4]

Nevertheless the majority of the new Parliament were Free Traders, and the Government seeing that if they stuck to Protection, they must certainly be turned out, and having no fixed principles, became Free Trade also. In the Queens Speech they announced as ambiguously as possible that they intended to continue free trade, though they would consider how best to give compensation to those who had suffered by it.

As soon as the session was properly begun Mr Villiers[5] moved a resolution in the plainest language, to support Free Trade. There were very long debates on this and a resolution of Mr Disraeli, which ended by an intermediate resolution of Lord Palmerston's being passed, by which the ministry were enabled to remain in, that their standing or their fall might be decided on the question of Mr Disraelis Budget.[6] In this he proposed to remove the Tea, Malt and other duties, and to make up the difficiency by doubling the house-tax, thus affording no relief to the farmers. The house-tax certainly appeared to me the fairest and most easily collected of all taxes, but the Budget was very much opposed by Mr Gladstone and others, and a majority obtained against it, not perhaps so much on account of the faultiness of the Budget itself as from a wish to turn out the ministry. Almost every body considers the Earl of Derby and Mr Disraeli to have earned nothing but disgrace by their taking office.

---

[1] 'pass' in the text.

[2] The election of William Forbes Mackenzie, Member for Peebleshire 1841–52 and for Liverpool 1852–3, and of Charles Turner, Liverpool merchant and chairman of the Dock Board, Member for Liverpool 1852–3, was declared void on petition. Horsfall and Lidell were elected in their place, July 1853. (The editor is indebted to the City Librarian, Liverpool, for this information.)

[3] Edward (later Viscount) Cardwell (1813–86), a Peelite.

[4] William Ewart (1798–1869), like Cardwell a native of the city, had been elected Member for Liverpool in 1830, 1831, 1832 and 1835.

[5] Charles Pelham Villiers (1802–98).

[6] This is the Budget to which Jevons refers in the entry for 16 January 1853 (see p. 79 above).

After a few days a new ministry was formed containing all the best men, on the whole a Reform ministry but said also to contain some conservatives. The Earl of Aberdeen is Prime minister, Mr Gladstone, Chancellor of the Exchequer, Lord J. Russell Foreign Secretary for the present, Mr Cardwell President of the Board of Trade, Earl Granville, Chancellor of the Duchy of Lancaster, Lord Landsdowne without office.

The Parliament is not sitting at present, having been adjourned soon after the change of ministers.

Sunday, 30 January

Today at about this time, Louis Napoleon the Emperor of France is to be married to the Countess of Theba or Montijo. The civil part of the marriage was to have been performed yesterday. He has been engaged to her a very short time.[1]

*   *   *

On Friday night I was again at a lecture at the Royal Institution by Dr Williamson. The title was 'On Some recent Discoveries in Organic chemistry'. The discoveries being those of the anhydrous organic acids by Gerhardt[2] a French chemist. The greater part of the lecture was a consideration of the general tendency of these discoveries on our view of chemical change, substitution of one element for another being now[3] believed to take place rather than the addition or subtraction of elements. There were of course not so many people as on Faradays night.

At College, we have been doing very hard things in the Theory of equations, which puzzle me awfully. In Natural Philosophy, we have finished Electricity and begun Voltaic electricity which however Potter does wretchedly. I have nearly finished reading Electricity in Library of Useful Knowledge, am half through Sir Snow Harris's Electricity,[4] and am at the same time reading in Chemistry two volumes of Regnault, Liebigs Letters, now & then, a little of Graham, Schmitz Greece, &c &c, more than I have read for a long time.

[1] On 22 January 1853, the Emperor Napoleon III announced his intention to marry Eugenia de Montijo, Countess of Téba. The civil ceremony was performed at the Tuileries on 29 January; the religious ceremony took place the following day at Notre Dame.

[2] Williamson, before going to University College in 1849, had worked in the laboratories of Charles Frederic Gerhardt (1816–56) and was one of the first in Great Britain to teach his students the new philosophy of chemistry developed by Gerhardt and Laurent. See Collie, quoted Bellot, op. cit., pp. 285–6.

[3] 'no' in the text.

[4] Sir William Snow Harris (1791–1867). His *Electricity* was published in 1848.

Sunday, 17 February[1]

I have now a whole month to make up, although several important things have happened, which I ought to have put down long since, and would have done perhaps if my last one or two Sundays had not been rather engaged.

Soon after the beginning of this month, we heard that my uncle, F Hornblower was very ill of rheumatic fever, and as he had for some time been[2] very poorly and weak, it was considered dangerous. In a day or two he died,[3] from the complaint reaching the heart. This news was particularly sad on poor Aunt Jane's account. His funeral was from our house at Liverpool;[4] Aunt Jane has been living there ever since and I should think will continue to do so as long as she lives. I have known Uncle Hornblower better than[5] any of my Uncles, almost as much more as I have known Aunt Jane more than any of my Aunts, and he has always been particularly kind to me. Several years ago (I think about 5 or 6) I used to dine every day at his house in Falkner [Street][6] at the opposite corner to our present house, while I was at the Mechanics Institution.[7] Since that I have spent many weeks at his house at Nantwich, which have always been very pleasant ones. The last time was in October. Uncle H. was brought up to the tea business, and I can remember his shop in Newington.[8] Since he gave up that, he was share broker for several years and then became minister to the Unitarian Chapel at Nantwich, where he was very much liked.

About the middle of the month I received from Papa one of his businesslike letters,[9] which I like to get better than any others, on the important subject, of 'what I am going to be', as the phrase is. I had before made up my mind to be in some commercial business, but in this letter he advised me to choose some[10] which I should be more able to like for itself, and proposed the Iron trade. This letter of course set me

---

[1] 17 February 1853 fell on a Thursday. The correct date of this entry would appear to be Sunday, 27 February, as in LJ, p. 30.

[2] 'by' in the text.

[3] Reverend Francis Hornblower died on 1 February 1853 at the age of forty.

[4] 125 Chatham Street. (See Journal entry for 23 August 1852, p. 56 above.)

[5] 'that' in the text.

[6] This word is omitted in the text.

[7] The Mechanics Institute School, now the Liverpool Institute, was in Mount Street, near Falkner Street and Chatham Street. At the time Jevons was at the school (1845–7), his family were living quite a distance away at Park Hill Road, Toxteth Park. They moved to Chatham Street in 1848, after his father's bankruptcy.

[8] A street off Renshaw Street in central Liverpool, adjoining Central Station.

[9] See letter from Thomas Jevons dated 9 February 1853, Vol. II, Letter 21; also Journal entry for 17 February 1856, p. 117 below.

[10] 'some one' (LJ, p. 31).

to think very seriously, as now one of the greatest questions of my life was to be settled once and for all. I had before thought of some of the reasons which he gave, and having had the same advice from several other people, I was not long in fixing to be a manufacturer of some sort, putting however an ironmasters business out of the question, because it would not suit me at all well and would besides take me from home for the rest of my life. Now however, I have the great pleasure of thinking that, as, far as can be known at present, it is determined I shall not be away from home more than 6 or 7 months longer. It can hardly be conceived, I think, how many pleasures and still more how many real advantages I should have lost, by leaving or I may say, losing my home at once. The choice now is between a sugar refinery, and a soap,[1] chemical or some other sort of manufactory, and an indispensable condition is *that it be in Liverpool*. I shall probably go into the Birkbeck Laboratory[2] next term.

*   *   *

About a week ago there was a rather hard frost, and skating began vigorously as soon as the ice bore. On Saturday 19th[3] I skated for two hours on Regents Park, where the ice however was very bad; and in the afternoon for about two more on the Serpentine. At the latter place I enjoyed it especially, as besides plenty of tolerably good ice, there were crowds of people everywhere, which always I think increases the fun, and the excitement now and then of somebody falling in and getting saved by the Royal Humane Society's men. On Sunday I went with Harry to some ice near the railway station at Barnes, where we skated for some time. The Monday before last we had some capital fun at College with snow balls, chiefly in the stormings of the Portico which was defended by another party of the students. The medicals had a fight in the streets with blackguards which ended in rather a serious row.

On Friday 18th I went over a lucifer match manufactory, which I thought very well worth seeing though it was a dirty, low hole. Harry wanted some specimens of matches in different stages for a lecture which he gave last Monday at the Spicer Street Domestic Mission,[4] on

---

[1] See letter of Thomas Jevons of 18 February 1853, Vol. II, Letter 22; see also Journal entry for 17 February 1856, p. 117 below.

[2] To study practical chemistry under Professor Williamson. The establishment of the Birkbeck Laboratory at University College in 1845 marked an important step forward in the study of chemistry and of chemical research in Britain – such laboratories having previously been available only in chemical schools on the Continent. (Bellot, op. cit., p. 283.)

[3] i.e. 19 February. This entry and the activities described can be dated by reference to the list on pp. 83–5 above.

[4] See Journal entry for 31 October 1852, p. 68 above. Social and educational facilities were provided at the Mission, including courses of public lectures by well-known people, which attracted large audiences. At the time of Harry Roscoe's lecture a distant relative of

the 'use and importance of chemistry illustrated by the improvements it has produced in *lucifer matches*, *bleaching* and other things.'

I have got into rather a lazy way of working lately partly I think on account of the skating &c. but am going to set to work seriously for the chemistry[1] examination which is only a month off; we are now going through the organic and the metals at the same time, on different days of the week and get on very well. I had hoped that when we began algebraical Geometry as we have done now, we should have had a little rest in mathematics; but the exercises seem only to get harder and harder. The Natural Philosophy also is very dull, being on Hydrostatics, and worst of all, the History class begins tomorrow morning at 8 oclock.

I have been one or two good walks lately, chiefly among the manufacturing parts. One Saturday I went from Waterloo Bridge, eastwards along the wharfs on the Surrey side, as far as Jacobs Island, which I found much improved since my[2] visit about a year since. The ditches had been filled up or arched over and the streets were beginning to be filled.[3] Another Saturday I started from the same place but travelled west as far as Vauxhall bridge, where I again crossed the river, and proceeded again in the same direction nearly to Chelsea, whence I walked straight home. Belvedere road[4] is full of small wharfs and manufactories, such as drain tile potteries, gas works, slate works, bone mills, glue, whiting, &c manufactories.

Yesterday afternoon I accomplished still more. Starting from College a little after two, I walked through the city and along Whitechapel and the Commercial Road almost to the West India docks. I then turned up

---

his, Henry Enfield, was its secretary; his brother, Edward Enfield, who was also closely associated with the Mission, later married Harry's sister, Harriet (see Harry Roscoe's letter of 21 February 1854 to Jevons, Vol. II, Letter 35). The annual reports of the Society's missionaries provide valuable information about the distressed areas of London during the last century. See V. C. Davis, *The London Domestic Mission Society: Record of a Hundred Years 1835–1935* (1935) pp. 1–30.

[1] 'chemical' (LJ, p. 32).

[2] 'I' in the text. LJ, p. 32 substitutes 'I visited it'.

[3] Jacob's Island was a notoriously squalid part of London on the borders of Southwark and Bermondsey. The tidal streams from the Thames provided water for the Bermondsey tanneries (see under Journal entry for 3 April, p. 91 below): 'the main ditch was Folly Ditch which surrounded Jacob's Island and which filled with water every high tide . . . we find that a stream, about twenty feet wide, entirely encircles a cluster of mean and dilapidated houses to which access is gained by about a dozen bridges from the 'terra firma' on the other side of the stream. The stream is bounded on the four sides by Mill Street, Bermondsey Wall, Nittiam's Court, and London Street; and from the east end of the latter Jacob's Island can be seen in all its glory' (Knight's *London*, Vol. III, pp. 17 and 20). *Oliver Twist* (1838) and Kingsley's *Alton Locke* (1850) contain descriptions of the area. It will be noticed that in most of his walks Jevons found that improvements had been or were being made in the poorest parts of London in the early fifties.

[4] On the Lambeth side of the river, between Waterloo Bridge and Westminster Bridge.

and passing a good many manufactories, reached Bow, and got home by the railway. I feel as if I could see nothing with so much pleasure now as a dirty pearl-ash manufactory or tar-distillery. I have remarked that in Bermondsey, Tower-hamlets and most of the parts east of London Bridge, the streets are wide and open, showing I suppose that land is cheap, but that the houses are very low, not always unhealthy or dirty, seldom more than two low stories in height. These parts are very low, and wretched, but are not as far as I could see in the day time, half so full of busy vice and crime as St Giles, Drury Lane, &c.

Sunday, 3 April[1]

On the 12th March, I had a pleasant walk from London Bridge through the close parts of Bermondsey and among the tanneries till I came into the middle of the market Gardens. I went down Blue Anchor Road, and returned up the Deptford Road to the Thames Tunnel,[2] whence I came home by the railway.

Before Easter, we were going through the Conic Sections in the mathematical [class][3] and I kept up pretty well in them till near the end when I partly left off working at Mathematics that I might have more time for chemistry. In Natural Philosophy we went at a great rate through Pneumatics, the Air-pump, The steam engine, heat & part of accoustics, to none of which I attended much except the last for which I am reading a little.

A few weeks before Easter I got a letter from Papa[4] with some money, and asking me to go to Liverpool for the Easter holydays. I was very much astonished at it, but of course said immediately that I would, though I should not have more than a week.

Thursday, the day before Good Friday[5] was the first day of the holydays, so on that day I went down. I fixed at first to go by the 7 oclock train in the morning, but when I awoke I found it was 6.45, so I went to sleep again and set off by the 12 oclock train.

[1] Part of this entry was written later since two of the events mentioned are shown by the list of activities (p. 85 above) to have taken place on the 12th (the chemistry examination, see p. 94 below) and the 17th (the walk to Hampstead, see p. 95 below).

[2] At this time the tunnel was virtually a 'white elephant'. It had been opened in 1843 but only for pedestrians, as Brunel's project for carriage ways had not been accepted. In 1865 the tunnel was bought by the East London Railway Company and adapted to railway use. See L. T. C. Rolt, *Isambard Kingdom Brunel* (1957), p. 313. An earlier visit to the Tunnel by Jevons is referred to in a letter from his father dated 19 November 1850 (see Vol. II, Letter 5).

[3] LJ (p. 33). This word is omitted in the text.

[4] This letter has not survived.

[5] 24 March.

I had a comfortable journey reading on the way nearly the whole of 'Les Corps gras', in Regnault. I got in at about 9.20 and found them all well but Lucy who was ill in bed from a cold. Uncle Richard[1] was there but not Aunt Richard. I did not find the house turned so much topsy-turvy by Aunt Janes ilness as I had expected, and everything seemed as cheerful as usual. I soon found however that music was not allowed and in fact neither the organ nor the pianos were opened all the time I was in Liverpool. Herbert had to sleep in the Drawing room that I might have the small room.

The greater part of the first morning I spent in a walk with Tommy at Birkenhead, but I began a few chemicals, practising a little at crystalizing, on nitre. The solutions I left to crystallize spontaneously viz. $CuO.SO_3.FeOSO_3.MgO.SO_3$. Alum. Nitre[2] &c, I found in a great mess; the solutions appeared to have run over the edges of the jars & bottles, and some of the jars were broken.

On Saturday morning I went with Papa to call on a Mr Nevin, the manager of Steeles Soap Works in Sir Thomas' Buildings. Papa had seen a letter of his in the newspaper on Penal Jurisprudence, so he sent him one of his books,[3] and getting to know his address, called on him. Sunday morning, to chapel and the rest of the day at chemicals.

On Monday Morning, Willy Jevons[4] & I went over the soap works with Papa. It consisted merely of a room with four or five immense boilers in which the soap was boiled, and tanks in which the solution

of soda was made caustic by lying for a few days[5] on lime in the cold, the lime being thrown up into a higher tank & used again with fresh soda which is then poured down into the lower tank.

[1] Dr Richard Roscoe.
[2] $CuO.SO_3$: probably copper sulphate (Cu_2SO_4).
  $FeOSO_3$: probably ferrous sulphate ($FeSO_4$).
  $MgO.SO_3$: probably magnesium sulphate.
  Alum: probably aluminium sulphate.
  Nitre.: probably potassium nitrate.
[3] Presumably his booklet entitled *Remarks on Criminal Law, with a Plan for an Improved System, and Observations on the Prevention of Crime*, published in 1834.
[4] His first cousin, William Edgar Jevons (1836–88).
[5] 'day' in the text.

One of the boilers was being emptied and hoisted into the room above to solidify while two others were being boiled. The soda ash used is that evaporated in the last part of the reverberatory furnace; it therefore contains much soot from the flame and is very impure.

In the upper room the soap is poured into large rectangular chests, in which it solidifies. The top part which is moister is scraped off as

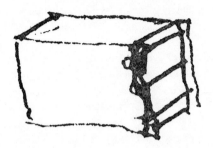

being heavier and therefore more heavily paid for in duty and this is thrown again into the boilers. We saw some of the soap cut up by wires, which is a very neat operation. The emptying of the palm oil barrels which is done by inserting a steam pipe into the bung-hole of the barrel turned upside down was carried on in the top room but we did not see it. 90 tons of soap were made per week but it was not of the best quality.

On Tuesday morning[1] I went over an Iron ship-building yard at Birkenhead with Willy & Uncle Timothy. The Punching & shearing were neatly done, but the carpentering machines were not at work.

Mr Steele['s] head clerk, Mr Nevin had given me a letter to see a soda works of his at Prestatyn near Rhyl, and on Wednesday, Papa and I went to see them, and it was fixed that I should go straight to London from Chester. We crossed to Birkenhead by the 9.45 boat, and got to Prestatyn about 1, going by railway to Chester & from there by the Chester & Holyhead railway along the Wales shore of the Dee. We saw over the works very completely (see *Soda* C.p.6) and I got specimens of the materials & the soda ash in different steps of the process. The process was almost the same as I had learnt it from Graham, but the only way to gain a good idea of the manufacture is to see it. After a dinner we returned to Chester by the railway and Papa there left me while I went on at six to Crewe, passing Beeston Castle, and the Nantwich station. From Crewe to Birmingham I went by the South Staffordshire Railway except between Crewe & Stafford, passing through the middle of the iron district where there were numberless

[1] 29 March (see list of activities, p. 85 above).

iron furnaces two or three together, blazing away on either side of the railway, and lighting up the sky; this part of the journey was long & troublesome but pleasant because it was new to me. Getting to Birmingham after ten I found that the train for London started from another station, and I was perhaps nearly an hour walking about the streets (which did not appear to me at all fine) to find it. I then exceedingly enjoyed some tea & ham at a coffee house I found open and set off for London at 12.15 getting home, without further trouble at about 5 in the morning, having been out quite 18 hours, the greater part too on the railway.

Till the next Tuesday[1] I had none but the Chemistry class to attend, and I had then great doubts whether I should go into the chemistry examination or not. At last, I resolved I would make an effort, and go in come what would, and the result was that I answered the 11 questions in 8 hours, quite I believe to my own satisfaction, but I do not yet know how much to the satisfaction of Graham.[2]

The next day I entered the Laboratory[3] to which I had been looking forward some time, but I did scarcely anything the first day but get my apparatus, clean my bottles & arrange my bench. The next day I was set to try the reactions of antimony, tin and arsenic, and after being a few days over those I had to separate them from a common solution which I found a long & troublesome process. Altogether I was very much disgusted with the laboratory at first, and particularly with Williamsons way of teaching, as he asks hard questions on purpose to puzzle you. One day while making arsenietted hydrogen, I suppose I breathed a little, for I was ill and sick after it, a real case of poisoning by arsenic.[4] After this I began the regular course of analysis which I found far better, having merely to find out the salt in a particular solution, and then try its reactions.

I expected Potters class would be better when on Light but it is duller than ever. In Mathematics we are just beginning the Differential Calculus at which I am going to work very hard at nights. I am seriously thinking of making an effort for both the Natural Philosophy & mathematical examinations seeing how well that for the Chemistry succeeded, but I have very little time to work and can only expect a low certificate in the latter class.

Aunt Jane who since Uncle Hornblowers death has been dangerously

---

[1] 5 April.

[2] The chemistry examination was held on 12 April and Jevons received the Gold Medal.

[3] The Birkbeck Laboratory. (See under Journal entry headed 17 February 1853, p. 89 above.)

[4] Arsenuretted hydrogen (arsenic hydride, As_3H_3), also known as arsine, is an extremely poisonous, colourless gas; it can be used for military purposes.

ill, has almost entirely recovered and we are looking forward to her staying at our house for good.[1]

I took my first proper botanical walk yesterday[2] in some fields at Hampstead, where I got 4 Ranunculaceae, Primroses, and a specimen of daisy. I have bought a map of the environs 15 miles round London, which distance only I intend to be the limit of my numerous projected excursions this summer.[3]

29 January 1854[4]

From several causes among which laziness, business and the want of the book are some, I have not written a word since last April. I must now therefore give a history of these last 9 or 10 months, about which I can perhaps remember as much now, as I shall ever want to read again.

During the last two months at College, I attended chiefly of course to the laboratory, though working for[5] Potters and trying to keep up in De Morgans. With analysis, as has always happened to me in Practical chemistry, I did not succeed quite as well as I might have done, much to my own disappointment, and I had regular periods of disgust with the laboratory. As at first I never answered Williamsons questions well, I never for the whole time became free with him, and could not but think he had a low opinion of me, which is the contrary however of what he has always showed. I think he is one of the most extraordinary men I have seen, very clever and exceedingly original, being quite free from all common prejudices. Neither I nor Harry thought him sufficiently mathematical & deep to settle the questions he wanted but still if he had a little more business in him he might be the first organic chemist. His freedom in religious and other opinions is what I chiefly admire. Though always thinking he is going to be the greatest philosopher in the world he has not any disagreable conceit or any humbug of that sort in him.

In the laboratory, I got through (rather slowly however) nearly all the 'bottles', and did several quantitatives[6] which were neither very bad or very good, which with a few preparations was all my work. But I consoled myself with thinking that it was the first three months I had learnt.

I worked up well for Potter's examination, not keeping merely to what

---

[1] His Aunt Jane died a few months later on 1 August 1853, aged fifty-six.
[2] The list of activities shows that this walk was made on 17 April (see p. 85 above).
[3] Jevons left the rest of this page blank.
[4] This entry was written at Liverpool after Jevons had left University College (July 1853).
[5] 'at' (LJ, p. 36).
[6] 'quantitative' in the text.

was sufficient to get the prize, and having De la Rive's Electricity,[1] I learnt much more on that subject than was necessary. There were very few in the examination and only one or two that answered any quantity. I had no difficulty with the mechanics, sound light, electricity, except a little I missed in hydrostatics and a mistake or two about telescopes, but was not so well up in Astronomy a newer subject to me. On waves I answered a good deal.

Mathematics was a much harder affair of course; some time before the examination I formed some desperate resolutions as to the place I would get, and I did work up a little. I tried very hard in the examination, but spent too much time on the hard ones and came out fourth.

I went to chapel but little generally taking walks or working and I got a few plants.

Since Easter I had been thinking a great deal of again living at home, and looked forward to it as a great happiness, for I thought that having a regular employment in the day, with the evenings and other time to myself would keep me in much better health and greater activity than[2] in the holydays when all the time was upon my hands.

Now came the most sudden and important change of prospects I have ever had.

One Friday afternoon about a week before I was going to leave the college and go home, Harry said he had a very excellent and unexpected thing to tell me. This rather excited me, as I hoped it would be as pleasant as good, and I was rather horrified, and disappointed when he told me going home, that it was the offer (as I understood it then) of the assayership to the new mint in Australia. There was scarcely anything that could be more distant from my wishes then, than to emigrate, and that together with the responsibility & difficulty of such a place made me think at one that it was *perfectly impossible*. This I told Harry at once, and I even made him partly agree with me; I also remember congratulating myself for some time after upon the very quick and strong decision I had shown myself capable of making upon any great occasion.

I at once of course wrote to papa about it, but had the disagreable job next morning of speaking to both Williamson and Graham about it. Williamson it appeared had recommended me to Graham[3] as the one

[1] Auguste de la Rive, *Traité d'Electricité théorique et appliquée, etc.*, 3 tom. (1854–58); *A treatise on Electricity, in theory and practice* [translated from the French by C. V. Walker]. 3 vols. (1853–8). In LJ Mrs Jevons has substituted 'De la Rue' (p. 36).

[2] 'and' in the text.

[3] In his autobiography Harry Roscoe gives a somewhat different account of how Jevons was offered the assayership: 'Graham . . . sent for me one day and offered me the post of Assayer in the Mint at Sydney, which had just been established. It was worth £600–£700 a year, and was a post which many young men would have jumped at. I felt, however, that I could not leave my mother and sister, as they did not wish to go to Australia, so I declined it with thanks, but told him I knew a young man who was singularly well fitted for the posi-

best fitted in the laboratory for the place. I thanked them both but said I thought I should hardly take the offer as I did not wish to go so far from home and hardly felt old enough for the place, but I said that of course I must hear from my father before deciding. This it afterwards turned out was a very necessary provision. On the Sunday, I went a quiet walk and thought but little about the affair, considering it quite impossible. Once or twice perhaps a sort of vision came into my head, of independence, a large salary, a position in society &c &c at [the][1] age of 18, but did not make much impression.

Harry told me next morning that Williamson had been speaking to another student about the place, and that if I had any thoughts whatever about it, I ought to say something more decisive. I did not think that there was the slightest chance but about an hour afterwards I got a letter from Papa,[2] asking me to consider, and saying that though he would hesitate as to my taking it if I had to leave England for good, he did not see such a great obstacle in leaving for some years together. I told this to Graham and asked for a few days to consider and decide, and as my Father wished packed up at once and[3] left for Liverpool. I remained at home from about the Tuesday to the Saturday a sufficient time as it appeared, for me to change my mind as to the leaving home but not to get rid of another objection, that of not thinking myself quite old enough for & equal to the position. I talked very little to any of them and they said very little to me, so that I also was convinced merely by knowing what my father and the others thought and by thinking about the thing myself.

On returning to London, I lived again for a short time at Aunt Henry's. On the Monday I saw Graham with whom I wrote a letter of application to Captain Ward the Master of the new Mint at Sydney, through whom the appointment would be made. I at once went into Grahams own assay laboratory[4] which I had fully expected would be the case though it was merely from his own kindness and at considerable expense & trouble to himself. On being taken over the rooms and seeing

---

tion, and who I believed would accept it. This young man was Stanley Jevons. Graham saw him, was pleased with him, and gave him the appointment' (*Life and Experiences*, p. 39). It is probable that both Williamson and Harry Roscoe (then working for Williamson as private assistant) mentioned Jevons's name to Graham, but Graham would already have been well acquainted with Jevons, who had been his student.

[1] This word is omitted in the text.

[2] Letter dated 10 July 1853 (see Journal entry for 17 February 1856, p. 117 below; and Vol. II, Letter 26.

[3] 'at' in the text.

[4] Jevons stayed on in London all through the summer holidays of 1853, working in the assay laboratory of Professor Graham, who was non-resident assayer to the Royal Mint and in 1854 became Master of the Mint in succession to Sir John Herschel. See Jevons's letter of 28 August 1853 to Harry Roscoe, Vol. II, Letter 27.

the quantity of particular apparatus necessary, and the number of things to be attended to I felt very much alarmed so much so that at last I determined to put as much of the responsibility of the acceptation off my own shoulders by telling Graham plainly that I was afraid of undertaking it, after seeing in what the work consisted and the extent of the arrangements I shall have to make for setting up an assay office in Australia. He only laughed and I did not know how to make any further operation.[1]

Accordingly I set to work to learn the assaying after a little joining in the regular business of the laboratory. At this time I lived in solitary lodgings at Camden Town, (No 13 Albert Street) and though rather troubled with business I remember the time without displeasure. Occupied during the day at College or about town buying apparatus – I spent the evenings very agreeably in reading – Geology was the subject I chiefly attended to & De la Beches work[2] on Geolog. observation, & comparison with the changes now going on, the work I chiefly read.

*   *   *

During this part of my life[3] – as I can now (October 1862) distinctly remember, I used to think that physical science was the true field of knowledge & enlightenment. Classical, historical, poetical studies etc I regarded as at the most elegant, & interesting. Possessing no certainty & being unprogressive they could not compare in usefulness with anything sure & progressive. Some other branches of study such as antiquarian research, history of art, I looked upon as the merest trifling – at any rate I used often to say to myself, it is useless to study an[4] old stone or old piece of armour. There can be neither profit nor good amusement from such fanatical interest as[5] some show.

To every one it must happen to be callous to some sources of interest, & pleasure & profit which others enjoy. Not even Aristotle or Plato was quite universal in his tastes – and thus at present although I have learnt to value many things which I formerly despised, I am unable to feel any enthusiasm in others, especially in those works of the painter's art for which some profess such admiration. Turners Landscapes & other pictures especially are either altogether above or below my powers of

---

[1] 'objection' has been substituted by Mrs Jevons in LJ (p. 38); in the original text, the word is 'operation'.

[2] Probably H. T. De la Beche: *The Geological Observer* (1851).

[3] In the original journal volume the following two entries, made in October and December of 1862, after Jevons's return from Australia, follow on the entry for 24 January 1854, and as they relate to this earlier period it has been thought best to place them here in their context instead of in their date order. See p. 184 below.

[4] '&' in the text.

[5] '&' in the text.

appreciation. Several of them, indeed, such as the Garden of Hesperides seem to me finely conceived, but far from surprising in any way.

* * *

When quite young I can remember I had no thought or wish of surpassing others. I was rather taken[1] with a liking of little arts & bits of learning. My mother carefully fostered a liking for botany giving me a small microscope & many books which I yet have – Strange as it may seem I now (Dec 1862) believe that Botany, & the Natural System by excercising discrimination of kinds, is the best of logical exercises. What I may do in logic is perhaps derived [from][2] that early attention to Botany. My Uncle Richard also gave me Henslow's Botany – He presented me with certain bookbinding tools which I had the greatest pleasure in using or trying to use. I am yet partial to bookbinding, & shall some time perhaps begin it again.[3] I used to think I should like to be a bookbinder or book seller. It seemed to me a most delightful trade, & I wished or thought of nothing better. More lately I thought I should be a minister – It seemed so serious, & useful, a profession and I entered but little into the merits of religion, & the duties of a minister. Every one dissuaded me from the notion – & before I had arrived at any age to require a real decision science had claimed me.

Now when I must look upon Christianity from a very exterior & critical point of view – it is amusing to look back on times when I reverenced christ[y] like most others – read Channings Evidences[4] with admiration & wonder. I was not without a tendency to inquire into the subject. The Gospels seemed worth more than reading – they were worth analysing & making into a rigorrous history of Christ. And this I actually undertook to do – while living in Chatham Street perhaps about the year 1850. I began the work during the quiet of Sunday afternoons in my small bedroom where I had a very diminutive table with an ink-stand and a few little things in a study like array. By noting down the facts as stated in the Gospels & comparing them & arranging them in chronological order I intended to form a regular life. But altogether apart from any difficulties which older persons might meet, I found the task very perplexing for my then powers. What most impressed the work on my memory is that on the second or third Sunday my father appeared suddenly in my room. As this was the very top of the house & he was usually sitting during the afternoon after dinner in the parlour, I suspect he must have missed me, & come to see my occupation. But

[1] 'taking' in the text.
[2] This word is omitted in the text.
[3] Some of the small books bound by Jevons still survive.
[4] William Ellery Channing: *A Discourse on the Evidences of Revealed Religion delivered before the University in Cambridge at the Dudleian Lecture* (1821).

finding me writing he pressingly inquired the subject, which I was at last almost forced to confess to my entire confusion & dismay. It seems curious now some 12 years later to reflect how long I have been reading, & writing, & thinking – Surely it ought not to be without result.

It was during the year 1851 while living almost unhappily among thoughtless if not bad companions at Mrs Mackenzies at No [*blank space*] Gower Street – a gloomy house on which I now look with dread[1] it was then & when I had got a quiet hour in my small bedroom at the top of the house that I began to think that I could & ought to do more than others. A vague desire & determination grew upon me – I was then in the habit of saying my prayers like any good church-person – and it was when so engaged that I thought most eagerly of the future & hoped for the unknown.

Then and before as well as after even up to the present time – I have had a strange habit of lying in bed awake for hours – dreaming in full wakefulness, imagining myself in all sorts of positions – always doing something very clever & extraordinary but sometimes very good & other times quite as bad, in short inventing endless novels with myself as the constant hero of them. Many of these dreams were so agreable that I continued or repeated them night after night or recurred to them after considerable intervals. One especially in which I was prime minister – far the most celebrated that ever was – In others I was a prince, a king – leader of armies, people – etc etc. at other times of brigands, or thieves & murderers.

My reserve was so perfect that I suppose no one had the slightest comprehension of my motives or ends. My father probably knew me but little – I never had any confidential conversation with him. At school and College the success in the classes was the only indication of

[1] Jevons lived at Mrs Mackenzie's boarding house from December 1850 until July 1851. His extreme disquiet about the place, even twelve years later, appears to have been connected with three other boys from University College School who also lived there, though there is no direct evidence to show its precise cause. According to his brother Herbert, in a letter to their father dated 23 November 1850: . . . 'Stanley does not like any of the three boys who would be his constant companions and does not like the prospect of being thrown so much into their company . . . he says he has nothing to say but that they are *nasty boys*, boys with tastes and pursuits not congenial with Stanleys'. . . . Jevons himself wrote to his father on 11 December 1850: . . . 'You want me to tell you something about my companions but it is not very easy to tell exactly what I think of them'. (See Vol. II, Letters 8 and 9.) One of the boys, Bolton, belonged to a prominent Liverpool family and if, as is possible, he knew of Roscoe's insanity, Jevons's great unhappiness would be explained. His brother's illness affected him particularly deeply at this period of his life, which saw the beginning of his determination to try and complete what Roscoe could not do. (See Journal entry for 23 May 1864, p. 195 below; also Biographical Introduction, p. 7 above.)

my powers. All else that I intended or did was within or carefully hidden. The reserved character as I have often thought is not pleasant – nor lovely. But is it not necessary? to one such as me. Would it have been sensible or even possible for a boy of 15 or 16 to say what he was going to do before he was 50. For my own part I felt it to be almost presumptuous to pronounce to myself the hopes I held & the schemes I formed. Time alone could reveal whether they were empty or real, only when proved real could they be known to others.

I do not remember that at College I had any fixed notions of how I would apply my labour ultimately. To increase my knowledge was my present task. But I early began to try some slight original research. When in the chemistry class of Prof Graham in 1852 & 3 I began to collect notes about a few little points, such as solution and the decomposition of water by heat. I also speculated concerning the ultimate molecular constitution of matter and began a formal little theory on the subject probably wholly absurd but still a connected & independent argument & tried to reconcile the deductions of the theory with the coefficients of expansion of the several metals. Some slight but probably accidental coincidences which I met immensely encouraged me. These notes I have yet.[1]

The ship *Oliver Lang*
September 11th 1854

Dearest Father,[2]

As we are now in pretty nearly the last week of the voyage to Melbourne, it is high time to be beginning some sort of an account of it, to let you know how pleasantly it has been passed by myself or how unpleasantly by others.

I will first give you a short account of our course up to here and the weather we have met with.

As soon as ever the steam Tug left us, (in sight of Tuskar)[3] we had a very fair wind which soon took us clear of Ireland, and we then sailed southwards on the ordinary course, till we passed on July 9th almost in sight of and to the westward of Madeira. We kept westward of the Canaries & Cape Verd Islands till we reached Latitude 9° N where we

---

[1] These notes are still extant. Jevons never ceased to be interested in this subject. Cf Biographical Introduction, above, p. 15.

Jevons left the next seven pages blank.

[2] This letter appears to have been a draft for the letter dated 11 September 1854 published in shortened version in LJ, pp. 40–4, with minor textual differences (see Vol. II, Letter 45). For an account of the earlier part of the voyage, see his letter of 3 July 1854 to his father, Vol. II, Letter 42.

[3] Tuskar Rock, off the south-east coast of Ireland, near Rosslare.

were obliged by a very bad wind to run due East, right up to the Coast of Africa. This we thought good sailing compared with the week before, the whole of which had been a calm often *a dead calm*, the average rate being 2 knots an hour.

After tacking about down the African coast nearly in sight of land we at last got S W and crossed the line (Aug 4th) in Longitude 20W. Reserving the account of the *shaving* which was first-ratedly performed, we made a very good south westerly run, till just westward of Trinidad or Ascension and 600 miles east of Rio Janeiro (Aug 12th) The weather was now again extraordinarily calm for another week, during which we went southeast, passing & passing to change our course to avoid, Tristian d'Acunha, on the 22nd August.

We had then been just 8 weeks out, a very long time for such a ship as this, and the only excuse for which is that we had most extraordinarily calm weather. Only twice till then do I remember anything like a fair wind, such as we have seen enough of since, and several times it was so perfectly calm that barrels thrown overboard floated out to the side of the vessel, instead of astern.

About the 21st or 22nd August began our heavy weather, with a gale, during which several studdingsail booms were carried away, and the main topsail split. On the 24th at night, a still heavier gale came on, when, partly through mismanagement, a large number of sails were torn. We then sailed about 10° south of the Cape with capital winds, but were afterwards obliged to sail rather northerly to Lat. 41°S, Long. 43° (about Sept 1st) and lastly not far north of the Marion Islands, & SSE to our present position, Lat 49°S & Long 97°E where we are tonight, most unexpectedly in nearly a dead calm.

I must not however forget a very sudden & rather serious squall which took us July 5th at 10 oclock at night, and rather frightened us. Sail was got in pretty quickly, and we then saw the first quick sailing, the log giving 17 knots an hour, though I doubt now if we ever went so much. I saw that night also a very distinct & beautiful *lunar rainbow*.

From that day to the 20 Aug. we had only 5 or 6 days with rain, and that only light showers, which will give you an idea of the fineness of the weather. In the tropics it was certainly often extremely hot, but we felt it less than I expected, and the delightfully cool evenings made up for the days. For two or three days near the tropics we had rather curiously, in the middle of a dead calm, a very large but low swell, which shook the ship about in a most uneasy and uncomfortable manner; it must have been caused by a storm just before.

I can remember perfectly some of the splendidly fine days we had in the tropics when we were lying on the deck under the awning all day, reading, playing cards, or draughts &c, after tea watching the sunset & the moon rise and then sitting out in the night till late.

Sometimes the sun went down all alone without a cloud in the sky. More often there were clouds of all varieties of shape; one time the sky all round was covered with bright fiery coloured clouds, which being of a scattered shape, looked exactly like ridges of flames; another time there were splendid mountainous masses of cloud about the sun, with others of very different shapes & colours about the sky. Besides the clouds there were the tints of the sky which were very beautiful, chiefly singular greens, every variety of reds & oranges, and a little time after the sunsets a very beautiful rose or pink tint.

Not to tire you, as we were tired, with too much fine weather, I must come to the gales. We saw a little of the sort on 22nd Aug. but on the 24th at 10 PM began the strongest. Though the Captain had fully expected it, he had, according to his usual custom, kept all sail out. One topsail was reefed by the men very slowly, but they as good as refused to reef the two others, though ready hauled up, & accordingly they were both soon torn; three of the staysails had been split at the first, and the three jibs had been torn completely to shreds. These, with one royal, made 9 sails more or less injured.

The next day, a second & different gale came on at 10 AM, and we ran all day before the wind with only the mainsail & foresail set, looking more like a wreck than anything. A very heavy sea of course rose and the large waves rolling in astern & leaving us by the head looked very grand, and more like rather distant mountains and valleys than anything else.

On Sept 4th and the night before we had another tremendous gale during which 5 or 6 more of the principal sails were more or less torn, including the mainsail and foresail. About this time too we had plenty of hail & snow, & water often froze on the deck. Since then we have had only one other gale worth mentioning, on the 9th, but the Captain had taken in sail before it began and we ran quite safely and without injury, through it, with close reefed topsails. Studdingsail booms have been carried away without number from time to time, and two of them from dipping in the waves and snapping off with the force of the ships motion.

I always said that the ship could not be rigged well in such a short time as it was, and it is quite proved now, by many things which are defective. Most of the ironwork is of the most horrible iron, and this is the chief cause of the loss of so many sails as well as of the falling of two of the topsail yards, though luckily they did not come down to the deck.

We have of course had the usual succession of fishes & birds to amuse us. We wondered for a long time at the porpoises until at last some dolphins were seen, a small one of which was caught by a line. We saw thousands of the small white flying fish, sometimes chased by porpoises. At length, in the tropics, a shark appeared and swam several times round the vessel on the look-out for someting to eat; he was hooked and harpooned after some trouble. The same afternoon another was caught, as well as one or two more from time to time. We had however the best sport with the last one, just on this side [of]¹ the tropics. He appeared in the middle of some Cape Pigeons which he was chasing, but some came up to the ship. The hook with a large piece of pork was put over the stern at once, and we saw him turn over twice and take it in his mouth. He was not hooked till the third time when he was hauled straight up and dragged off to the main deck. He had a Cape Pigeon in his stomach, swallowed whole. He was about 5 feet long (the same length as all the others) and of a fine blue colour.

We have had Cape Pigeons following the ship now for nearly a month. They are very pretty black & white birds of the shape of a pigeon & fly about the stern in great numbers. Among them are nearly always several albatrosses; we have seen none of a pure white colour all over and most are of a dull black. Still they are magnificent birds, floating about in the air with the greatest ease, without ever moving their wings; in fact I have hardly ever seen one flap his wings. How they keep up their speed none of us can make out. There has been very poor luck with my lines; I hooked an albatross a few days ago and a Pigeon or two, but they all got away, (and it has been the same with everybody else [as]¹ well.

Neptune's visit on board on crossing the line was very well carried out among the ships company. Neptune & Amphitrite first made a procession round the ship on a gun-carriage with all the rest of their men, very cleverly dressed, and then set to work shaving on the spars above the main deck. The apprentices, stewards & musicians were the ones shaved; the clerk called over the name of each from the book in which they were all set down, the inspector & his policemen brings him from any part of the ship where he may be, he is then well tarred and the brush shoved into his mouth when he opens it to answer the regular questions put to him. The barber then shaves him, the doctor gives him a pill & a dose of medicine besides a smell of the smelling bottle with pins in the lid, and the man who is always by this time in a tremendous rage is overturned into a sail full of water where the two *bears* duck him so long as they think proper. It ended by one of the policemen himself

---

¹ This word is omitted in the text.

being seized and shaved on the pretext of his not having crossed the line before. The whole was one of the funniest things I ever saw.[1]

To come now to the first cabin passengers,[2] it is no easy matter to know exactly how much to tell you about the continual quarrels there have been. They have affected me very little as I have been on friendly terms with nearly everybody, but even considering that we are all Australian Emigrants and that most are only second cabin passengers turned into the first cabin, I could scarcely have thought it possible that so much jealousy and hatred as well as petty quarreling could have been crammed into such a small space as this cabin during three months.

I should think it was part of the duty of a good Captain to prevent and to smooth down all such affairs as these, but Capt Manning on the contrary was the first to raise a quarrel.

Mr Lane, an Irishman, and a French Professor, two Irish ladies, & the Captain (who is, I should think, going to marry the younger of the ladies) were those most concerned and it resulted in a very strong dislike between Mr Lane & the Captain and a separation of the Cabin into those who *would* and those who *wouldnt* speak to Mr Lane. This feud has been kept up particularly well among the ladies and has been the chief starting point for all subsequent quarrels.

I kept clear of everything, till finding that Mr Lane was a gentleman well worth knowing and certainly not the most in fault of the two, I became more intimate with him & consequently incurred the dislike of the Captain and one or two of the others. Mr Lane is from Cork, but has lived 20 years in different parts of France so as to have taken completely the appearance of a Frenchman. He has been lately, Professor of Literature (English literature, I suppose) in the college of Amiens. He is therefore a very well educated man and knows a great many of the first men of France. I have had a great many very pleasant talks with him, but he has rather extraordinary political opinions being a regular Republican, engaged a little in the Revolutions at Paris, as well as in the Irish Rebellion. He is going to Sydney to see his family and I shall therefore probably see something more of him, though I shall take care not to be more intimate with him than I wish. He is very much offended at the Captains conduct and even intends publishing something against him at Sydney.

[1] Jevons left half the page blank after this.
The following passage included in the letter actually sent to his father does not appear in the Journal: 'We had some very pleasant meetings with ships till the bad weather began, since which we have not seen one. On the 23d of July the *Fletcher*, from London to New Zealand, came up to us, and ran a race for several days, falling back at last. There were often two or three in view at the same time, but there was no chance of sending a letter back.' See letter of 11 September 1854, Vol. II, Letter 45 .

[2] There were 24 first cabin passengers out of a total of about 400. See Jevons's letter to Harry Roscoe, dated 25 June 1854, just before he went on board, Vol. II, Letter 41.

Mr Newton is the one I care most for after him. He is a working engineer, at one time an enginedriver, but a very superior man of his sort. He has been engaged making the Mint Machinery, and is sent out to see it put up. After that he will remain there on his own account, but will probably be employed occasionally by the Mint. As he is such a sensible, pleasant man I shall try to get him to let me lodgings in the house he is going to take for his wife & family and I should then, I expect be comfortable enough. I should even, if possible, like to have my laboratory in the same house but I cannot tell how it can be settled till it comes to the fact.

About John Anderson,[1] my chum, I need only say that he is as good a fellow in every way as I could wish to know, but he is going to a farm near Sydney and I shall not see much of him after we land.

Mr Day, [is][2] a retired old grocer & butter dealer from Shoreditch, London, but one of the kindest old men I ever saw. He has told me so many tales about all he has seen and done in London that I think I could write his life. He is a great cribbage player, and I have had some very pleasant games with him to help over the long evenings, reading being impossible. Mr Day is going to Melbourne, as well as a Mr Grylls, a young solicitor and a sporting gentleman, but a very good fellow. Mr Clarence (alias Joseph) Holt[3] is a very amusing sort of man, but not from his acting which is all tragedy. He is very greedy at dinner and in a state of the greatest fear during gales, standing in one corner of the Cabin and asking everybody who passes what they think of the danger.

The second cabin passengers are on the whole a very disagreable set, though Chas Bolton's[4] chums are among the best of them. The third cabin and intermediate passengers on the contrary are the best behaved in the ship, but nearly everybody on Board agrees in disliking extremely the Captain, doctor and purser, and finding fault with the arrangements of the ship generally. To begin, the ship is much too crowded in all the cabins, it ships a great deal of water in the storms & wets every place through, while the main deck is kept in the most horrible state of filth; the provisions though good, were tossed in such a hurry that nothing can be found when wanted and accordingly the provisions were not given out according to the scale. The Captain never listens to a complaint

---

[1] The Scottish boy who shared Jevons's cabin. See his letter of 25 June 1854 to Harry Roscoe, Vol. II, Letter 41.

[2] This word is omitted in the text.

[3] Clarence Holt of the Royal Lyceum Theatre, London, tragedian and theatrical manager. He and his wife, Mary Holt, were well known in Australia during the middle years of the nineteenth century. He was the father of Bland Holt (1853–1942), actor and celebrated producer of melodrama in Australia. (The editor is indebted to Professor J. A. La Nauze for this information.)

[4] The young man whom Jevons took out as an assistant for his assay office. He was a younger brother of the Jevons family's nurse, Ann Bolton. Charles Bolton settled in Australia.

reasonably and never goes at all to see that things are properly and comfortably managed, and altogether there is so much said against the way in which the ship has been sent out, as I am sure would injure James Baines & Co, if it were known in England.

The doctor too, is a young man who has just got his diploma, and he treats everybody in such a manner that he is universally disliked and despised and is therefore quite unable to manage the third cabin passengers properly. Whether through his attention or not there has not been a death or a serious illness on board, while there have been three or four births.

The Captain is very much disliked by the crew for the manner he treated them during the gales, keeping them up for nights together, taking in sail. The first mate is the only one liked on board and the only testimonial that has been or is likely to be got up, is to him.

I have now said enough about the complaints and quarrels, but they have been so much the subject of talk on board, that I cannot help saying something. I rather think you will hear of them somewhere else, as the passengers do not intend to remain altogether silent about the things.

I, however, have passed the voyage pleasantly enough, and the complaints have served only as something to interest me when there was nothing else. I have read very little, a thing nearly impossible on a ship, but have spent the time chiefly in watching the weather & such things, talking & playing draughts & cards. In the fine weather, especially in the tropics, this was all very pleasant, but since the stormy weather and long nights began it has got more tiresome. Twentyfour hours of some of the gales we had is enough to tire anybody out, from the motion of the vessel, noise & wet, and I can give you no idea of what scenes there sometimes were at dinner, when with a sudden lurch, hams, fowls, loaves or cheeses would roll off the table, water soup gravy &c would spill over you and the knives & forks would regularly fly into the corners of the cabin.

Off Port Phillip Heads.
Sept 22nd 1854.

At last we are in sight of land and lying some miles outside of the Harbour with the pilot on board and all anxious to get in but without a breath of wind to take us in. We were expecting land all yesterday and at seven oclock in the evening, the revolving light on Cape Otway[1]

[1] The lighthouse on Cape Otway, a promontory on the coast of Victoria about 70 miles south-west of Port Phillip Heads, was completed in 1848.

was seen right ahead of us, the first land or mark of any sort we had seen since we lost sight of Cape Clear.[1] You can imagine what a pleasure it was to watch it as we hove to 10 or 15 miles from it so as not to reach the heads too early. About twelve oclock we set sail again slowly and this morning I was called up as soon as it was light to see the land, the Heads being then just on sight. The pilot came on board at 8 oclock but I begin to think now that we shall hardly get to Melbourne to night as it is a calm.

The coast on the western side is very like that near Liverpool in appearance with a hill exactly like Dinas Dinlle;[2] on the other side it is more rocky & uneven with a range of hills in the distance. With the telescope I can see very plainly the scrubby dark coloured trees and the dull grassy hills just above the beach. There are certainly trees enough for anything all over the land. The day is what they call regular Australian weather, a very fine & warm though clouded and the air very pleasant. There are beautiful large pieces of sea weed floating about which show me what to expect.

Since I wrote last we have had some more stormy weather particularly a very heavy gale on the night of the 14th and a very sudden & violent squall on the 18th which surprized them a little. One day a shoal of large grampuses passed us which looked very singular with their great round snouts slowly rolling out of the sides of the waves. On the 14th & 16th we had fine displays of the Aurora Australis which were much finer than anything I have seen of the sort in England.

Melbourne
Sunday. Sept 24th 1854.

Here we are, anchored a mile or two from Melbourne[3] and waiting to land the passengers tomorrow & to be off again as soon as possible. We sailed up the Harbour yesterday morning and had some very pretty views of the land & the hills as we came along. We saw also the first signs of life, men sitting at their tent doors getting breakfast, wooden houses, &c &c.

---

[1] Off the extreme south-westerly tip of Ireland.   [2] Near Caernarvon (LJ, p. 44).
[3] The following rather different description of Melbourne was included in the letter actually sent to his father: 'Here we are, anchored a mile or two from Melbourne, and near enough to the shore for us to examine by the telescope the manner of life in Australia. The appearance of the houses in Richmond and Williamstown which we see, is very strange and ugly, and tents are very common. The land round Melbourne is flat and not very inviting, but there are ranges of hills all round in the distance very similar in appearance to the Carnarvonshire mountains. I shall very probably go on shore tomorrow, and I have rather luckily made out Caldwell, Train, and Company's name on a large building at the water's edge . . .' See below, letter of 11 September 1854, Vol. II, Letter 45.

The shipping lies in a small bay at the head of Port Phillip, and Melbourne rises from the beach to the eastward of this bay. The appearance of the town is very curious; it looks like a crowd of ugly buildings of every size chiefly iron & wood arranged as if no two houses were in one street. There seem to be very few large buildings & these are as ugly as the rest, but we can make out by the telescope, an Exhibition building, 2 or 3 churches, & so on, with a railway station on the other side of the bay.

The country is flat for many miles round Melbourne, and covered with the usual quantity of trees, but in the distance there are several ranges of hills very similar in appearance to the Carnarvonshire hills but not quite so beautiful.[1]

8 Church Hill,[2] Sydney.
Jan 5th 1855.

Time gets on fast & I begin to feel the necessity of doing something satisfactory, and of carrying out to some small extent all the fine things I have imagined. For the last 18 months what serious advance have I made in knowledge. I made some progress in Geology of which I was before that time quite ignorant, and I am gradually getting some ideas in Meteorology and such half-sciences, but that good solid foundation of all other scientific knowledge, mathematics, I have attempted as yet in vain, and I am afraid that I have lost the habit of studying and cannot concentrate & direct my thoughts as I used. Still I think this is no wonder, considering the worry, anxiety & labour after common things and arrangements that I have had to go through.[3] These may have been usefull to me but any advantages I may have derived from such changes & troubles must[4] be set down under a different head for they have not helped me on with study. For many months yet too I cannot look forward to being settled and to have my mind free for the subjects I wish.

Of one thing however I am glad; I begin to feel that liking for and

---

[1] Jevons landed for a short while at Melbourne. He reached Sydney on 6 October and was met at the ship by the second assayer to the Mint, F. B. Miller, and by Sergeant Trickett who was also to be on the Mint staff. (See letter from Thomas Jevons, dated 31 January 1855, Vol. II, Letter 53.) The journey had lasted a hundred days, an exceptionally long one, seventy days being considered a reasonable duration for the passage (see letters from Thomas Jevons dated 10 July 1853 and 30 September 1854, Vol. II Letters 26 and 46). below.

[2] The cottage where Jevons had established his assay office and where he and Charles Bolton were living. The full address was 8 Charlotte Place, Church Hill, Sydney.

[3] For Jevons's father's remarks on this subject, see his letter of 1 August 1855, Vol. II, Letter 69.

[4] In the original text, Jevons has written 'much'.

interest in history poetry & literature in general which I always expected would come to me some day. It is certainly a much less severe exercise of the mind than the mathematical sciences & I hope I shall not get to indulge too freely in it.

It[1] seems rather strange to say so now, but I cannot see that coming on such an errand as this to Australia will at all benefit me ultimately. It is a perfectly decided thing in my mind to be at home again in from 5 to 10 years, and as I have no intention of being nothing better than an assayer or chemist all my life, I shall have to begin life again on a new bottom. Only I shall begin this second time under considerable advantages, backed by a small capital (supposing everything to go on well here) my mind wellformed and its direction clearly determined, with a good many years *colonial experience* of the world which will be equal to double as much *home experience* and I hope with knowledge and abilities which will enable me to get a good stand wherever the standing-place maybe.

* * *

From time to time, there is a thought which presses upon me and it is one of the most unhappy & discouraging thoughts I have ever felt; it is the inalterability of a mans disposition & character, and of my own in particular. That saying, 'man is a bundle of habits' always occurs to me as particularly true[2] and I will add, that these habits are generally very oddly & oppositely picked out and tied up together to form a man, and that it is very difficult if not quite impossible to rectify completely any mistakes that may have been made in picking out the habits. For myself I know that I continually & habitually do things that I totally disapprove of when fully considered and which are also in opposition to my general principles & conduct. Yet I find myself doing the same things again & again in spite of all wishes and efforts. This is bad but it is not the worst or most painful part of the subject. Two things I believe quite necessary to a successful man, or a successful mind in whatever line it lies, *firstly ability* or *talents* and *secondly diligence* & *perseverance* in applying them. The last lie in mens own power in most cases and I am not much afraid of being found wanted in this respect. But how is anybody to ascertain truly whether he has ability or not; before a man has made a discovery or improvement, or done some deed which at once establishes his reputation and gives him data from which in his own mind to estimate his powers. But he may & most likely does think but little of what he has achieved and imagines he has powers for much more.

[1] Jevons has written 'I' in the text.
[2] Jevons first wrote '. . . particularly happy & true . . .'

A paragraph in Whewells Hist of Induce Sciences vol 2 p 184[1] expresses best the thought that I intend

'The hidden fountain of our unbidden thoughts is for us a mystery; and we have in our consciousness, no standard by which we can measure our own talents; but our acts & habits are something of which we are conscious; and we can understand therefore how it was that *Newton* could not admit that there was any difference between himself & other men, except in his possession of such habits as we have mentioned, perseverance & vigilance. When he was asked how he made his discoveries, he answered "by always thinking about them"; and at another time, he declared that if he had done anything, it was due to nothing but industry & patient thought: "I keep the subject of my enquiry constantly before me, and wait till the first dawning opens gradually by little & little, into a full & clear light". No better account can be given of the nature of the mental *effort* which gives to the philosopher, the full benefit of his powers; but the natural *powers* of mens minds are not on that account the less different. There are many who might wait through ages of darkness without being visited by any dawn'. – How painfully but with what truth does this last sentence fall upon your mind after reading & being encouraged by the first part.[2]

I now feel[3] called upon to carry out without furthur delay all the plans & designs which I have been for so long contemplating; I can no longer put them off till some futture time when I shall have more leisure or more spirits. The experiment must be tried now, now or never, as to whether I can get any good out of my books and my shows of study. I find however that my habits of study are really changed since I was at College and that it is really not so easy to apply myself to a book as it was then.

On looking back at the time I spent in Church Hill, it does not seem to me as if there was any great displeasantness in the life except in the state of continual dissatisfaction & annoyance in which I was kept by having my time so unemployed. This wearied me and made me anxious about the finishing and success of the Mint and this uneasiness of mind again kept me from applying my mind to any thing seriously. As to not succeeding in my business as an assayer, I never had intended to undertake work for the public and never in Sydney set my mind upon getting it.

Annangrove Cottage – Sydney.[4] June 10th 1855

---

[1] William Whewell, *History of the Inductive Sciences* (1837) Vol. 2, pp. 184–5.

[2] The top part of the next page has been torn off. The rest was left blank.

[3] The top part of this page, on which Jevons appears to have written, has been torn off. The place and date of the entry (see note 4), at the bottom of the page, were possibly added later.

[4] Since the beginning of May 1855, Jevons had been living with Mr and Mrs Miller. 'I live out here very comfortably . . .', he wrote to Harry Roscoe on 11 July 1855, 'having a

I was not very disappointed at not getting much but it was disagreable to think that other people were setting you down as unsuccessful & incompetent.

It is impossible now to prevent[1] oneself casting out some thoughts a few years in advance, when with one or two thousand pounds at my command I can fix my own course freely and make a move in the direction I should wish to go. Unless the Mint is found not to succeed it will be several years before I shall feel myself justified in giving up a salary of £500 and going home to look out for something else. But what occurs to me now is to make a sort of speculative investment of a part of my money say £1000. The means of investment I would propose is perhaps rather singular, I mean to *spend it on myself*. Say I leave when I have saved £2000. Instead of paying £60 for a passage home, make up my mind to spend £200 before getting to England and see if I could not see something worth seeing. For instance first of all, a tour through NSW or Victoria to learn a little of Australia scientifically & socially. From here to Ceylon, & India, Overland route to Europe and a tour through some of the principal towns. Then in England suppose I spend two more years at College or improving myself in some other manner so that when again I have to earn my bread, it may be by some employment at which I can permanently remain & rise as I hope.

Now that I think about it how it seems as if the keenness of my anticipations & hopes as to my life & position were blunted now that I am really engaged in pursuing my intentions. I have lost & forgotten all my first feelings & motives and I find left only a sort of ambitious impulse. It is disagreable to me to examine the nature of this impulse for I always find in it so little but what is selfish & I always used to ground my principles on unselfishness. That latter thing is indeed a rare thing. I suppose what I find taking place in myself is merely the effect[2] of growing older and having a business to attend to, and it is only what I have found in smaller affairs. For instance you plan out a piece of carpentry work, draw it & determine all the dimensions. While busy in the midst of the practical work, the principles & plans upon which you began to work are forgotten and you find yourself working blindly and without much comprehension of what you are about

This sort of feeling ought[3] not I think to cause any anxiety for if a man begins with true motives but in following out the course at first determined on does not continually keep these same motives before his eyes

---

little sittingroom and bedroom and everything in fact as well as I could wish it. It is four miles from Sydney, therefore regularly in the country and surrounded by woods, but upon a turnpike road on which omnibuses run continually to Sydney.' Cf. Vol. II, Letter 66.

[1] In the original text, Jevons wrote 'present'.
[2] 'affect' in the original text.
[3] 'out' in the original text.

he can hardly be blamed; the motives once existed & he remains under the impulse they produced. Worse motives however may of course present themselves.

Annangrove Cottage
Petersham Near Sydney

4 November 1855

Now and then I get it into my head that I ought to write something in this fragmentary journal. On thinking what to say I cannot help feeling that everything that occurs to me is too egotistical, vain, boastful, or whatever may be the proper word to apply. This is the chief reason that I dislike writing. I will try and avoid this by the choice of subjects.

For pretty nearly as long as I can remember I have been accustomed, as a habit I believe, to the pursuit of some particular subject, and when I think about it, it occurs to me that I have had a regular succession of subjects each of which has had my *voluntary* attention for a year or two at a time. Botany is about the first subject I think of, and to this I very distinctly recollect my mother, of loved memory, trying to direct my liking. In fact at home are all the books, each of which I remember her giving me, and of the little microscope particularly I can remember every circumstance. Botany was for a long time, in fact till within a few years since my only voluntary study. From want of any other help than books, I got on very slowly and I never had more than the slightest knowledge of it, though a practical one. Still I liked it exceedingly, and no doubt the time was not lost time.

Up to the time of my going to London, what a little I knew of any science but botany; I had tried to read a book or two on parts of Natural Philosophy (Libr. of Useful Knowge)[1] but I knew not one fact

[1] *Library of Useful Knowledge:*—

NATURAL PHILOSOPHY I

Objects Advantages & Pleasures of Science, (Ld. Brougham); Mechanics, (D. Lardner); Hydrostatics, (Brougham); Hydraulics, (J. Millington); Pneumatics, (D. Lardner); Heat, (Ogg); Optics, (Sir D. Brewster); Double Refraction & Polarisation of Light; – with an explanation of Scientific Terms, and an Index. (1829.)

NATURAL PHILOSOPHY II

Popular Introductions to Natural Philosophy, (J. Marcet); Newton's Optics, (D. Lardner); Description of Optical Instruments, (A. Pritchard); Thermometer & Pyrometer, (J. S. Traill); Electricity, (P. M. Roget); Galvanism, (P. M. Roget); Magnetism, (P. M. Roget); Electro-Magnetism, (P. M. Roget); – with etc. etc. (1832).

NATURAL PHILOSOPHY III

Astronomy, (Sir B. H. Malkin); History of Astronomy, (R. W. Rothman); Mathematical Geography, (E. Lloyd); Physical Geography, (H. J. Lloyd); Navigation, (Lord Wrottesley); – with etc. etc. (1834).

NATURAL PHILOSOPHY IV

Chemistry, (J. F. Daniell); Animal Physiology, (J. S. Smith); Animal Mechanics, (Sir C. Bell). (Bound separately.)

of chemistry except the recollection of one or two of Roscoes experiments which I treasured up in my mind.[1]

At University College School I took to chemistry and went on fiercer & fiercer at it till I got the gold medal at College; the part of chemistry I liked best was Molecular Philosophy and this I followed out a little; though from its branching out into nearly all the other sciences, it was a serious affair. Crystallography in particular I liked.

While learning assaying in London, another science rose to the top, i.e Geology[2] and I followed it through a few books and two or three excursions near London and Paris. Finally I have come to and am pretty hard on Meteorology. A few pages in Grahams Elements which I used nearly to learn by heart for the examination was the beginning of my meteorology; Buffs Physics of the earth, recommended to us by Graham the first book I read on it. And my first thermometer observation was made in the half year before sailing for Australia.

I had a thermometer with me and intended taking the temperature of the air on the voyage several times a day. However I broke it in taking the temperature of the sea a few days out, and then I was obliged to content myself with what I could write down of the weather. A very short meteorological journal I carried on throughout the voyage but I was ignorant of the proper meanings and distinctions of the common names of the clouds and had no means of any exact description. Nevertheless I saw enough to interest me very much in the clouds and several parts of meteorology and on landing I determined as soon as possible to begin a proper series of observations.

In the middle of January about three months after arrival I began buying a Maximum and Minm ther.[r] In such a place as Church Hill I was awfully puzzled to know where to place [it];[3] at last I put it in a thick flat wooden box fixed against the wall of my cottage and surrounded on all sides by walls. There if any where it was first-rately protected from the suns direct influence, but what fraction of the daily range it showed I cannot say. I made my own barometer and used it for

---

[1] Chemistry was taught at the Mechanics Institute High School, and the teacher, Balmain, made an impression on his students, of whom Harry Roscoe was one. There was also a chemical laboratory, which was unusual for the time (*Life and Experiences*, p. 15). Jevons, however, must have been too young to take chemistry, as he was only eleven when he left the school. For Jevons's description of working with his brother who had studied chemistry at the school – see Journal entry for 23 May 1864 (p. 194 below).

[2] In 1902 Jevons's son, the late Professor Herbert Stanley Jevons, became Lecturer in Geology at Sydney University. He held the post for three years and during this time his interest turned from pure science to economics, as his father's had done and he resigned in order to return to England and devote his whole time to the subject. Before leaving Australia he gave a course on elementary economics, much of which was incorporated in his book *Essays in Economics* (1905).

[3] This word is omitted in the text.

some months not caring much for the bubble of air at the top. Two observations a day I took from the first at 9 am & pm.[1]

17 February 1856[2]

A sorrowful duty and pleasureable pain I now have to undergo in arranging and reading the letters of my father who is no longer present on earth but in the recollections of his children & others who loved him, & of whose affection & goodness, particularly as shown towards myself, these letters from the best record & evidence.[3]

    1. 1849. July 7 th4 Written to me while staying with Henny & Tommy at the house of my Aunt & Uncle Hornblower,[5] at Nantwich Cheshire, & during the midsummer holyday, of Mr Beckwiths school at which I then was. My father seldom gave *set* advice by viva voce, & chiefly trusted[6] for their improvement to the example of his own character & actions.

    In this letter however, he seizes the opportunity of my being from home to give me the excellent & *reasoning* advice which the letter will be found to contain on the 'worst weakness' I had, viz '*bashfulness*' (not exactly *timidity*.) I believe & trust that the advice has been *somewhat* followed but it has not been *much*

    2. 1850. October 28 th At this date I was living with Herbert[7] for a month or two at 23 Harrington Street Hampstead road; I felt the first

---

  [1] Jevons has omitted the two following pages, which contain some pencil jottings relating to legal problems, apparently made before the book came into his possession.

  [2] A cutting from a printed diary for Thursday, 14 February 1856, pasted into the Journal between these two pages bears the following note: '10.0. Recd. intelligence of my fathers death. Went home at 12.30 only doing ingots.'

  In his proper diary for 14 February 1856 is the following entry: 'On getting to Mint at 10.30 a.m. found two letters awaiting me from mail per "Mermaid". A black seal, the seal of sorrow, indicated the nature of the news, the *death of my father*. This is about the heaviest sorrow of a man's life and when the object on which one's thoughts and happiness so much centred has been so suddenly removed, it will require much thinking and much *faith* in the goodness of Providence to rearrange one's motives and designs.'

  [3] The work of summarising the letters was done over a period of several weeks.

  [4] Jevons began his summary of his father's letters by setting out the page in columns, on the left headed 'No. Date', and on the right hand side his account of each letter written under the heading 'Contents, remarks &c.' However, over the course of the next seven pages, he gradually evolved the simpler style adopted here.

  [5] His aunt, Jane Roscoe – Mrs Francis Hornblower (see Journal entry for 17 February 1853, p. 88 above).

  [6] 'trused' in the text.

  [7] His elder brother Herbert was at that time studying medicine at University College. Jevons shared lodgings with him during his first term at University College School, before going to Mrs Mackenzie's boarding house. (See Journal entry for December 1862, p. 100 above.)

sentence somewhat for I had really delayed writing much longer than I should have. As to prizes I have much pride in feeling that the advice was scarcely necessary or at all events well followed, for I got 5 prizes first or second, & first mention in the only other examination I attended.

He speaks next of Henny & Tommy and it is pleasant to think that his satisfaction in them can only have been multiplied since.

3. 1851. May 18th[1] Written without any special object, except to please & encourage me; for he says 'go on in like manner & prosper you must in whatever walk of life you select.' It shows too the interest he took in any new undertaking as the Crystal Palace.

The second part mentions two things; the 'usual rubber' that he played *every* night for the amusement solely of his own father in his last year or two, and his setting out to Crown Street[2] for his regular Sunday's visit to & walk with, his *least* happy & fortunate though eldest son Roscoe.

4. 1851. June 28th Showing apparently but poor spirits at the time of writing and he speaks of two things that must indeed have sorrowed him, Roscoe's permanent helplessness & Herberts unhappy illness.

5. (1851)[3] September 26th Written likewise in no cheerful tone, for it was very likely soon after Herbert's sailing for a long voyage to recover his health when my grandfather required 'much attention', & when we seem most of us to have been away from home on visits.

6. 1851. November 19th[4] He first answers a letter in which I had mentioned my first long walk through the city of London. It is true I am never quick in appreciating nor fond of expressing my feelings & wonder, but if he had lived longer he would have perhaps sometime have found that no *sight* or object of interest had been thrown away on me.

He next adverts to a few things as to the change from Lodgings with Herbert to a boarding house. Next the Crystal Palace, then buildings which was one of the things he had the great possible interest in & admiration of.

7. 1852. January 14th A beautiful and valuable letter, written very soon after my grandfather's death, and showing how well prepared my Father was in his mind for the great change which has since come upon him. Somewhat curiously this letter refers to both my grandfather &

---

[1] The date of this letter is 18 March, not May.

[2] Crown Street, Liverpool, is close to Chatham Street. According to R. B. Muir, *A History of Liverpool* (1907) p. 334, 'University College was opened in 1882 in a disused lunatic asylum, in the midst of a slum district'. As the original University College was in Crown Street, the asylum was presumably the one of which Roscoe Jevons was an inmate.

[3] In the text Jevons used ditto marks in his dates column.

[4] The correct date of this letter is 19 November 1850 and Jevons should therefore have placed it third in his list.

great grandfather and proves how well their son's duty to them was performed; may it now only prove the same of mine.

8. 1852. May 3rd Expressing his happiness at my obtaining a silver medal.[1] One sentence speaking of humble (unnoticed) effort I can well understand.

9. 1852. June 8th On many little business & home affairs, for instance speaking of his *planning a house*, a favourite occupation; Herberts voyage &c.

10. 1852. November 17th Speaking first of the Duke of Wellingtons Funeral, second of the slight earthquake in Liverpool the sensations of which he describes Thirdly about my settling to a business.

11. 1853. February 9th Entirely occupied with the question of what business I was to enter at the end of the current session He proposes an iron-masters.

12. 1853. February 18th A second letter entirely on the subject of my future business, which it seems he as well as I then wished to be in Liverpool, as a soapboilers for instance

13. April 2nd. Giving me some ideas he had about a manufactory I went to see with him at Prestatyn N.W.[2] This visit I well remember.

14. May 6th Congratulating me on the result of the College examinations 1853.[3] and mentioning a few other matters, especially the 'success of another aspirant' Tommy, at school in which Papa evidently takes as great a delight as Tommy himself, who was always his favorite son, being the youngest.

15. 1853. July 10th This letter commences the present era of my life viz the Assayership. It can not be said to press upon me the Australian appointment, but assuming the excellence of the opportunity, lays before me all I should lose & suffer by leaving home (& what too he would suffer) for so long a time. He makes it a condition of my accepting it that I should return to see him again within five years, and now before two of them are nearly gone, he is himself no more.

16. 1853. September 17 Chiefly occupied with matters connected with the Assayership which have long since been settled but ending with a very warm expression of his affection.

17. October 17th Containing a statement of the terms on which he advanced me money to purchase apparatus &c. & also explaining fully & openly his motives the provision in his will and his views as to our circumstances in case of his death. It is a letter excessively interesting to read, now that he is indeed dead, now that Herbert has 'to maintain himself', that Tommy is left a 'delightful charge to his brothers &

[1] In the college examinations at Easter, 1852.
[2] Cf. entry for 3 April 1853, p. 92 above.
[3] Cf. entry for 3 April 1853, p. 94 above.

sisters' and that all the other provisions he makes have to be carried into effect.

18. 1854. February 15th The only letter I possess written to me while staying for about two months in Paris during February & March. It is about merely passing matters.

After my departure for Australia.

19. 1854. July 6th Written soon after I sailed in order no doubt that I might receive a letter very soon after arriving in Sydney. Even here he speaks of the pleasure of communicating thoughts by letters, even 'if it should please our Heavenly Father that we should never interchange them personally on Earth.'

He writes a deal describing the scenery near Dolgelly where he was staying, and with which he seems extremely pleased; also referring to his favorite Geological theories on the formation of mountains, and the agency of water.

He then advises me to endeavour to obtain private assay work in Sydney, which I did but without success. Before arriving in Sydney & seeing the backward state of the preparations for the Mint I had never any serious intention of undertaking more than the Mint assaying. I was not therefore so much disappointed at not finding myself equal to the business when obliged by a temporary want of money to take whatever chance employment I could get.

The rest is about general or family matters.

1854

20. Sept 1st A long letter written upon my birth day, again pressing upon me to try for private assay work, and advising me about a few other little things.

A large space is occupied about the swindling Gold mining companies & engineers, in which he unfortunately became interested & eventually lost a little money.

21. Sept 30th Mentions that he had heard of the Oliver Lang being spoken at sea. Recommends very forcibly great care of my health, which I must say I begin to feel is more necessary to be attended to now than formerly. It is then occupied nearly to the end with accounts of the Meeting of the Brit. Assoc. at St George's Hall Liverpool, experiments lectures &c &c.

22. January 31st 1855. Answering some of my first letters and occupied by a few ordinary business affairs. He seems to have been a little anxious about my money affairs and tells me to draw freely upon him to the [extent?][1] of £200 at least if necessary

[1] A word is omitted here in the text.

23. April 1st 1855. Written under the disappointment of not receiving a letter from me by the Overland Mail & showing what a large space I filled in his thoughts. Telling me of a few little presents they were going to send

24. April 18th 1855. An extremely interesting letter He first mentions two iron ribless boats[1] that were turning out very successfully and which were built on a plan which I believe he really originated; I remember myself the *model* he speaks of but whether the principle is a correct one I am not so sure; iron ship building was one of the things he was much interested in.

Next he refers with evident pleasure to the improving condition of their iron business and also to his plans, which have since acquired such a melancholy interest, of extending their business to the Continent. It is evident in fact that he had already made up his mind for a continental journey which he had long looked forward to as a crowning pleasure of his life. In reading it, however much I might wish that he were still living, I feel not even the[2] slightest possible tinge of regret at the plan. After many years of anxiety, trouble, & sorrow he found his affairs continually growing more & more cheerful in aspect, and he died at a moment when every thing was prosperous & satisfactory and himself in the midst of the truest enjoyment.

He speaks of my engaging a little in iron or other business, but this was no doubt written rather *talkatively* and only half seriously, and he says indeed that to suggest speculation to any of the same age but myself would indeed be injudicious.

25. May 3rd 1855. First refers to a number of unimportant matters. He mentions the Poltimore Mine again and I may say here what I always felt about it, and which I can say without the least violence to my love or respect for him, viz. that this interest in a mere speculation showed a slight falling off in his judgement caused by his advancing age.

He speaks with great satisfaction of Herbert & Henny and calls Lucy his 'right hand'.

The letter is in a very different tone from Nos 4 & 5.

26. May 9th 1855. He speaks of Tommy being ill of the 'mumps', and appears to think him of a less strong constitution than the rest of us. The Iron business with America had very good prospects at this time and his satisfaction is evident; the rumours of war with the United States would doubtless have caused him the greatest anxiety had he lived, while on the other hand a war would have proved the correctness of his judgement in opening a European trade of which he again speaks, as before.

---

[1] See Biographical Introduction, p. 4 above.
[2] In the original text, Jevons wrote 'not the even'.

27. May 18th 1855.[1] A long letter fully answering all I had written home, & talking of all my prospects & of Sydney Affairs. He again offers me money to set up some sort of a house or office if I want, but of that I had no need on account of the change in my position with the Mint. This letter was no doubt a most interesting one to me at the time.

28. June 3rd 1855. In answer to my letter communicating the proposed change in the position of the assayers. My father seems to have had great expectations of my making a speedy fortune, and the reduction of this to a fixed £5 or 700 per ann. was a great disappointment to him, more indeed than to me, who never expected much more. His disgust at Capt Ward's conduct is perhaps not altogether groundless but how far the necessity of economy in the Mint in order to carry it on at all, was a justification, is rather hard to say.

He again speaks of the very prosperous state of the business of the Firm and of the press of work they were having and concludes with various pieces of Public news.

29. June 17th 1855. Written from Llangollan where Lucy Tommy & Henny & Ann Bolton[2] were staying 6 weeks, my Father spending a Sunday or two. Chiefly occupied with domestic affairs, with however a paragraph about his decimal coinage ideas, and one also intended to soften his expressions in his last.

30. July 14th 1855. Liverpool. A most happy & satisfactory as well as long letter. Having been to Birmingham to attend the Iron-Masters meeting,[3] he had seen Roscoe,[4] and still expresses his belief that he was better than he had 'seen him for a very long time'. These false hopes, we may hope, somewhat lightened his affliction at Roscoe's state, but they would no doubt have grown less and less as he became older.

What satisfaction he seems to have had at the meeting which he says was 'to me a very cheerful & successful one'. The rest is filled with various agreable domestic news, written chiefly from Llangollan where he again went to stay some days.

31. August 1st 1855. Liverpool. An answer to one written by me after moving from Church Hill Sydney, to Mr Millers at Petersham, and chiefly referring to my affairs. He speaks with great pleasure of getting back home again, with the house all painted and newly arranged. He checks himself however and reminds me that whatever be the comfort

[1] This letter is actually dated 18 March.

[2] The Jevonses' nurse.

[3] The Midland ironmasters held regular quarterly meetings in order to fix prices and regulate conditions of sale. See J. H. Clapham, *An Economic History of Modern Britain: The early Railway Age, 1820–1850* (1926–38).

[4] Roscoe was apparently in Birmingham at this time. (See Biographical Introduction, p. 8 above.)

& pleasure of a home, the truest happiness is in performing ones duties wherever they lead us and my duty, I almost feel with regret has always been away from home.

I am sorry to find, however, he still retained a feeling of disappointment at my prospects being in his opinion, cut down.

32. August 26 th Liverpool. Written on the day before he was going to start on his last journey, and therefore fuller even than usual, of the most affectionate feelings towards me, 'his far distant son'

33. September 2nd 1855.   à Paris.

Rue de Lille 59.

A letter to Henny, sent on to me in lieu of letters direct from my Father which he undoubtedly would not have time to write. It merely gives a pleasant account of the chief things they had seen & enjoyed up to that point on their journey.

34. September 9th ditto. A short letter written from their lodgings at the same house in Paris as I lodged in during my stay there. He briefly explains what they had done, and then speaks of his interest in the NSW contributions to the Paris Exhibition[1] particularly the specimens of colonial timber.

He also tells me of their visit to the French Mint, to get my Assayers Diploma & stamp, in which as well as buying me a small specimen of aluminium he succeeded at once. One feels a pleasure in knowing that even on this, his last journey, he met traces of my efforts & my successes and that they must doubtless have afforded him satisfaction.

This is his last letter addressed to me except one from Rome.

35.   September 25th 1855. Faido
                                                       Canton Tessin.

A long letter to Herbert written after passing the Alps from the above place & Lugarno. It is an interesting and well written account of the most noticeable points in the splendid country they had just past through. His complete absorption in the grandeur of the scenery & the real enjoyment of travelling is evident.

36. October 29 th 1855. Rome. The last letter which he wrote to me and as his death by cholera took place so soon after as the [*blank space*]th of November, one of the few last he could have written at all.

Near the beginning he speaks of a letter from me which had followed him to Rome, having 'added greatly to the pleasure and delight I am

---

[1] At the end of this page in the original Journal, the sequence of some entries becomes confused. Continuation of this passage is to be found 92 pages further on in the book: here the editor makes it follow on directly. Further entries have been rearranged, where necessary, in chronological order. (See note to p. 130 below.)

constantly receiving on this grand tour at this *climacteric* of my years'. To know that within a few days of his death he received satisfaction from a letter & intelligence from me, must ever form a pleasant recollection connected with this tour. Looking out the word *climacteric* in the dictionary, I find it means a critical year of life, 63 being the grand climacteric; to him indeed, within a few days, it proved so.[1] This is a singular coincidence, but I see no indication that his use of the word was more than accidental, or more likely arising from that due sense of the constant nearness of death which all good & thoughtful men continually have, and which in the minds of such, does not detract the least from the cheerful enjoyment of all true pleasure to be obtained here.

He then gives merely a list of the chief places they passed through on their tour, in crossing Switzerland & visiting Italy. He also refers to a few things that had excited his interest in Rome particularly the Decimal system of coinage; of the latter he put by 2 small 1 Scudo gold pieces together with a 10 and 5 franc French gold piece saying 'they are for Stanley' and I now have these small coins through Lucy's care as a last & pretty memento of my father, on his last journey He says, 'I must now turn to your letter and congratulate you on the altered position in which you find yourself, and express my fervent hopes that health and happiness may long continue to be your lot, though I can never forget' &c. And again he expresses disappointment at my prospects here not being better even than they are. I am indeed sorry to observe that this seems really to have caused him some amount of disquietude; whether in any part of my management, I committed an error of judgement, which I do not believe, my sorrow will really be that he did not live longer that this feeling might be effaced by one of more complete satisfaction at the sucess I look for, and I may almost say confidently expect.

Again 'I see that you purpose sending me back the money which I invested in your outfit; I shall receive it from you with grateful and thankful feelings but' &c. And there again seems to be some slight regret or some 'itch' which I do not understand, unless it be at his having ever spoken of its repayment in any manner at all, or added term, even though those were on account of his eldest son.

In an Hotel at Pisa, just at the commencement of his return journey he was suddenly seized on the night of the 7th November 1855, with an attack of cholera and after severe severe suffering soothed only by the presence of his most dearly loved daughter Lucy, he died on the morning of the 8th leaving us, while fully feeling and appreciating his loss to rejoice that his last few years were those of continually increasing happiness & enjoyment, arising partly at all events, we should be glad

---

[1] Thomas Jevons would have been sixty-four on 27 November 1855.

to feel, from our own love & devotion and to our dispositions & conduct being partly such as would please & satisfy a Father.

These last thoughts may perhaps be rather unbecoming but I give them because they are what seem naturally to occur, concerning the memory of one that is gone; to know that one had given pain unatoned for by after good conduct would indeed have given me cause for sorrow that I should never have effaced. While on a contrary the evidence that the foregoing letters give that I though so much away from him was still as much a source of pleasure to him will leave an ineffacable impression of delight & satisfied affection about his recollection.

Account of an Excursion to the River Hunter, & to Maitland

It happened that Friday May 23rd 1856 was made a holyday in the Government Departments on account of the opening of the New Parliament,[1] while May 24 being the Queens Birthday & Monday a holyday for the assayers, I had 4 clear days and determined to go a second trip[2] to some part of the colony. The Hunter being undoubtedly the second most important district in almost every point of view,[3] & being also very easily reached by a daily steam communication, I arranged on Thursday to start at once by the boat the same evening, and in preparation had only to pack up a small carpet bag with a clean shirt & a few things, which after all I did not use.

The steamers, of which two are always run together in opposition by two Companies, the old or Australasian Steam Navigation Co & the new one or Hunter River New Steam Navigation Co,[4] always start from Sydney at the extraordinary hour of 11 at night, and I reached the

[1] The New South Wales Constitution Act, 1855, granted some measure of self-government to the colony. Jevons is referring to the opening of the first session of Parliament under the new constitution.

[2] The first had been to the gold diggings at Sofala, northwest of Bathurst, where the first great Australian gold discoveries had been made in 1851. The account of the tour was written up in a separate diary (see Appendix, p. 213).

[3] At the time of Jevons's visit, the Hunter River district rated second only to the gold-fields in importance to the colony. The coal measures there (see below, p. 125) were being mined only on a small scale at Maitland and at Newcastle, where the river enters the sea. The port for the Hunter Valley was upstream from Newcastle, at Morpeth, where the navigable passage for steamers ended. (See below, p. 126.) See Oswald L. Ziegler, *Symphony on a City, The story of the City of Newcastle, New South Wales: its birth, its development and its place in Australia* (1957).

[4] Before the development of overland routes, communication between Sydney and the other coastal settlements was by steamer. The reason for the competition on this route was that the merchants of the Hunter River thought that the Australian Steam Navigation Company (dating from 1839) had grown too big to serve their interests and they therefore formed their own company in 1854. The *Williams* on which Jevons returned from Maitland, and whose fare he found to be cheaper, was one of their steamers.

wharf of the former in good time by omnibus from the Glebe. The time being close on Ten oclock, I of course had the usual dispute with the *driver* for an extra sixpence, but I take these occasions to exercise my resolution and came off successful with the amount in question still in my pocket.

The steamer was the 'Collaroy', (paddle-wheels) and was moderately good in every respect. Having engaged one of the sofa-berths for the night, there would have been nothing to occupy one's attention if a drunken passenger had not taken an accidental plunge overboard & thus run the risk of his life. After a deal of exertion on the part of those about & especially of a seaman who jumped[1] in, but whom one admired rather than envied, he was hauled out completely helpless and in a curious state of *foolish* drunkenness, and had to be taken down stairs & undressed by some friends he seemed to have.

Soon after this we started and steamed quietly round out of Darling Harbour & down Port Jackson of which the stillness was quite undisturbed except by ourselves and the opposition steamer a little a head of us. From the darkness the shores & Points could scarcely be made out except by the lights, & this mid night sail down the Harbour was much less pleasant or interesting than I expected.

We felt the swell of the ocean as soon as ever we got between the Heads in a manner which showed strikingly the shelter afforded by a Harbour like this Most of the passengers retired at once but I first waited till we had lost sight of the Heads and till I had enjoyed sufficiently the pleasant sensations of being again on the open Ocean and looking round on an unlimited horizon (the coast indeed partially visible to our left.)

The close Head to Head sort of opposition between the two steamers was soon apparent, for though the rival one, the 'Williams' had a start & rounded the North Head inside, our captain was evidently resolved to race it, & seemed to have every chance of winning. The fares, too, were reduced on both, to a rate quite insufficient I believe to give any profit, viz 7s to Newcastle, 8s to Morpeth by the Collaroy first cabin not including meals &c.

I did not wake till about six oclock when it being yet dark we were steaming inside the Heads just up to Newcastle. Of this place I could see but little now, and will leave it to be described on the downward trip. Though we had gained a short distance on the Williams during the night the latter was quicker in discharging cargo etc at the wharf & started a few boats lengths ahead of us. We soon entered the Hunter river which just above Newcastle expands into wide Flats or Shallows. The navigable channel is very narrow I believe, & bordered by shoals

---

[1] In the original text, Jevons wrote 'to jumped in'.

often appearing above the water, while several considerable flat Islands rise here & there dividing the river into separate branches. The Islands as well as the Mainland are covered with close & rather low bush, of disagreable unpromising appce so that altogether the place seemed useless to man & beast. One remembered however that beneath lay stores of that 'hoarded labour' or 'solidified power', coal, now every where so justly considered as scarcely second to any other source of National Wealth, and that it is in places like this that one of Nature's greatest engineering operations is visibly going on, & that alluvial lands, or various sedimentary beds are being formed which may some time produce the sustenance[1] of future generations or puzzle future Geologists as to their cause & nature.

We steamed however rapidly & safely along, under most careful pilotage and soon [reached?][2] the *River proper* which was a moderately wide & very much curved, but muddy-looking & disagreable stream. The banks were of earth, rising perhaps about five feet above high water mark. Coarse large grass or reeds grew along the edge of the water, while on the land nothing but unusually ugly or stunted gum trees or tracts covered with dead Indian Corn Stems were seen, not calculated indeed to improve ones impressions of the beauty of the scenery. The style of navigation was novel to me, viz two considerable steamers racing at full speed up a narrow winding river, in which the two could only just pass, the back water from each spreading out in beautifully curved waves[3] and breaking in a uniformly advancing swell upon the alluvial banks. These breakers must exercise considerable levelling power on the bank, and the matter worn away from these will settle into the bed of the river & render the channel shallower than it is, or will be carried out to its mouth to form new expanses of flat land.[4]

The flat alluvial lands of the Hunter are evidently the product of an estuary of the sea when this stood formerly at a higher level.

We stopped for a few moments at Raymond Terrace, a dirty looking place like a large wharf on the side of the river with a few public & other houses, but certainly a most embryo town.

The country changed but little as we approached the landing place, Morpeth, except that huts and houses & other appearances of improvement were more frequent and that the flat alluvial lands became narrower and the country more nearly picturesque from hills & ranges being visible. Morpeth when reached about 9 am (we had had breakfast on board about 8 am for which we paid dearly) appeared to be a

---

[1] In the original text, Jevons wrote 'sustaniance'.
[2] A word is omitted here in the text.
[3] Jevons wrote 'waved'.
[4] At this point Jevons turned back 50 pages in the book to continue the account.

prosperous business like town built upon sloping land occasioned by the raised & more ancient geological lands extending themselves to the side of the river. The river was here very much narrowed, and of such small width that the steamers can scarcely be turned. I watched the operation of warping one of them round, and it was a very close fit. The River Hunter is not navigable I believe any further up hence Morpeth is the Port of Maitland.

Landing was soon accomplished, but although several excellent inns were in view, I did not see anything of sufficient interest to induce me to stay here and therefore mounted one of the busses which were in waiting, to carry the passengers to either East or West Maitland. The rest of the passengers I should have mentioned were a pretty respectable but heterogeneous lot when examined by the light of day, chiefly well to do publicans, tradespeople, and farmers, also several Sydney gentlemen going on visits.

The busses, which appeared as if they had seen much work in this or other parts of the world, proceeded at a leisurely pace for they were unusually crowded along roads, moderately good though stoney, which passed chiefly upon the border between the raised & flat alluvial lands. The river appeared to spread out in many flat channels or swampy low flats, though the main body of the river continued a considerable stream. Two or three miles travelling brought us to East

Maitland, a town, chiefly of good sized houses, Inns & other establishments very regularly and *roomily* laid out on a flat convenient site.

My omnibus, however, proceeded with but slight delay to the other portion of the town called West Maitland and I continued with it. We crossed a creek (?) by a well made wooden bridge, then continued about half a mile over ordinary cultivated country till we entered one end of a long and nearly level street, which by degrees became bordered by log huts, or decently built brick or wood cottages. These gradually thickened, then streets and lanes branched off at right angles and lost themselves in open waste spaces with an irregular assemblage of less desirable dwellings. By degrees numerous public houses, tradesmens shops, agents & auctioneers establishments, a 'Mercury' office, Schools of Arts, Chapels etc were passed and we were in the heart of Maitland. Most of the passengers were dropped at their respective destinations, I and another gentleman & lady proceeded right through on the omnibus to a very large red brick building the Northumberland Arms which was the principal hotel, where I engaged a room and then looked for something to do. I started to walk up the road into the country. I found it first crossed by a long wooden bridge a flat low space of land bounded by steeply sloping banks. The whole was now dry and covered by fields of corn etc with here & there log huts, but it appears that when floods occur, which is generally about once in 7 seven years, the *back water* of the river runs up these low flats & floods a large portion of the country & some portions of the town. It even runs into the cellars of the inn in which I slept which was built on the very edge of the raised ground.

On the opposite bank, so to speak, beyond the bridge were several very large Inns, several large flour mills of red brick, with tall chimney & machinery-like appearances, and a tanning establishment in an extensive log construction. The road was good passing over gently rising or undulating ground of a hard clayey or stoney appce. This was soon covered by tall fine gum trees but these were placed further apart & the intermediate spaces less occupied by bush than in other parts of the country I have seen. At one place coal mining was being carried on on a small scale. I saw some good cannel coal and the pit seemed not very deep nor had much expense been incurred in raising it.

Several ranges of rocky hills were in view in different directions; towards one of these, deceivied as to the distance I directed my way, leaving the main road and passing through woods of tall gums. The country seemed by no means attractive, the ground being hard dry clayey earth and the appearance of the whole more monotonous than usual. At last however I came to a large flat open low treeless space, a portion of which was cultivated & bore potatoes & other crops, or was in fallow but on attempting to cross this I found it was in fact little better than a swamp or lagoon. An old woman who was working in the fields told me there was no way across it and the only road was back to Maitland and after full examination of the nature of this inconvenient obstacle, I had to change my direction. This flat, I found, extended a great distance in every direction, probably communicating with those near Maitland. In many parts there was evidently great depth of water though entirely filled up with luxuriant rushes & similar water plants. It was in fact a swamp or half drained lagoon, but the whole land being owned by various farmers, they were trying to reclaim & cultivate the drier portions. Indian corn seemed the main crop. Several considerable farming houses, and a gentlemans residence were visible at different places. I got back to the hotel without seeing anything more worth noticing.

A good dinner, although there was only one other gentleman Mr Vincent Dowling, & a boy to eat it in addition to myself. He was a squatter, who had come down to sell a mob of (400)?[1] horses which he had bred, in order to remove to another part of the colony. I had some talk with him about the country floods etc.

Afterwards I attended the finishing of his sale of horses, sauntered all about the town etc. I saw a brewery and many corn steam mills of which the largest an immense brick building was only just being finished. The Indian corn grown in the neighbourhood here meets the coal from Newcastle I presume, and this seems the main trade of Maitland.

In the evening there was much letting off of fireworks by the juveniles, an additional percentage of drunkards etc, all denoting the day to be a holyday and time of license, (the shops I should have mentioned were chiefly closed throughout).

As I found nothing at all of especiall interest here and felt very dull in fact, I determined to return by the steamer of the following day, and retired to bed rather early to a small remote & not very comfortable bedroom in this large establishment in order that I might be up in time for the omnibus for Morpeth, the steamer starting from there, I think at 7.30 am.

Found myself in good time on top of omnibus & in progress through the long single street of West Maitland, which to tell the truth appeared to me a quiet respectable still very business-like & important town, much superior to Bathurst[2] or anything else I have seen here. It being the Queens birthday many of the tradespeople and their somewhat good looking daughters were going off to Newcastle to spend the holyday at the Regatta there. Both our own and the opposition bus, (for there are opposition busses corresponding to the opposition steamers, and I chose the other Company returning) were therefore soon full and we arrived at the Morpeth wharf only just in proper time. The fare of this omnibus to Maitland is included in the fare of the steamers but omitting to get a ticket I had had to pay 2s extra going up. This I of course avoided a second time.

The Williams steamer was very fully of holyday people and was dirtier, rather smaller and less delectable than the Collaroy, still it started quickly got well on its way and we had a pleasant sail down the river, nothing further being noticeable, except it be several villas or gentlemans houses here & there on the banks which I forgot to mention. I paid 12.6 fare but this I found included breakfast & dinner, while on the other steamer, eatables were charged extra & 2 cups of coffee which

---

[1] This is Jevons's query.

[2] Jevons passed through Bathurst on his way to and from the Sofala Diggings. His description of the town ends with the comment: 'In my life I never passed through streets with less interest and pleasure and in the people, untasteful situation and everything the feeling was fully borne out' . . . (See journal of the trip, Appendix, p. 226 below.)

I had taken early & breakfast had cost me 4s leaving a balance on the side of the Hunter River Company.

We stopped a short time at Newcastle while some cargo, chiefly a number of bags were discharged, and I now observed Newcastle to be the dreariest, most barren place I ever saw. It is built on the North sheltered side of a bare brownish coal-measure-like rock of which detached & singular shaped portions extending out into the sea form the *Nobbies*. There were some appearances of coal mines, also of manufacturers on the opposite flat banks of the Harbour, if Harbour it is to be called, being only the open estuary of a river.[1]

Most of our passengers landed here and we proceeded to sea with more convenient freedom of room. On rounding the Nobbies and standing on our course along the coast we found that the wind was dead a head viz |S and not a little fresh so as to occasion a rather large swell and make the steamer pitch most uncomfortable. The ladies vanished at once, and thoughts of that terrible malady sea sickness now entered the head of every one for the the first time. Some felt some slight affection of the sort immediately & quickly knocking under retired to the cabin and a berth at once. Others pretended indifference, and walked about on their sea legs to show their seamanship. And the remainder, among them myself, combined prudence with valour, & choosing comfortable stations on the paddleboxes where the sickening motion was diminished and an unfailing supply of the purest sea air is obtainable if anywhere in the world, prepared to enjoy the pleasures of an open sea voyage, with a view of an interesting coast & other usual remarks of travelling with as few thoughts or feelings of sickness as possible.

The first category were no doubt well attended to in due time by the steward, the second set were sooner or later, more or less, violently affected, & sank into helpless dead like attitudes on the seats, or rushed from sudden necessitous motives to the windward bulwarks to —————— Even most of ourselves on the paddle boxes confessed to symptoms of nausea, but using prudence & foresight equally meritorious chose new stations where certain functions might be discharged if necessary with least annoyance to other parties. Myself, though sometimes sorely tried, bore it all without flinching, as if I had passed my life at sea. As the day wore on and 3 or 4 oclock came, an appetite came, and I enquired for dinner. At last the bell rang and I prepared to rush to a seat but Lo! no motion occurred among the passengers, and all lay still as if the bell had not sounded or had not awakened them. Could it be dinner? Still on descending I found a very extensive & good one laid out but no one but the Captain and his wife and another

[1] i.e. the Hunter.

young fellow to eat it, the last even retiring after soup. I enjoyed it however, from ship soup to pie & pudding, and felt my self for once remarkable (as a sailor!)

The coast is rather peculiar; low after leaving Newcastle but becoming bold & broken near Broken bay. We entered Sydney Heads about 5 PM, the pitching motion ceasing immediately we quitted the ocean swell, and the effect being almost instantly perceptible on the sick. and after a pretty sail up the Harbour came along side the wharf at 5.30, all the passengers appearing suddenly resuscitated and rapidly disappearing on shore. So ended my second trip.[1]

29 July 1856

Lately I finished reading Bulwers book 'My Novel'[2] which though an incongruous and, especially in latter parts, a trashy work, has however suggested to me several serious reflections of which I will relieve myself by putting them into writing. The First vol. is generally sincere and truthful in its style and I felt some degree of interest in the characters of Leonard and Randal so well contrasted (at all events to the end of this volume) as they are and so applicable to one in my circumstances. Ambition was the characteristic of each, and knowledge or ability was the instrument to which each principally looked to raise himself in the world. From the first every one approves of Leonards disposition, and equally detests that of Randal; in which really consists the difference. I cannot see that it is in selfishness and unselfishness for each had an equal family affection and beyond that neither could be said to labour with a view to other than their own benefit. It *might* happen too that both should gain equally high stations and to all app[ce] be equally praiseworthy, still the difference, the direct opposition of characters remains unexplained. I cannot quite understand the exact difference which lies perhaps under the same mystery as *selfishness* does in my mind.

Is it that Leonard was prompted & urged on by an inward, perhaps innate sense of the *Good & Great*, an idea which working within him, leads him, without any positive view to his own or others mere happiness & comfort; Continually on an[3] upward path to stations of eminence

---

[1] It was Jevons's habit to take a small notebook with him on his excursions and to write up the full account from these notes afterwards. This would explain the confused sequence of entries in this section of the Journal. The account of this second trip was actually written up some months later, as we know from the following entry in his diary for 16 February 1857: 'Finished account of trip to Maitland which I had not written though it is now 9 or 10 months since.' The next Journal entry is found to begin 43 pages further on in the book.

[2] Bulwer Lytton (1803–73); *My Novel* was published in 1853, in two volumes.

[3] 'a' in the text.

& influence. He looks not to the pleasure of receiving praise for this probably is distasteful and the exercise of power would be merely a burden. But it is in satisfying this natural appetite and feeling himself continually moving in an upward direction that the exquisite happiness of a person like Leonard would consist. Randal Leslie on the other hand has not the slightest appreciation of the meaning of Good or Great; his satisfaction is in continually approaching the same goal of eminence, esteem, & power but for the sake of the mere reward of these: hence he is always ready to take a short cut in which he thinks he will be unobserved though it be by a *dishonourable step*. Leonard & Randal are indeed something like two men setting off to circumnavigate the Globe for instance one with the genuine love of travel & improvement, the other for the sake of the name he will obtain on his return; each might visit the identical same places, yet the one find everywhere gratification and interest whereas the other perhaps detests each place he comes to, counts up the stages of travel still remaining, and arriving home again, gains a suitable reward by being discovered and his superficialness exposed.

'Knowledge is Power' is a very frequent phrase throughout the book; as is said it is scarcely intelligible unless more expressly applied. I look upon knowledge in two lights, either as an agreable intellectual *exercise or sport* or as an instrument for the improvement of the mind and the application of its powers to the general improvement of the condition of the human race. It is an instrument for the attainment of the Good & Great, but the idea of the latter must be the moving cause.

My principle of action, indeed of life is this, and it has been growing more & more defined for some time; I aim at qualifying myself for any object I desire in life, I aim not at it and try no means to obtain it but those of being fit for [and][1] worthy of it. Witness my almost total & partially intentional neglect of ties of acquaintance ship & interest, and my habit of total reserve. It originated a deal no doubt in mere bashfulness or a nervous want of confidence which I really have no want of but I now begin almost to esteem this property in myself and should feel utterly wretched if I knew another to think me better than I was. Persons older & more *experienced* than myself might perhaps shake their heads and say it would never do; I however feel inclined to regard *worth* as synonymous with *success* and though not independent of the *chance* & unavoidable & inexplicable *evil* of this world still by far the best armour against it.

Speaking of experience of life as we find it in old people, is it indeed at all [a][2] desirable thing and is it not the absence of it that makes youth

---

[1] This word is omitted in the text but is inserted in LJ, p. 66.
[2] This word is omitted in the text but is inserted in LJ, p. 67.

daring enterprising and happy? Is not the old man speaking to & warning the youth something like a dull, worn out, old carpenters chisel with a rounded edge speaking to a new & fine one just sharpened and in the Carpenters (God's) hand about to enter on its tough & woody work, saying 'Oh it is of no use your beginning your work with such a fine edge as all that; I was just as sharp when I was as new as you and you will be just as[1] dull & useless as me before you have been long at it'. It is perhaps true that a chisel dull all its days might be contented and happy, nay even as happy as the sharp and therefore always busy chisel just as a quiet country life may be pleasanter than a busy public one but when would Gods work or the Carpenter's either be done if men & chisels were always dull.

13 September 1856

Last week there was a lecture given at the School of Art[2] by Dr Woolley[3] of the Univeristy of Sydney, on 'The Selfish theory of Morals'. The subject is a good one and of interest, to me at least. The printed lecture is very difficult to understand, and the only point of importance that I gained from it, is the following arrangements of the various theories of morals.

1. Selfish.	a.	Man purely selfish & unrestrained in the pursuit of pleasure only by force.[4]
	b.	Selfish but deriving his highest pleasure from benevolence which is therefore identical with his own benefit.
2. Benevolent.	c.	Benevolent from a sense of duty merely which becomes often a real pain.
	d.	Benevolent by duty, but always finding his highest enjoyment in the performance of this duty.

[1] In the original text Jevons here wrote 'a'.

[2] The Sydney Mechanics School of Arts, founded in 1833, ran a lending and reference library and classes for Matriculation. It also organised public lectures – 21 were delivered during 1856, a number being on subjects of literary interest and on social questions (Annual during 1856, a number obeing n subjects of literary interest and on social questions (*Annual Report of the Sydney Mechanics School of Arts to 31 December 1856*). Jevons attended some of the classes as well as lectures, and he was a frequent user of the library and reading room.

[3] Reverend John Woolley, M.A., D.C.L., was Principal of Sydney University (inaugurated in 1852) and Professor of Classics. He took a prominent part in the social life of the colony and in the running of the School of Arts – of which he was Vice-President in 1856. He delivered many public lectures on education and other subjects. (H. E. Barff, *A Short Account of the University of Sydney in connection with the Jubilee Celebrations, 1852–1902* (1902).)

[4] This should read 'Man purely selfish and restrained . . . etc.'

There is an evident counter connection between a & c and between b & d. I must acknowledge my opinions rank, if anywhere in b, and having reflected a little on the subject I have come to a complete conclusion quite satisfactory to my mind.

I regard man in reality as essentially selfish, that is as doing everything[1] with a view to gain enjoyment or avoid pain. This self interest is certainly the main-spring of all his actions, and I believe that it is beyond a mans nature to act otherwise, just as food, his *fuel* is the source of all his bodily actions, and his only possible maintainance. But he is not necessarily what we should call an avaricious, interested or in fact in its full sense a *selfish* man. It is by the quality of those pleasures which he is continually seeking and by the causes of pain he equally flies from that he is to be judged. It is quite possible that one of his chief pleasures may be to see another person happy, or that he may have a friend connected to him by such intimacy, similarity of feelings, and in short complete *sympathy*, that pain to the friend is pain to himself. Towards such a one his conduct will undoubtedly have the appearance of unselfishness, and be for all common purposes, called so, still pain to himself or pleasure in prospect was not less really the *prime mover*. In its action on the body the mind must follow a simple & universal law of seeking the most pleasure, and follow it as implicitly as[2] the railway train follows the curves & turns of the line upon which it is running, but it is in the nature & spontaneous impulses of the soul itself and its relation, by sympathetic feelings to other souls, that what we shall call, unselfishness, disinterestedness[3] or benevolence consist. It is these impulses and these feelings which actually form the pleasures & pains, and constitute the iron line, on which our railway train has been running. The truly selfish man will be he who has no such connections with the souls of others, and whose enjoyments are completely[4] or material or perhaps misanthropical.

To close with another, and I think a rather apt comparison, a mans mind and character may be likened to a complicated piece of machinery moved by steam. All his feelings, love, likes or dislikes, in fact the whole of his thoughts & feeling with respect to other men, are represented by the frame work, the slides, guide-rods, and the whole regulating portion of the machine; the steam, the prime mover of the whole, the actual *motive*, is the mans unavoidable, and half animal instinct of self interest, which is his only intimate & ultimate *motive* or cause of action. But just as the machine may turn out the most beautiful work from the rudest material, so is the man, under the influence of his guiding passions

---

[1] Jevons wrote 'everywhere' here in the text.
[2] In the original text Jevons wrote 'and the railway trains' . . .
[3] 'disintesedness' in the text.   [4] A word appears to be omitted here.

capable of the noblest, the most disinterested & the greatest actions. As well might we complain of the coin, when we see it flying out bright, beautiful & perfect from between the dies, that it was made by the aid of dirty coals & muddy water, and is therefore itself filthy, as to object to this theory of this human machine that it is false because it represents the noblest of actions, which whatever theories we may adopt, we cannot deny to be anything but noble & disinterested, as springing in the first place from an ignoble & half animal instinct of self interest.

Petersham near Sydney
January 1st 1857

My dearest Lucy,[1]

Christmas comes, still, once a year in Australia, but when it comes it hardly brings the same good cheer as we all know it does in England. Nevertheless it brings a holyday or two even here and it happens I have passed my Christmas holydays in a manner as agreable, as well as novel, and which I think worth being made the subject of a letter to you. I have in fact been a three days walking tour over the country about 50 miles to the West of Sydney, and I wish to describe all the particulars of the country as well as of the people and the usual incidents of travelling because you will I think get a better idea of Australia and Australian life in this manner than in any other. So here I go straight into it.

Christmas day being on Thursday, Boxing day being a public holyday and the Saturday a holyday also in the Mint & some other public offices, I thus had four clear days[2] which I soon resolved not to lose but to devote to a trip, contemplated for some time previous to the Richmond district[3] and to waste no time I settled to go by railway & coach to Windsor on Wednesday night.

[1] The text of the final letter sent to Lucy is much shorter than this draft (see Vol. II, Letter 95). Although the entry is dated 1 January, we know from Jevons's diary that it was only begun on this date and that it was continued on the 2nd and 8th and finished on 11 January. [2] 24–8 December 1856.

[3] This district, about forty miles to the north-west of Sydney and noted for its rich fertility, has from the early days of colonisation been one of the chief food-growing areas. It is watered by the River Hawkesbury 'a fine broad stream, the Thames of New South Wales' (see LJ, p. 72); the scenery is lush and verdant, and nowadays there is to be found here a mixture of old-world charm and modern development which is unique in Australia.

On the morning of the first day of the tour, Christmas Day, Jevons walked about the agricultural plains near the town of Windsor, the fourth largest country town of New South Wales at that time, and in the afternoon he walked to the nearby town of Richmond (both towns being named after their English equivalents because of their situations on the 'Thames-like' River Hawkesbury). The extremely winding course of the river makes the route Jevons took rather complicated to follow, for he crossed the river three times.

On Boxing Day, Jevons left the rich plains and walked south-west to explore the mountainous fringes of the Blue Mountains, and the following day he joined the Great Western Highway (which crosses the mountains) and returned to Sydney.

My outfit I may state before starting was of the slenderest possible description, and my clothes of a happy degree of coolness & lightness which it has required three summer's experience and much deliberation to attain to. For most Englishmen I may tell you never seem to be aware of the difference of 10° between the mean temperatures of Sydney & London or Liverpool, and may accordingly be seen encountering the hottest of hot winds in black cloth suits of clothes, black hats & everything complete. On the present occasion I luxuriated in a grass-cloth coat as thin as a ladies gauze dress, trousers & waistcoat but a shade from white, and a cabbage-tree hat, which latter article being remarkable in itself and the universal mark of a true colonial I figure here.

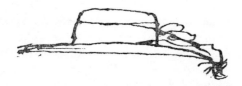

I carried with me one shirt, pair of stockings &c. packed up in my Botanical tin collecting box (for I intended to botanize) and to make this a less remarkable object to such vulgar people as do not comprehend its use, (do you remember it at Bryn Rhedyn) I made it up into a most shapeable and respectable brown paper parcel.

Well, having happily finished my assays in good time on Wednesday (for assays often prove stubborn unobliging things when one is in a hurry) I rushed home, changed my clothes, ate[1] my dinner and rushed off in time to catch the 5.52 railway train from the Newtown station to Parramatta.[2] I always find that it rather shuts one up on recounting ones Australian adventures, to begin[3] with starting by the railway, it is such an unromantically civilized and easy manner of travelling. But an excellent line it is, however, and no different from an English one except that one pays 2s. 9d for being carried 13 miles in 45 minutes, through flat country covered by bush or gum-tree woods of a very uninteresting & unEnglish appce.

Arrived at Parramatta about 6.30, I singled out from several omnibuses in waiting, the one going to Windsor, and found it, of course, to be the most wretched & uncomfortable of all of them, and the top seat being already crowded I had to creep in[4] to the inside of what was nothing but a square box with four air holes and to give up once

---

[1] In the original text, Jevons wrote 'eat'.

[2] The short railway line from Sydney to Parramatta was the first to be opened in Australia, in 1855, not long before Jevons's trip.

[3] 'beginning' in the original text.

[4] 'into' in the original text.

and for ever my intended remarks en passant, on the country from Parramatta to Windsor.

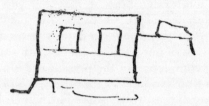

The inside too was soon crammed to full high pressure point and we then proceeded at a good slow rate to the town of Parramatta which is about a mile from the station. Parramatta is a pretty nice little town, built very regularly but[1] still picturesquely on a slightly hollowed space near the Parramatta River which is the extension of Port Jackson.[2] It boasts a church with a pair of wooden spires which would make the cats laugh, but which if I remember right, look quite architectural in the Australian Keepsake.[3] The first part [of the][4] road seemed as far as I could distinguish quite uninteresting passing through gum trees & pretty bushes, but in descending the Baulkham hill we passed through the largest orangeries in the colony, consisting of an large number [of][5] acres on both sides of the road, closely & regularly planted with the rounded, well-kept orange trees which have such a rich, and beautifully green appce. from a distance.

It soon became pitch dark when my chances of perceptive enjoyment were restricted to listening to the remarks of a fellow opposite, much of my own sort only 5000 times more talkative, who wandered at last, to my amusement, as far as Liverpool & St. Georges Hall (which he said was a very fine building) but he was in reality one of those intolerable nuisances one has often to put up with. By means of the slowest possible travelling and frequent stoppages at each inn for the sake of those who took nobblers, we thus contrived to pass away four hours in a dark

---

[1] Jevons wrote 'by' in the text.

[2] In 1790 a regular town was laid out at Parramatta which had been established in 1788, a few months after Sydney. A Government House and barracks were built and a park was laid out which is still admired to-day. The town was in fact the real capital of the colony in the early days.

[3] Landscape Scenery, illustrating Sydney, Parramatta, Richmond, Maitland, Windsor and Port Jackson, New South Wales (1855), also known as The Australian Keepsake.

[4] These words are omitted in the text. Jevons first wrote 'The road seemed . . .', then inserted the words 'first part' above the line.

[5] This word is omitted in the text. Jevons first wrote '. . . consisting of many acres . . .', then deleted 'many' and substituted the words 'an immense number', finally substituting 'large' for 'immense'.

crowded omnibus in accomplishing 20 miles of road, and for which we paid 6s a piece.

However about 10.30 pm the driver fulfilled his contract by delivering us at an inn in Windsor,[1] where I as soon as possible retired (??) to bed in a small two bedded garret[2] very respectable fellow fortunately dividing the bed with me while two other highly unrespectable and objectionable ones filled the other. To describe the temperature & closeness of this room during the night would be impossible and as I cannot state the degree of either temperature or dewpoint I must leave you to estimate from the conditions given the effect likely to be produced, viz from four sleepers in beds covered by excellent close green mosquito curtains with calico tops in a small garret room after a hot day during which the sun had been in full play upon the roof.

Early next morning the low lands near the river were covered by beds of mist and the sky was thickly covered by low cloud of a vapoury misty appce. This did not immediately forbode rain though their appce. was dark & thundery, for having formed during the night & near the surface of the earth, they were probably caused by the cold night air off the mountains flowing down onto & running with the warmer & damper air of the valleys. The first rays of the sun in the morning by warming the earth and the air immediately up quickly redissolves the vapour and [the][3] sky is soon quite clear. So it luckily turned out soon after starting, which I did about 8.0 am after having had breakfast. Turning my back upon some very tempting high-lands and mountains, but a few miles off, I proceeded, according to a programme I had marked out, to walk through the splendid cultivated lands for which the Windsor distict is celebrated and to make myself acquainted with two or three places which though figuring largely on the map are nothing but small villages.

The nature of the country I can best explain by a[4] an imaginary section, which gives a sort of general view of the form of the valley of the Hawkesbury between Wilberforce & Penrith.

The plains are formed of a rich, and exceedingly deep natural earth which seems to require nothing but the sowing of the seed to bring forth corn or anything else without further preparation. No wonder that this

---

[1] Windsor was one of five townships which Governor Lachlan Macquarie (1762–1824) established in the Hawkesbury Valley in 1810 on land above the level of the periodic floods. The others were Pitt Town, Wilberforce and Richmond (see below); also Castlereagh, which Jevons does not appear to have visited.

The inn, where Jevons was also to have his Christmas dinner (see below, p. 140) was presumably the Macquarie Arms. It was destroyed by floods in 1867.

[2] Jevons first wrote 'one' after this, then deleted it without substituting any other word.

[3] This word is omitted in the text.

[4] At the end of this page in the Journal, Jevons turns back 100 pages in the book to continue the account. The first word to be written on the new page was 'small', which he then deleted.

narrow strip of land has been greedily seized upon, divided up and cultivated as closely as in any English model farm, while 20 or 30 miles of busy and woody country between it and Sydney lie comparatively

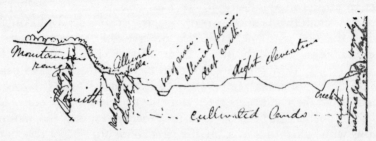

uncleared & wild. Indian corn, oat, lucerne, & crops chiefly intended for horses occupied most of the land and are often cut when young for green stuff of hay and it is singular how seldom wheat is seen growing near Sydney. The Indian corn was in all stages of growth for crops are not in this climate so much confined to one regular & fixed period of the year, as at home; when tall & planted in a wide regular manner it has a handsome & beautiful green appce. Granaries full of the pods here & there showed its great productiveness.

In this part the country might have had the homelike appearance of your English fields & meadows, but for one or two striking deficiencies viz hedge rows and trees. Ditches are not at all required in this country since there is seldom any excess of water to drain off, except during our regular heavy rains when your[1] ditches would go for nothing, and hedges which are the natural accompaniment of ditches are replaced here by the universal three-rail fence. This railing which is I believe, the only sort used throughout Australia, is very curiously & ingeniously made from the trees growing upon the spot by the use of the axe & saw alone and without a single nail or any other fastening so that [it][2] is well worth a description. It is made entirely of split-wood, for the most of the timber here is of such a stringy coarse texture that it can be split up by a good workman in any manner. The tree is first of course cut down, the bark is carefully removed in sheets about 6 to 8 feet long which being flattened out are used for roofing, and the trunk having been first sawed into lengths of about 6 feet, is completely split by the axe & wedges into rails & posts. The former are then mortised into the latter in such a manner that each rail is wedged in by those at each end of it, and the whole is thus more firm & durable than any amount of nails & carpentry work almost would make it. If a close *paling* is required, the timber is split up into thin narrow boards which can be either

---

[1] In the original text, Jevons wrote 'you'.
[2] This word is omitted in the text.

jammed in between three rails as in the figure or as is more common nailed on to a two rail fence. Additional rails may also be added as closely almost as may be desired, until the railing becomes quite a wall

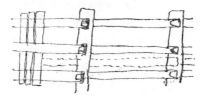

of wood. Log huts in which a large part of the population of Australia lives are made of similar roughly split logs of wood placed on end closely together so as to form a strong wooden wall, the chinks being plastered up with clay or mortar, but often so imperfectly as to make[1] the walls rather transparent.[2] You people of the old world perhaps few of you know what a shingled roof is; as shingles are also made by this process of splitting I may here describe that they are short little boards (about 12 inches into four) of split wood which being nailed on the battens of the roof like tiles or slates form the more watertight covering than anything else I believe, since the rough split fibres of the wood, I suppose, hold the water and prevent it running any way but downwards.

But to return from my digression, the thousands of miles of this railing that fence off all the roads, where they are fenced off, and separate all farms, properties, or fields whatever, form a feature of the country quite as monotonous as the gum tree woods from which they are formed, but being intended only to retain cattle & horses and not to keep out trespassers, they offer very little obstruction to men, and I never have the least compunction in going straight across any bodies property if it is the shortest way; I have seen trespassing boards in Australia but they are rare, as they ought to be.

Well I walked from Windsor to Pitt Town, a distance of about 4 miles, and this place may be described as only a very straggling & rather small village. The houses were either small farm houses or very neat comfortable cottages generally of wood. They are often distinguished for very pretty little gardens filled with rose trees, oleander bushes, orange trees and all the ordinary garden flowers, while passion flowers and other creepers, cover the walls or verandah, with almost too great luxuriance. Too much credit must not be given to the Colonials for this care and tastefulness, considering that the plants once set, grow almost without further care.

[1] 'made' in the text.
[2] Jevons inserted these two sentences at the bottom of the facing page of the Journal and overleaf and then continued the narrative around them. Here the editor places them where they seem most relevant.

Pitt Town is placed on a slightly elevated piece of ground on the edge of the uncleared bush, to be out of the way no doubt of floods. At its extremity I found the road to lead down to the River Hawkesbury where the old punt-man took me across in a boat for 3d. The river was here wide and deep with fine clear fresh water, which is tidal and was running in. The cleaness of his element seemed a standard[1] subject with the old boat man, and he appeared complimented by my drinking an inordinate quantity of it and praising it. The river had a very circuitous course about here but its beauty was spoiled by the almost total absence of trees and shrubs. After leaving it, I walked about two miles through cultivated plains or woody country to Wilberforce,[2] which was even a still more straggling insignificant village and as a road of about four miles in length lead direct from here to Windsor I determined on seeking my Christmas dinner at the latter town but being by this time very tired hot & thirsty I first took a 'downer' about noon under an unusually thick tree on the bank of the river to one of the numerous bends of which the road closely approached. The ground was likewise covered by unusually thick grass which formed a soft seat, and everything conspired to form a perfectly delicious resting place. Seeing several people bathing in the river at different points, I thought I might enjoy the same gratuitous pleasure, and I soon had a dip in a shallow flat part, hardly the less delightful for being solitary.

A few miles of a dusty, hot, uninteresting road, on the sides of which however several market gardens seemed to be flourishing amazingly, I reached the river again, and crossing by the punt for 2d. this being a clumsy old floating contrivance worked along a rope which is stretched across from bank to bank.

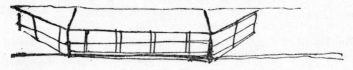

Being denied a dinner at the first Inn I met, I had to seek it at the one at which I slept;[3] here the servant quickly conducted me to an upper room where the family & strangers were just in the middle of their Christmas feasting. Such a funny christmas dinner I never had before, for I found myself in a long but low & oblique angled ball-room, evidently the Banquetting hall & chief assembly room of the good town of Windsor on all public occasions. A long table reached from one end to the other, one half of which was now covered by miscellaneous lumber

---

[1] Jevons first wrote 'standing', which he corrected to 'standard'.
[2] Wilberforce lies on the opposite side of the river from Pitt Town and Windsor.
[3] The Macquarie Arms.

(among which a terrestial globe of all things in the world) while on the other half a very tolerable dinner was laid. The fat old host sat at the bottom the hostess at one side, (their portraits hung conspicuously at the end of the room and were unmistakable likenesses of their large English faces, if not very admirable works of art) while three extremely common looking strangers, and three or four of the hosts children half grown up and all singularly exact images of the parent countenance, filled up the occupied portion of the table. I evidently excited considerable amusement as I entered with my mysterious brown paper parcel & cabbage tree hat, which I deposited among the lumber; my clothes, too, were not at all in Sunday or holyday condition, their whiteness being much marred by stains of red iron stone dust from the road as well as perhaps other unlucky patches of dirt, while the folds of my shirt & collar were sadly relaxed or distorted by copious perspiration. Upon taking my seat on the border of the lumber, I was somewhat dismayed to observe their fair daughter of the house, facing me, in a scanty gauzelike white muslin nondescript dress. She was proud and handsome (in her own opinion) and favoured poor itinerant me with attentions amounting to Nil, which she would scarcely have done if she had recognised in me a salaried officer of Her Majesty's Mint. However, a feeling of great amusement at my novel position soon occupied me and drove out my previous dismay, & I commenced the ordinary operations of eating dinner with as gentlemanly an air as I could assume.[1] To raise myself if possible in their estimation, I called for a bottle of stout (the most impressive order you can give I think (1s. 6d) unless it be a bottle of wine), but not without considerable misgiving as to the effects it might have. With most men, to drink a bottle of porter is no difficulty in truth; to me it is easier to pay for it than to drink it, for fear of those symptoms of incipient inebriation (called by ladies 'getting in their head') which always remind me of Paris & the unavoidable portion of vin ordinaire at the restaurants. However I escaped the dilemma safely and enjoyed considerably my dinner of turkey and plum pudding.

Shortly after finishing I went to pay the landlord the charge which was altogether 4s & 6d, when he observed looking at my *respectable brown paper parcel*, 'been doing business this morning?' The horrible suspicion crossed my mind that he thought I was some sort of travelling hawker and that my tin box contained my wares, probably in his opinion false jewellry. How much better, I thought if I had boldly passed it off in its scientific character, but then again as yet I could not have shown him any specimens of Natural History but a little manufactured cotton and a little wool.

[1] In the text, 'as assume'.

In spite of intensely heated air and a still powerful sun, I walked clear of Windsor as rapidly as possible, in the direction of Richmond. I hate almost all interior Australian towns that I have seen from Sofala downwards. They are so utterly untasteful, so utterly destitute of any object on which the eyes can rest with pleasure not to speak of the churches usually present of which the Parramatta one with its[1] two wooden spires, mentioned before, is almost a favourable type; they are so bare of trees although but a few years since trees & bush alone covered the ground and have been purposely cleared away; so ill situated upon some slightly raised, sun-baked space of ground, and finally they seem to me in general to have such a vein of licentiousness & drunkenness running through them, that I utterly hate them & always try to be as much as possible in the open country, and among the country people whose manners seem so much simpler & more pleasant.

New-South Wales towns may I think be divided into two classes, those that are just being put up, and those that are just tumbling down. The first comprises those mushroom like collection of temporary dwellings which are sure to arise where population is increasing so rapidly and is settling down on new lands with all the prospects of wealth before them. The latter of which Windsor & Parramatta are examples, as well as some parts of Sydney are perhaps only apparently so, and the appearance is produced by the very temporary character of the best colonial style of buildings. Well finished & often large houses, of red brick, & with beautiful gardens or perhaps grounds may be seen falling in ruins but have still none of that picturesqueness, though perhaps imaginary, which attaches to old things, especially such as appear to have long successfully resisted the approaches of decay.

Well after leaving Windsor behind me with an inward prayer that this might be another Australian town I might never see again, 'the force of nature could no further go' and I lay down in the shade till the sun might descend lower in the heavens and the air be more tolerably cool.

Afterwards I walked among fine but not very closely placed trees towards Richmond. This land formed I believe a common, and part of it had been cleared & was covered by a thick soft & bright green grass, which from a distance had a singular but beautiful appc. I did not believe that it could be grass till I saw it close; cattle were grazing on it, perhaps on *commonage*.

Richmond which I reached about five PM. was a long & very regular town. The cottages or houses were large & good & surrounded more generally by fine gardens than in any town I had seen. There was a square open space in the centre about which were several respectable

[1] In the original text, Jevons wrote 'it'.

inns &c, and there was altogether nothing that one could find fault with in it. It was placed upon the edge of a sort of high & extensive bank of earth which borders the plains at the distance of about a mile from the river. This position is doubtless to secure it from floods which I dare say cover these plains when severe.

But I liked not the idea of remaining over night in Richmond and therefore after obtaining information as to the fact of there being a public house further on I proceeded about two miles along strait dull even roads and among numerous fields of corn & various crops till I reached the river. This I crossed by the well known Richmond-punt & found a good convenient public house on the top of the opposite bank, and in a situation most nearly approaching the romantic & beautiful that I had yet met. Here I engaged a bed and was soon sitting at[1] tea, a meal however I should not have much enjoyed but after such a day of open air exercise, for there was only damper, some well picked bones of goose, which others apparently had relished before me and some tea, which had mostly the flavour of hot water, others again having evidently had the full benefit of the herb. This was my first introduction to *Australian damper* or the *bush bread* of Australia. It is like very close-grained unfermented bread, and a first one expects to find it heavy & disagreable, but I was surprised that it turned out not at all dry nor yet pasty, but certainly very satisfying; here they appeared to have no bread.

I afterwards turned out in the cool & half twilight of the evening to enjoy the calmness & beauty of this country place so contrasted with the noisy half drunken jabbering & wrangling of the men who filled the Inn and were trying I suppose, to take out in spirits the full benefit of the season & day. This place, Enfield, I found situated among low swelling alluvial hills which border the West side of the Hawkesbury even here, extending a great distance uninterruptedly towards Emu,[2] while North they[3] increased in height & even formed tall perpendicular cliffs at the side of the river just where it bends off towards Windsor. On the opposite side the plains were seen extending in a narrow strip along the river south & becoming wider near Richmond & then likewise curving off towards Windsor. All along it was bordered by a sort of bank of raised & less fertile land, allowed as we have before said, to remain still covered by the primitive woods & bush. But to the South-west lay the place of my desires, viz the vast mass of sandstone ridges & mountains which rising close to the Nepean[4] R stretch uninterruptedly

[1] Jevons wrote 'a' in the text.
[2] Emu lies south of Richmond at the foot of the Blue Mountains, near to Penrith.
[3] 'the' in the text.
[4] The River Nepean flows along the coastal plain from south to north at the foot of the Blue Mountains and for part of its course becomes a continuation of the Hawkesbury River proper. Penrith is the most important town on this river.

to Hartley on the west & extend North & South with greater or less continuity, through a great part of the colony as the Great Dividing Range. But the river was the great attraction near here, with its broad, generally straight tranquill stream, deep sunk between great banks of earth, here and there covered by dark acacia? trees or orchards of peach & apple trees &c. These high alluvial banks, generally 30 feet or 40 I should think, give it a peculiar romantic appearance, and I can well conceive that if this river were adorned by beautiful neat villas, and its[1] bareness covered by fine trees & more frequent gardens & orchards that it would much surpass in loveliness even the Thames. The banks are often hollowed out by floods, during which the river even overflows these immense bulwarks; (it had recently risen about a third of the height) & these spots seemed favourite places for gardens & orchards, doubtless on the joint account of the moisture & the concentrated heat of the sun rays. It[2] occurred to me that the composition, origin, and capabilities of such a vast mass of alluvial vegetable earth as forms these banks and plains would be very interesting and I therefore finished my days work by collecting three samples from the bank near the punt & three different elevations above the water of the river, which I packed up and carried with me for examination & analysis at the Mint. (for results see General Notebook) Bed was then grateful to me, and even my usual late habits did not prevail.

December 26th In descending from my room about 5.30 am I observed the strange route by which I must have ascended the night before. My room which was mine alone for a wonder, though of course double bedded, was large uncomfortable, of disagreable odour, and

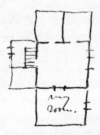

with a small window on one side[3] only to be reached by a small pair of steps. From this you passed into a sort of general dormitory (evidently well occupied during the night) into which two other rooms also opened, thence into a sort of side garret, & down steps in a pantry whence by another door, an open passage was at last gained. All this was evidently available sleeping room, but how pleasant supposing one

---

[1] In the original text, Jevons wrote 'it'.
[2] 'I' in the text.   [3] 'sided' in the text.

had by some chance to make ones way over all the rooms full of reclining figures, and how singularly awkward if ladies formed part of the party.

I had breakfast, paid about 4s. 6d for my total accommodation, with which I had received gratis the costless but valuable consideration of civility & attention, & after a little enquiring about the roads started SSW over the hilly country before mentioned.

I soon met however a good road leading in a W & SW direction & followed it up as quickly as I could walk among scattered or close gum trees with various simpler flowering trees or shrubs beneath, on the whole of a rather novel & therefore pleasing appce. The sky was yet closely covered by clouds, which reached the earth in the shape of mist; the air was damp & cool but this was the greatest of all delights in walking.

The wild flowers became now interesting & abundant in their forms, and tempted me here for the first time to open my box & commence collecting. Among the gum trees were also interspersed many acacia trees, of a small size compared with gum trees, but of neat rounded shape, with very small pinerated leaves, & quantities of small yellow sweetly scented balls of flowers, all stamens, which gave the whole a very fine appce.[1]

I walked a great distance through these solitary woods the beauty of the view gradually increasing till about 8 am the sky began to clear, and a fine hot day to announce itself, while at the same time, I reached an open cleared hill, and discovered, as an explorer would say, a wide extent of very hilly but beautiful country to the West, cleared, or timbered in a light & varied manner, and altogether strongly contrasted with the dark mass of precipitous, rocky mountains, covered with thick gum trees & bush, which stretched in a long range out of sight to the Westward, and formed a barrier which it would take almost weeks to cross except by a track or road. Still my ambition was to cross this country over to some point on the Great Western or Penrith road which would easily lead me[2] back towards Sydney and be much preferable to retracing my steps.

I therefore proceeded but with continually decreasing hopes as the road provoking[ly] turned more & more West^d. Comfortable neat cottages lay here & there surrounded by fields or pastures of encouraging appce, & the country seemed to me a delightful & peaceful spot. I frequently enquired for a road across the ridges, but the people could

---

[1] Jevons inserted this paragraph at the top of the facing page overleaf in the book and drew a line apparently indicating back to the previous page. Here the editor has placed it where Jevons probably intended that it should go and where it seems most relevant.
[2] 'my' in the text.

only tell me that this road led to Hartley[1] (small consolation), till at one small cottage an old bushman, after much conversation, told me of a track across to Springwood and directed me 2 miles back on the road & then to cross the R. Grose,[2] at 'Ben Carver's'. After a long walk and tedious enquiries of every cottage or person for 'Ben Carver's', during which I came upon a nicely situated gentlemans residence, and met to my great surprise three young ladies in large fashionable hats, I reached the river Grose.

This ran in a flat, & rather low sunken sandy bed, the banks on the side I first reached being alluvial & covered with luxuriant bush & other vegetation, & on the other side of sandstone rocks. The winding course of the river prevented me seeing far but tall almost perpendicular ridges of sandstone could be seen within a mile or two up the stream between which I have no doubt it runs from the centre of the Blue Mountains. The R. Grose is in fact a mere mountain torrent composed of the innumerable creeks draining all the gullies that one meets on the road from Springwood to Blackheath.[3] After heavy rains it must therefore contain an immense rapid body of water, as indeed its unequal bed of coarse sand impeded every where by trunks of trees borne down, showed. I was greatly surprised to find that the small quantity of water that was now running down was of a brownish colour and distinctly disagreable taste, as one always supposes a mountain torrent running over sand and sandstone to be pure as crystal. Its impurities may have been derived from the *gum foliage*.

It being yet very early in the day (10 am) and my legs much fatigued by having walked so far without,[4] I rested for a short time under the shade of the banks, digesting a little damper I had pocketed at the Inn, with the aid of the bad tasted water. I then took a turn at botanizing on the banks and found a large number of plants chiefly shrubs quite new to me. Among these was a large Euphorbiaceous flowering bush, a true Ribus, which was bearing blackberries not very unlike those at home, a very small & modest but true violet &c &c.

In passing the identical Ben Carver's, I had found a large number of colonial men who had however civilly directed me on my way. On wishing now to cross the river to the other bank & proceed I was dismayed to find the whole of these with an equal proportion of females, deter-

---

[1] A settlement on the western slopes of the Blue Mountains, 85 miles from Sydney on the Great Western Highway.

[2] The River Grose runs from east to west through the Blue Mountains in a series of dramatic sandstone gorges to join the River Hawkesbury near Richmond.

[3] Blackheath lies in the western portion of the Blue Mountains on the Great Western Highway, north of Katoomba, whilst Springwood lies on the same road, about 49 miles from Sydney. Jevons wrote 'Sprinwood' here in the text.

[4] Jevons then wrote 'stopping', which he deleted without substituting another word.

minedly encamped in a sort of pic-nic manner just where the track crosses. They were in this remote spot as elsewhere keeping Boxing Day an absolute holyday, and were evidently in great want of something of an amusing nature & capable of being joked up. Imagine me then, a somewhat remarkable figure with the box at any time, obliged to pull off my shoes & stockings in face of them, to tuck up my trousers, & to ford boldly across; the bed, too being very *holy* it was natural that I should deviate more or less from the exact path of the ford, and sink a little too deep which I soon did, to their very uncivilly expressed amusement. However, it did me little harm and I proceeded along the best track I could find through undulated land with tall sparse trees & abundance of flowers, similar to that nearer Richmond Punt. I was greatly disappointed to meet no Mountains, and every now & then, I passed enclosed land, often cleared & improved, but only to my left hand or to the Nepean River.

I had been told that it was 12 miles from Grose River to Springwood but before I had gone 4 of them, unmistakeable signs of a thunderstorm appeared to the West. Long radiating arms of cirrostratus rose over tall woody ranges of sandstone which now lay a short distance on my right, while connected masses beneath these, exhibiting the appearance of *dropping folds* of clouds, absorbed rain, and the irreg. loose thundery 'ascitizi', showed a well *organised* and therefore severe storm to be approaching if indeed frequent low rumbling thunder did not sufficiently prove it. The air had by this time become exceedingly sultry and there was little wind, still I proceeded rapidly uncertain how to shelter myself.

The ground by degrees became more uneven, rocks showing themselves here & there and I at last approached quite close to the steep sandstone ranges which seemed chiefly parallel with the River. The thunder now produced an almost continuous *rumble* which was quite peculiar & very impressive, the cause being as it were invisible. Scattered drops of rain too began to fall, and I then looked eagerly for shelter but finally seeing a fence, determined on following the path up & seeking a cottage.

Within about half a mile I came on a large cleared & very open space of ground with a prosperous looking collection of cottages, barns & cattle. An old woman came out on the barking of the dogs, which were nearly biting me, and granted me the shelter which no one could have refused, looking at the heavens.

The cottage was of course a true specimen of colonial log building, but was neatly kept & comfortable. The windows, contained no glass, but were either opened or covered by a linen curtain, & closed at night by a wooden shutter.

The old woman, who seemed very particular, and severely religious but withal very truly respectable told me much about the place. This it seemed was a farm, her husband had occupied for 20 to 30 years, on the banks of the Nepean, which river lay to my surprise within a few

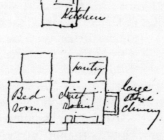

hundred feet, as shown by the flourishing orchards & gardens here again at its edge. They made their way to Sydney by fording the river & then making for the Penrith road. She had many sons who were chiefly carriers, and there was another boy with her now, her husband being out engaged.

Presently she laid the table which I watched with hungry eye, and the storm seemed to turn out quite a godsend for I had a substantial good dinner, still upon christmas remains, with rice pudding & tea, which I was truly in want of.

The storm advanced but very slowly though the motion of the clouds was distinct |90° and the whole sky was becoming covered in every direction by cirrostratus or dense masses of stratus & other storm cloud. Rain indeed though continually threatening in large scattered drops never commenced properly but passed to the Northward where, about over Richmond, exceedingly heavy rain was to be seen, with frequent immense flashes of forked lightening extending often over the greater part of the sky. A separate but much smaller fall of rain too appeared past us, and in the direction of Sydney, and the whole heavens appeared nothing but a universally threatening storm. It seemed to me however to be a sort of stationary or very slow moving storm, and rather to form spontaneously on the spot, as indeed some of the lowest scudlike thunder cloud overhead could be distinctly seen in the action[1] of doing. At this stage [a][2] sudden violent squall came on from the West of a great degree of warmth, swaying the trees about and causing a great branch of an old dead tree to fall with a crash, in a manner rather disheartening to one who had to cross six miles of solitary mountain forests.

Besides the danger from falling trees, accidents from lightning are exceedingly common in N.S.W. I hear of them everywhere, and the old

[1] Jevons wrote 'acting' here.
[2] This word is omitted in the text.

woman told me of an instance she was acquainted with lately in which a boy sitting by the fireplace was killed, other persons in the house stunned, and many dogs and animals either in or out of the house stunned or killed.

The storm having to all appece abated for some time at least though the clouds were nearly unchanged in appce & many now rapidly |40°, I determined about 2.30 PM on making the least of my way to Springwood, and furnished with minute directions from the old woman as to finding the proper track up to the top of the nearest ridge which then lead direct to Springwood, I thanked & left. My directions failed at once, and I had to depend entirely on my discretion in finding a faint track which ascended the termination of a steep rocky & woody hill.

Reaching the summit I could not help but pause a minute on an open point to admire the view.[1] The Plains lay in a narrow strip,

[1] The view from this spot was thus described, almost one hundred years later, in a letter to Jevons's daughter: 'I think you might like to know that my husband and I paid a pilgrimage to the spot high on the mountain overlooking the Nepean River where your father climbed on his Christmas walk so long ago. The beautiful spot is a reserve . . . and as we looked down over the lovely plains spread out below us, with the river sparkling in the sun curving away in the distance to the blue hills beyond, the thick gumtrees and eucalyptus and underbrush, with great outcrops of rock down the mountain side, it was all very lovely. Cultivated patches, cows grazing on the paddocks below. And great groves of citrus trees. We know with certainty how much Mr. Jevons would have enjoyed that same scene – very little altered today from when he knew it . . .' Letter to the late Miss Winefrid Jevons, dated 15 May 1955 from Mrs Iris Burke, author of an article on Jevons as a photographer: 'Australia's First Pictorialist', *Australasia Photo-Review* (January 1955) pp. 6-23.

In the article referred to above Mrs Burke briefly describes Jevons's walking trip to Windsor and the lower slopes of the Blue Mountains and comments '. . . Even to the modern bushwalker this appears to be a somewhat unusual route for a Christmas holiday walk, and one quite remarkable for Jevons' time' (op. cit., p. 21).

bordering the river & stretching away to the Northward, while beyond were nothing but dense dark coloured mass of gum trees; rain could be perceived in many places driving about & everything promised a very unquiet walk. On the other side were[1] several other adjoining ridges separated by steep gullies, all densely covered & almost obscured by gum trees & bush. Falling rain soon appeared to be approaching over them like mist and a heavy shower followed, from which I had to shelter myself as I best could. I then walked rapidly on; the track at first was the faintest possible path, often hidden entirely by some bush or by a sudden turn; on every side lay the interminable bush and except upon the spot no one can imagine the instinct with which one clings to a small path amidst boundless, trackless & nearly impenetrable bush. In this case the road was naturally walked on for it lay along the very level top of a continuous narrow ridge, which lead in a nearly straight line to Springwood. On either side lay deep gullies, and it was in fact just like an enormous railway embankment overgrown with trees & bush. A great source of discomfort too were the wet bushes which almost covered up the way & which continually drenched one from the waist downwards in passing.

Nevertheless this mountainous part of my walk, is what I looked forward to with most pleasure and now look back upon with most satisfaction. There is to me a kind of delight in the very being among these scenes of wild, remote, untouched nature, indigenous vegetation above below & on every side of you, gullies, full of mist, rendering the country impassable but by nicely chosen paths, and occasional views of other distant ridges, only impressing you the more strongly by their dark, & steep, closely timbered sides, and their general appce. of monotonous wildness, that you are in an uninhabited and almost uninhabitable tract of country only within a few years crossed by any but aboriginal savages. If there is one thing, too, that adds to the[2] romantic wildness of these woods, and impresses one with the feeling that destruction & decay are proceeding simultaneously with the productive processes of the vegetative force, it is the number of fantastic, shapeless, trunks of trees, true ruins of nature which lie around, eaten into by ants, blasted & shattered by lightning or bearing the marks of ancient bush fires. Huge branches, too, may be seen, either supported by a mere stick of remaining solid wood, ready to fall at a puff of wind and impressing the traveller with sense of the continual nearness of accident or death, or perhaps, suspended in an inverted position among the branches of a

[1] In the original text, Jevons wrote 'where'.

[2] Jevons broke off the sentence at this point, marking the place with an asterisk, and turned four pages further on in the book to continue the paragraph. In doing so he wrote the words 'to the' twice and 'as' instead of 'adds'.

neighbouring giant of the forest which has as yet felt less severely the effects of time & weather. Often one trunk, burnt & dead, had fallen, as it were into the arms of its brother tree, and there remains supported.

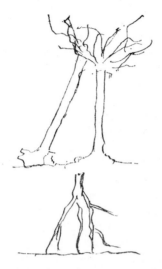

In one case a large branch in falling had alighted as it were on its legs, and still stood upright, and finally in the woody country on the further side of the Grose I saw an immense gum tree of which the trunk was a magnificent long straight & cylindrical piece of timber, which had been loosened in its roots and falling over down a slight hollow, had snapped [and][1] broken off in its *course* the timbers of two other considerable trees as well as stripped to mere bare poles a number of saplings as many in fact as lay within reach of its widely spreading branches. These latter too from their weight & the violence of the fall had been shattered and the whole lay in one great ruin of the most genuine picturesqueness.[2]

Besides the usual variety of gums, the vegetation was composed of the species of *tea tree* or other mystaceous bushes, quantities of small yellow *goodeniads*,[3] & similar herbs, tall white Composite plants, and one composite bush, an occasional orchis, some papillionaceous creepers, Etc.

The walk seemed long and tedious; my anxiety however diminished as the track became more distinct or even widened into a road, *barked* or felled trees likewise indicating that I was approaching a great thoroughfare. The *barking* of the trees is done to get the sheets of bark for roofing; a tree selected for straight cylindrical trunk is nicked round at two

---

[1] This word is omitted in the text.
[2] The account is now continued five pages further back in the book.
[3] Species of herbs, widely distributed in Australia.

places 6 or 8 feet apart and the bark being removed in one or two strips is easily flattened out by pressure for a short time. The tree soon dies, and these dead, barked trunks form a rather mournful spectacle along these roads. At last I passed one or two of those singular bare round mounds or knobs of clay earth so frequent on the sides of the Western road which I used to think were graves of Convicts dying in the making of the road. I believe however they are surveyors marks, and the convicts as many as were buried here, probably lie in an even more solitary mournful manner, unmarked.

I passed at last some ground of richer appce and slightly cleared and then was rejoiced at the sight of the broad highway of the Hartley road, and a cottage on it. This I found to be a boarding house $\frac{1}{4}$ mile short of Springwood, and a woman provided me with tea. She too asked me 'is it jewellry or what is it.' but I assured her thereupon I was collecting specimens of Natural History.

Afterwards four more miles of this well known & monotonously picturesque road brought me to Wascoes old Pilgrim Inn[1] about seven oclock, having been out 13 hours, about 10 of which I was on my legs, so that I must have walked fully 30 miles under by no means favourable circumstances. A glass of hot brandy & water, and an early and long sleep set me all right after wet & fatigue, and I rose next morning quite fresh.

Dec 27th. Getting out about 6 oclock I could have enjoyed sitting in the verandah for any length of time, looking round on the woods and on the mist only just rising out of the hollows. This is to me a Meteorologist a distinct pleasure; to others it might only suggest damp disagreable travelling. So probably thought the *gold escort*[2] which now drove up in the little mail coach from Penrith. It consisted of four fine tall well armed troopers, with their sergeant, the seats being filled up by 2 passengers, a lanky strange looking chinaman, and a little delicate & not bad looking girl.

I knew myself what it was to start about 4 am of a cool damp misty morning and ascend these wild mountainous roads on a jolting and altogether most uncomfortable open car, and the wearied pale half sleepy appce of this little girl as she timidly sat in her seat and watched the troopers enjoying a cup of coffee in the Inn, excited my pity and moved me to the only galant act I ever did which was to send her a cup by one of the waiting girls. Her satisfaction and gratitude were evident, even as she scalded her mouth by trying to swallow rapidly the hot but reviving drink, and I felt in this as in many more things in the country how the natural courtesy true civility and good nature which

---

[1] The Pilgrim Inn at Lapstone Hill, the junction of the Old and New roads to Bathurst.
[2] The armed escort for bringing the newly mined gold from the diggings to the Mint.

always seem to prevail amid nature excel the studied etiquette, and the miscalled politeness of towns. I allude however more particularly to the universal habit up the country of speaking to each person you meet solitarily, even if it be only to say good evening or good morning, and of freely asking or giving all directions or information about roads distances, other travellers, or straying cattle or horses. Once when I omitted to say good morning on passing a remote cottage, they bauled it out after me, and I am sure that if I passed many weeks in travelling in this manner I should become the most communicative of persons.

I left Wascoe's Inn where I was civilly attended on and comfortably lodged &c for 4s 6d about 8 am, and was suprised to find myself none the worse in the legs for yesterdays walking, only a little sore in the toes. The road I was well acquainted with, but I did not the less enjoy my last few miles of the mountain ridge. Lapstone Hill where the road very ingeniously and expensively constructed winds down the side of unusually steep gorges into the Emu plains below was as romantic a spot as I thought it before, & the pleasure of collecting plants was added to the interest of my first trip along the road.

After reaching the bottom I wandered among the bush botanizing, visited a pretty spot where Oconnell & I had camped out our second night,[1] and then climbed a short way up the bed of another gully. Here I met a slight reverse, for as I was revolving in my mind how lucky I was not to meet any snakes, (I had seen no mammalia but a few lizards varying from a few inches to a foot in length) I was brought to a sudden stand by the sight of one of those detestable & deadly reptiles lying in my direct path, and with[2] about 2 or 3 feet of me, lying in motionless spiral coils. As it was not wakened but lay still motionless, I retreated and returning deliberately with a long stout branch of a tree suddenly dealt it such a blow as at once to disable it from leaping or moving to attack me. It wriggled itself about, bit at the air in every direction in infinite rage and inspired me if anything with an additional share of horror at these animals. It required a long beating & pounding to render it even harmless and a nervous motion as usual still remained when I[3] left it laid out. It was between 3 & 4 feet long, & very thick in the middle; of a reddish brown colour above, & whitish in the belly and if not a poisonous one, might have been so, and is none the less disagreable an object to meet under one's feet.

I gained Penrith by the usual road meeting many horse men &

[1] Jevons and O'Connell (the brother-in-law of F. B. Miller) had camped in this spot on their way to the gold diggings in March 1856. See Appendix, p. 216 below.

[2] Jevons evidently intended to write 'within' here as he deleted it earlier in the sentence in order to include the words 'in my direct path'.

[3] 'it' in the text.

women going to the races[1] held some where on Emu Plains, and dining at Perry's Inn, took a place in the Parramatta coach afterwards and reached home without further occurrences worthy of mention, about 7.30 PM.[2]

28 January 1857

I have been not a little disturbed lately by my reflections on religious subjects. This has been caused partly by a little religious talk I have had here, very wide of my own opinions certainly, but chiefly by an attempt I made to explain the general character of my opinions to Henny,[3] when they appeared to me so cold and abstract compared with her heartfelt realities.

But how can I help it; I was brought up in perfect freedom of opinion for though I can remember my mother teaching me my prayers, I was then very young, and what religion I have since been taught at school or elsewhere only lead[4] me to enquire whether the whole was true.

Natural science was my chief study and I may say that I have become so impressed with the general character of natural laws of fact and have become so accustomed to habits[5] of severe and exact thought, that I must have a solid foundation for my religion or I shall have none.

My father never so much [as][6] communicated his opinions to me in

---

[1] These would probably have been held at Homebush, about eight miles out on the road to Parramatta. (See Birch and Macmillan, *The Sydney Scene 1788–1960* (Melbourne, 1962).

[2] This walk is outlined by Jevons in his diary and the comment he makes on the day after his return (28 December) reads: 'I am somewhat surprised to find myself so strong and capable of bearing fatigue: yesterday I walked more than 30 miles through the most oppressively hot and close weather, and yet I feel no effects from it. With practice I believe I could become an immense walker'.

[3] In letters to Henrietta dated 3 May and 1 October 1856 and 4 January 1857 (see Vol. II, Letters 86, 93 and 96).

Jevons further expressed his religious views at this time in two diary entries: on 30 April 1857 he wrote: 'Many if they understood my opinions might call me a deist and say I was without faith almost in a God, but I have faith in Good and in good intention, and almost believe myself independent of others so as not to need or care for approbation but feel contented and moved by the love of abstract good and usefulness.' And on 13 June 1857: 'It is very singular but I am strongly inclined at present to take a view of religion fundamentally different from all others; to found my faith not on the universe and its design but on Man and his feelings. The world is a stupendous, in fact infinite and most wonderful, orderly machine but inanimate or destitute of feeling. There is no positive good in the world but the happiness of man. Yet as far as man is dependent on material nature he is equally subject to evil here; where is there a God here; it is only man's mental feelings, those of love and sympathy which triumph over evil and lead him to a conception of and faith in something free from it; an intention of *good* in the universe; an idea of abstract good which the mere machine like operation of material nature however perfect cannot give.'

[4] 'led' (LJ, p. 78).   [5] 'habit' in the text.
[6] (LJ, p. 78). This word is omitted in the text.

any way nor do I know them now; whatever they were they were founded in the truest and tenderest *humanity*.

Revealed Religion I had long since dispensed with; I know not how my doubts about it first began. It appears to me such a confession of imperfection in Gods works to suppose that it was necessary to break their order to reveal himself to us. God is seen if anywhere in the wonderful order and simplicity of Nature, in the adaptation of means to ends, and in the creation of man to which everything refers, with power[1] capable of indefinite improvement. To suppose all this inadequate, to suppose him leaving man confessedly without means of enlightenment for ages and then to suppose him only revealing himself by breaking the order of his own creation and speaking through the mouth of a man, appears to me a most awkwardly constructed belief.

I see no evidence whatever of the inspiration of the Bible; the humane & perfect philosophy of Christ is indeed astonishing amid so much corruption, but one very probable suggestion explains it all. Christ was no doubt a great genius and just as Newton was a genius of Natural Science, Mozart of Music, Bacon of general learning, Shakespeare of *humanity* &c, so Christ devoted his powers to *Morality* and wonderfully pure his teachings[2] no doubt were.

However this is not where my difficulty and doubts lie; I feel no conviction of anything because it is in the Bible and I examine Matter and Mind in order to found my conception of God.

I perfectly comprehend everything that may be deduced from Nature, as to *design, order,* unity of conception &c of the universe, and I confess that both the theory of *Chances* and that of *Conditions of existence* are perfectly inadequate as explanations. The world is evidently but one vast organism full of motion and intelligence; it is not mere matter, for the very order & form of it express intention & mind. God is identified and inseparable from his works. But again I confess I do not see that as far as man's condition is concerned that the world is perfectly adapted. Evil exists and I see no way of completely reconciling it with any religious theory. A man falls from a cliff, a branch of a tree falls on him, or on some other animal, or perhaps a man advanced in civilization fall into a course of those refined evils which always accompany it. How is creation perfect here, or how can any recompense hereafter remove this imperfection, however slight, which now exists.

I have been lead[3] to these remarks by reading two books, Whewells Hist of Inductive Sciences and Saintines Story of Picciola.[4] The first

---

[1] 'powers' (LJ, p. 78).   [2] 'teaching' in the text.   [3] 'led' (LJ, p. 79).
[4] Joseph Xavier Boniface otherwise Saintine (1798–1865): *Picciola* (1836); first English translation: *Picciola, or Captivity Captive* (translated from the French by Mrs C. F. Gore?) 2 vols. (1837).

proceeds systematically & profoundly through all the ideas of the mind, all the subjects of Natural Science, and having sufficiently grounded all this on the natural properties of man[1] reason, so that if mans existence be a reality, his deductions are equally real, he at last touches on the puzzling question of Geology & Scripture. How disappointed I here was to observe his change of tone; instead of *what is what must be*, what it is *in the nature of man to believe*, he here tells us what *ought or should* be. We must believe scripture till its plain and evident interpretation is contradicted by demonstrated facts, but we must not put these forward too *rashly* and we should endeavour to reconcile &c &c. He is no doubt obliged to prove to others that his book leads to no unorthodox conclusions, but to those who are already not orthodox its conclusiveness & value just ceases where he leaves the thread of his demonstration and attempts to show this.

In Saintines Picciola, read just by chance, I was surprised to find an instance of a man, full of science & knowledge, who like me felt that *chance & evil* exist in the world. The story is very pretty & very excellent. The demonstration of the order & adaptability of the creation proceeds in a very nice and clever manner merely from the observation of a single plant, and I thought myself almost as surely saved from dark cheerless thoughts as Charney himself, when alas, one paragraph ended all my hopes and formed as bad a conclusion to Saintines pretty managed tale, as Whewells concluding chapter did to his great Philosophical work; it is the following 'do not accuse God either of the errors of man, or the eruption of a volcano (why not?); he has imposed on matter eternal laws, and his work is accomplished without his being anxious if a vessel sinks in the midst of a tempest or a town disappears under an earthquake. What matter to him a few existences more or less! Thinks he then of death? No! but to our soul he has left the care of regulating itself; and what proves it is the indipendence[2] of our passions. I have shown you animals obeying in all things the instinct which directs them, having only blind impulses possessing only qualities inherent in their species, man alone forms his virtues and his vices; he alone has free will, for him alone this earth is a world of trials. The tree of happiness which we cultivate here below with so many efforts, will only flourish for us in heaven. Oh! do not think that God can change the heart of the wicked, and will not; that he can leave the just in sorrow, without reserving for him a recompense. What could he than have willed in creating us?' If Saintine had intended to write a sort of parody or caricature of such demonstrations he could not have written other wise. What matter a few existences more or less to God? But what matter they

---

[1] 'man's' (LJ, p. 79).
[2] Jevons apparently started to write 'indifference'.

rather to their possessors, and we are told from a much more *humane* authority that not a sparrow falls to the ground without Gods heed: again 'do not think that God can turn the heart of the wicked and will not'. Why does not he then, for there are certainly many wicked people in the world and they cause much evil. If he does it finally why does he delay. To explain it by free will and so on, is mere prevarication; for in granting that instrument of good or harm he grants it with perfect knowledge and is certainly 'to be accused' with all consequences, just as a man that would knowingly let[1] a pistol to a murderer would be implicated in the crime.

No, this paragraph is indeed lame if intended for a proof, clever if a parody and at all events, it has done more than neutralize the good effect of the rest of the book.

But though I find not God in this way, I find goodness in the human heart, I am susceptible of sympathy and love; I feel the dignity of man, the height he may attain, the final[2] happiness he may enjoy if he seeks it from a proper source and those if not standing in place of a distinct conception of God, produce equivalent good effects on my actions and intentions.[3]

April 5th 1857.

Remarks on Whateleys
Lectures on Political Economy[4]

Two of the chief arguments in this book seem to me worthy of a few written remarks, the first of them for its the truth and beauty, the other for its looseness and utter improbability.

1st. The exposition of that hidden and seldom noticed principle in the nature of masses of associated men, which leads each to labour on ceaselessly in that very pursuit which will most benefit the whole body though himself seeking all the while his own exclusive advancement is exceedingly interesting and most excellently put.

---

[1] 'lend' (LJ, p. 80). [2] 'pure' (LJ, p. 81).

[3] Jevons left the rest of this page blank. The next entry is to be found ten pages further on in the book.

[4] *Introductory Lectures on Political Economy delivered in Easter Term, 1831* by Richard Whately 1832). The passages here referred to by Jevons occur in Lectures IV and V; the *Lectures* do not in fact contain any 'Chapter' entitled 'Origin of Civilized Society'. Jevons mis-spelled Whately's name 'Whateley'.

Whately (1787–1863) Archbishop of Dublin, was also the author of *Easy Lessons on Money Matters for the use of young people*, which Jevons's mother had read to him.

Jevons had bought the *Lectures* on 27 March 1857, according to his diary: the copy is now in the possession of Mr C. F. Carter.

The principle itself, or a closely connected one I had roughly conceived beforehand and expressed under the principle of Individual Competition, and it was my intention to show how a number of men all really and entirely selfish might yet, by means of the advantageous & equitable arrangements which fair & free Competition always ensures work together unconsciously or at least unintentionally each for the good of all. I find this same thing explained by Whateley only from a much higher and more general point of view, and considered to be the result of a *Social instinct*, conferred by God on Man, the system of co operation, and exchange which civilized Society always presents, being a remarkable & very stiking because unexpected example of *design* in Providence. I cannot but concur fully in this argument, and I should be glad if I can in time more fully develope and demonstrate the causes mode of operation, and exact effects of Selfish Competition.

In the next chapter on the 'Origin of Civilized Society', he attempts to prove that man is utterly incapable of rising, that is [of][1] raising himself from a *savage state*, but that the first civilizing movement having been communicated from without (doubtless from the First Cause or God) he may then progress at a rate quite unlimited and to an extent quite indefinite without further help than the judicious exertions of those powers originally granted him by God.

He considers that he demonstrates this as a formal proposition by appealing to the past history of the human race. 'On looking around us and examining all history ancient and modern, we find as I have said, that no savage tribe appears to have risen into civilization, except through the aid of others who were civilized.'[2]

Now though Whateley has allowed and referred to the looseness of the term *savage*, he has not attempted to define it but adopts as *savages, some tribes in as low a state as we are acquainted with*. I maintain however that *savage* is a term necessarily indefinite and in fact only comparative; that all human beings known are in a greater or less degree civilized, and that the lowest term of the scale, which those perhaps intend who speak of the '*natural state*', is the *animal state* where man becoming a creature whose motives are only instincts, unguided by the light of *reason*, is in fact no longer a human being. I mean by this that *civilization* cannot be defined but as the effect of mans reason operating through a greater or less space of time, upon his material or mental condition, and as *reason* however primitive & undeveloped must I conceive produce some effect on the mans action & condition, we cannot lie entirely dormant, I cannot allow any man to be a complete savage but when devoid of reason, when of course he is no longer a complete *human being*.

---

[1] This word is omitted in the text.
[2] Whately, op. cit., p. 112.

History can give us no account of any tribe of merely *animal men*, on the contrary it presents us with the innumerable diversities of the human race, differing in bodily form & appearance as well as cranial or mental development, but all are certainly found possessing a few at least of such simple contrivances and customs as must result from the exercise of some amount of reason.

The proposition that none can raise themselves from the *savage state etc*, the first civilizing influence being the direct agency of God is changed to the prop. that none can raise themselves but by the aid of reason derived from God, but that having received this in their creation, all *have* risen to a degree of civilization proportional to their mental capabilities.

*   *   *

The indirect evidence of the truth of Genesis which Whateley evidently aims to establish thus in my opinion falls through. The gift of *reason* was necessary in the first place to make man man, but unassisted reason is I believe always capable of raising itself and has produced all the various conditions of the human race from the Australian aboriginal to the most refined & energetic Anglo Saxon, the ultimate limit of the advancement of the latter being as yet completely out of sight.

Account of a Trip to Wollongong in the District of Illawarra N.S.W.[1]
April. 1857.

Having five clear days before me during which my presence would not be necessary at the Mint, I left home at the very untimely hour of 10.30 PM on Thursday night, April 9th, the eve of Good Friday, and made my way with carpet bag and mountain barometer in hand, through the cheerless streets of Sydney to a still more cheerless wharf on Darling Harbour. Here were collected a large number of excursionists,

---

[1] A small map traced by Jevons and entitled 'The ILLAWARRA DISTRICT of New South Wales from Sir T. Mitchell's Map', is pasted on to the page where this account begins.

Jevons's MS. map, 'Descriptive Map of the District of Illawarra, N.S.W., April, 1857', is bound with his *Social Survey of Australian Cities*, MS.B.864, Mitchell Library, Sydney.

The Illawarra District is a narrow coastal plain beginning about forty miles south of Sydney. At the time of Jevons's visit, coalmining was just beginning in the mountain ranges which wall-in the coastal strip, and has since formed the basis of industrial development around Port Kembla and Wollongong. The historic dairying industry (see p. 169 below) still flourishes.

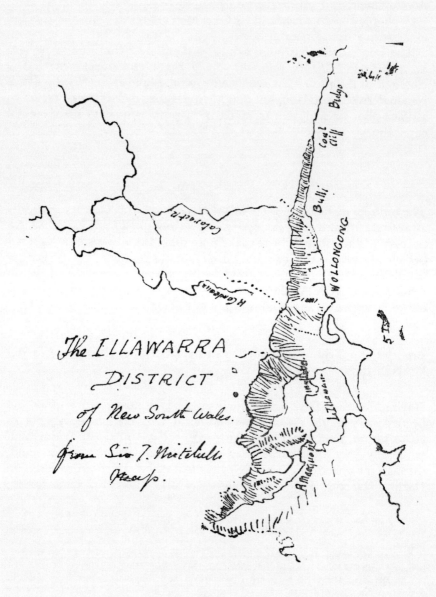

The ILLAWARRA
DISTRICT
of New South Wales.
from Sir T. Mitchell's
Map.

a great wonder indeed in Sydney where there is so little pic nic enterprise, and their numbers continually increased up to 12 PM, the time
when the steamer (Nora Crenia) should have started, but as there were
yet no signs of her arriving from Wollongong, the ardour of many was
damped by the chilly night air and the numbers now decreased as
rapidly as they had before increased.

About 1 am the steamer came along side and among all the abomina-
tions of a small overcrowded steamer I made my way to the cabin, to
lie in a far away corner for three hours, sleep being all along out of the
question both from the disturbance of a number of noisy passengers
below, and the overhead din of discharging & loading cargo on the
deck.

About 4.0 am when the splashing of the paddle wheels at last announced our moving, I went wretchedly on deck and found nothing
of interest till we were astride the heads and the morning was breaking.
The sunrise was of ordinary appce but dark masses of cloud hung over
the NE horizon while[1] much misty looking scud covered the land.

The coast was singular and worthy of much attention. The high
perpendicular cliffs of the South Head interrupted with pretty bays &
circular beaches, extended though of less commanding elevation to the
opening of Botany bay. The south head of the bay was low, many parts
sloping down to the sea as if the ocean breakers had there exercised little
eroding power. Outside the cliffs were again very high & nearly
resembling those near Sydney. They were less continuous, however, and
above them the land covered only by low scrub, took a singular shape,
probably from the formation of ancient sand drifted hills. We were at
last opposite the wide opening of Port Hagen or Hacking though its
shores were yet almost hidden in mist. On the left a long sandy beach
& considerable sandy tract stretched inland, affording an example I
expect of the manner in which the surface of much of the country near
Sydney & Botany Bay was formed by blown sand.

The left or southern side of Port Hacking appeared to be lower
country not bounded by cliffs of any size, but further south the coast
again became very bold, in fact in almost every respect similar to the
South head Cliffs, except that the sandstone appeared slightly redder.
At one part a curious white line against the cliff turned out to be a
waterfall which with two other smaller streams of water fell over the
cliffs from the height of perhaps 200 feet.[2]

Soon after passing these, the coast assumed and entirely new appearance, indicating our approach to a different geological district. Hitherto

[1] Jevons wrote 'which' here.
[2] This whole area round the waters of Port Hacking now forms a National Park, 18 miles
from Sydney.

the heads & cliffs had been caused by extensive but low ridges running in an east & west general direction, the east ward end of which was consequently cut away by the waves. Now an immense mountain ridge[1] was seen closely edging the coast & then running in a N & S or NNE & SSW direction. This was of a regular continuous form & of a general elevation of perhaps 700 or 1000 feet, it was so near the sea line as to slope down to it at a great angle and here and there small spurs ran out eastward & being eroded by the waves presented an immense arch like cliff of reddish sandstone (probably).

The steep sides of this range appeared every where to be covered by luxurious bush whereas so long as the coast remained of the same character as between Sydney & Botany heads, a low continuous scrub looking in the distance like a smooth grassy lawn was all that covered the ground.

As we proceeded, the range became more elevated & remarkable, and its sides, now less rapidly sloping into the sea were diversified at parts by clear grassy space.

At Bulli where the county of Cumberland ends & the district of Illawarra commences, the range receded or rather an alluvial flat stretched out about a mile to seaward, extending, with arched sandy beaches & slightly projecting rocky points, for about 10 or 12 miles to the more prominent rock which forms the boat harbour of Wollongong, where we soon arrived.

With my fellow passengers on a whole I was less pleased or more disgusted than any I have fallen in with before. Gentlemen they were not with few exceptions but noisy stupid colonial men out of offices & stores, with nothing attractive or pleasing about them. The ladies or women were no great shakes either, but fortunately most of both men & women were quietened for the time by sea sickness & to my delight very few landed at Wollongong the rest proceeding in the steamer to Kiama or Shoalhaven places of apparently equal attractions further along the coast.

Landing at the little pier which forms the boat harbour, I walked a short distance towards the town to Russell's Marine Hotel, a most quiet respectable & comfortable establishment, which however I was sorry to

---

[1] The Illawarra Range.

find had ruined the proprietor, from a sudden diminution of the number of excursionists the last two seasons.

After washing a little, I set out about 11 am with my barometer with a view of getting up the nearest projecting point of the range viz Mt Keira if possible. first taking a reading of the barometer on the beach.[1]

Wollongong is well situated upon hilly ground slightly raised above the alluvial flat country; its streets are broad & well laid out in rectangles, but the objection is that they are not filled up with houses and that there are no signs of any building going on yet. It does not appear retrograde but only stationary and though checked in its progress at present I have no doubt its excellent position in all respects will render it important sooner or later.[2]

The principal street of the town is prolonged into the main road of the district, leading to Dapto a village or town about 10 or 12 miles off in the centre of the grazing country and on the way to Kiama. Walking about 2 miles along it over pleasant cultivated hilly country, I turned off to the right into the Mt Keira road, being the mail road in fact which after ascending the high land at Mt Keira proceeds by Broughtons pass to Appin, etc.

The ground soon began to rise & slope up to the mountain in undulating hills & low ranges, formed, I believe, of some rock of the coal measures. The surface soil appeared rich & was entirely cleared & cultivated, houses & barns indicating the prosperity of the owners. As the steepness of the road increased, the ground becoming more & more uneven was less cleared & still covered in many parts with bush which gave me the first idea of the luxuriance of Illawarra vegetation.

To describe the nature of this mountain, I must mention that some

[1] On this walk Jevons was especially interested in surveying, presumably no official survey of New South Wales having been made at this time. The calculations he made after his return to Sydney of the heights of the various points at which he took barometer readings during the trip, are shown in a large sheet of blue paper, folded up and pasted into the Journal between these two pages and in a small sheet giving the main results pasted in on the following page. (See p. 165 below.)

At this time Jevons took many readings for calculating elevations in the neighbourhood of Sydney, and compared barometers both with Dr Smith of the University of Sydney and with W. B. Clarke. In his diary for 6 May 1857 is the following entry: 'Went out to North Shore to Revd. Mr Clarke's. Compared Barometer etc. and had much conversation on *elevation of the country*, sea-beaches, sun gauge, etc. etc. He invited me for a walk to South Head on Monday.' (See p. 167 below.)

[2] In 1856 Wollongong had a population of 846, but in comparatively recent times the population of the town and of neighbouring towns and settlements, now included in the area of the City of Greater Wollongong has grown to a total of 162,835 (in 1966). It has become the industrial centre of the southern coalfield, the principal industry being the iron and steel works at Port Kembla just south of Wollongong – the second largest in Australia.

distance off along the coast, faint lines of projecting rocks were visible at a certain elevation on the range. Preserving a somewhat horizontal arrangement that is appearing in any place at about the same elevation above the sea, they occurred more & more distinctly in the form of wall like cliffs as we approached Wollongong, till an immense projecting rock slightly detached from the range of a squarish form at the top & with a lofty perpendicular precipice towards the sea, & flanked by similar bold precipices in the range at either side appeared to form the termination or salient angle of the range. This was Mt Keira.

The perpendicular rock, I found, on approaching nearer, was perhaps

400 or 500 feet high, and almost flat & upright as a wall but from its base a very steep talus of broken blocks of stone sloped down to the undulating ranges before mentioned.

The road led at one point apparently close beneath the highest part of the rock, and diverging from it I reached the base of the talus and tried to climb up to the actual base of the cliff. I found myself however in the midst of a scene of Nature which surpassed all I had seen before in luxuriant beauty & wildness & the almost tropical novelty of the forms of the plants.[1] The large blocks of stone which had no doubt at some remote period fallen from a more elevated position on the cliff were now all covered by deep soft, moss, by small but exquisite & very various ferns, or by a number of other rock clinging plants with which I was quite unacquainted. The decayed remains of former generations of plants & trunks of trees so rotten & soft that they yielded to the foot filled up the interstices forming a rich mould which appeared to be always saturated with moisture, there being even such an excess of the latter that it trickled down at every part in small rills among the rocks, rendering the air deliciously cool & fresh, & affording at any moment such a refreshing draught of pure water as I had not tasted before in N.S.W.

From such a soil, large fine gum trees & bush of all kinds sprung, but I was especially delighted to find on all sides graceful tree ferns from 5 to 8 feet high, cabbage tree palms, with short stems indeed but large spreading fan like leaves, luxuriant creepers adorning the trunks of

---

[1] The slopes of the Illawarra mountains in this part are covered by an isolated belt of subtropical vegetation.

the trees climbing about in graceful curves & spirals or stretching from trunk to trunk in rope-like festoons. I could have remained long seated on a wet mossy rock admiring these beauties of the vegetable kingdom surrounding me above below & on every side, and as a botanist I could no doubt have found occupation for a month, but I had other objects before me, & no time to spare. Therefore not attempting to climb more than a few yards into such a thicket, where slippery rocks were piled up at an angle of about 45°, & no footstep or holding was secure from the rottenness of the fallen timber & sticks, I set up my barometer & took a careful reading or two.

Elevation calculated =

I estimate the height of the top of the talus or the foot of the cliff as 50 feet above my position here; its height therefore =[1]

Regaining the road through a thick mass of rank stinging nettles & other weeds which I observed to border a cleared spot (I saw the same elsewhere) but uninjured beyond a few scratches, I pursued the steep & winding & almost impassable road for some distance, it taking a direction rather to the rear of the mountain. Settlers were here and there with their log hut & small sloping cleared space of rich dark coloured soil partly covered in most cases by indian corn, potatoes or other vegetables. At last the road fairly entered a gully of great depth (Devils hole Gully) running up between Mount Keira & the steep slopes & precipices of the main range, the road winding round the sides & being cut out as it were through solid bush. I now met a house which seemed likely to be the last, and on enquiring if there were any track up to the summit of the mountain, I found that the man had been in the habit of taking people up, and he offered to send his son up with me.

My guide was a lad neither very sharp for a colonial nor remarkable in any particular; he took me a short way along the road then straight up the slope on the flank of the mountain, through bush at first of considerable density & beauty, but afterwards thinner & less luxuriant in appce. A very short distance from the top we had to climb up some irregular rocks which seemed to form a portion at all events of a crown round the summit. The top itself I found not far from level, & covered by close gum trees & moderate bushy scrub beneath. We quickly got to the edge of the cliff at a projecting point where the clearest view is to be obtained, where after arranging my barometer I leisurely enjoyed the extraordinary beauty & extensiveness of the prospect. The whole of the low district of Illawarra, lay in fact at my feet, a flat wooded alluvial plain, or low ranges of undulating & beautifully shaded hills bounded on the one side by a somewhat singular coast line of arch-like sea beaches, extending between low rocky points, which with five small

[1] Jevons did not enter the results of his calculations here. See note 1 to p. 163 above.

rocky islets, (Five Islands)[1] formed a pretty picture, and in the other direction running inland between two series of immense converging ranges, of one of which the rock I was on formed the commencement while the other rose some 20 or 30[2] off on the coast & continued in an uninterrupted confused series of ranges as far as the view extended. To the extreme right in fact the view was limited by another prominent rock or mountain of the same range as Mt Keira viz Mt Kembla, a large steep & somewhat sugar loaf shaped hill, of bold & picturesque appce, and partially detached from the more regular intervening ranges.

Most parts of the flat lands were extensively cleared, and the cultivated verdant spots and scattered houses & barns formed a sight unaccustomed but yet agreable to an Australians eye. A strong contrast to this existed however in the dark closely wooded & bushy ranges rising with confused outlines on every side, the wild monotonous appce of the vegetation being in scarcely any place broken but by the lines of perpendicular cliffs running in a horizontal manner beneath the summit of the long Shoalhaven ranges opposite, & like the *retaining walls* of some huge fortification or engineering work. On the steep slopes beneath these rocks, the deep brownish green of the bush was generally finely shaded & varied by the undulating surfaces of the hills & the lines of the watershed, or of the torrents & gullies descending from them. The *tout-ensemble* formed in fact a characteristic picture of the extremely wild & monotonous yet picturesque & interesting scenery of Australia and the feeling of awe & admiration is increased if, after scrambling through a few yards of thick & luxuriant scrub, looking down into the depths of a gully, or wondering at the height of a precipice, one considers that in these ranges, such wild scenes of Nature are spread out for many many miles unreached & unviewed by any intelligent man capable of perceiving the beauties or comprehending the moral deductions contained in every few yards of space which he passes over or every glimpse he obtains on any side.

I omitted to mention the large sheets of water of Lake Illawarra,[3] and the smaller lagoon called Tom Thumb which occupy the centre of the flat district near the sea, communicating with the sea by small sinuous channels. They are likewise characteristic of an Australian scene, and are also interesting from the reflections they suggest as to the alluvial formation of land.

By my spirit level I determined that this was by no means the highest point of the country, Mt Kembla, the ranges on this side of it,

[1] Jevons was here looking at what was to become the site of the man-made port of Port Kembla at Five Islands Bay, now second to Newcastle as a centre of heavy industry in Australia.

[2] Jevons then wrote 'miles to the south' but crossed it out.

[3] The great lagoon, now a renowned holiday centre.

& especially the great Shoalhaven ranges being much higher. I took two careful readings of the barometer, the elevation thence deduced being 1556 feet.

On looking over the projecting rock the precipice was seen to extend like a huge smooth wall, to a fearful depth, perhaps 300 feet beneath, nought being seen on the steep slope or talus commencing at its foot but an unbroken & close arrangement of tree tops, continuing to the limits which cultivation has reached. I tried to estimate the height of the precipice by the fall of a stone over it, which occupied on an average 4.1 seconds, which by calculation gives 270 or perhaps 250 as the actual height.

In descending I tried to get to the foot of the precipice so as to measure the actual height of the top of the talus but the least deviation from the track brought us to such precipitous rocky slopes as it would be most rash & dangerous to attempt to descend. We even had some difficulty in getting back to the road through a close growth of saplings, several kinds of tall stick like plants, (one of peculiar smell named Hinderberry) and their dead rotten but still standing stems. I drew considerable information from my guide about surrounding objects, such as that cabbage tree hats are manufactured from the soft young unexpanded leaves of the trees, which are found in the centre of the leaves, enveloped in a covering & forming a long straight sword like bud of about 3 feet in length.

On getting back to the road, I got the boy (who seemed rather surprised at my endurance of fatigue & the difficulties of the bush) to accompany me a short way up the road & into the sandy flat country which reaches from the edge of the ranges far inland to Campbelltown etc. The road cut out like a tunnel through the trees & bush which formed a beautiful arched canopy over it, wound up & round the top of the Devils Hole gully & then on to a wet sandy flat of land, where to my complete astonishment, I found the bush change character within the space of a few yards, so that now there was nothing but the sparse gum trees, stiff singular banksias, hakeas etc, & the scattered wild flowers of the ordinary Australian bush, especially indeed like that near Sydney. Crossing a swampy space overgrown with luxuriant grass I climbed a high rock, & took a barometer measurement which gave the elevation 1615 feet or considerably higher than Mt Keira.[1] This rock (as well as Mt Keira I think,) was composed of a very coarse sandstone so filled in some places with small white quartz pebbles as to form a conglomerate. The pebbly sand derived from the disintegration of this

---

[1] Pasted between these two pages of the Journal is a sheet of paper giving W. B. Clarke's readings of elevations at various points on Mount Keira, on which Jevons wrote: 'Determinations of elevations by the Rev. W. B. Clarke – as given to me by him.'

is all that composed the soil except the organic matter derived from decayed former vegetation. This accounts for the poverty of the soil and the fact that not an acre of it is cultivated for many miles.

On the rock the boy drew my attention to my trousers, which sufficiently covered & soaked with mud now exhibited large stains of blood. These were caused by four leeches biting & sucking my legs in a disgusting manner, a thing I thus learned to be very common in the bush; they do however no harm unless the bites be irritated into sores.

We were rather late in reaching Braces, the boys house again and his mother, being alarmed was heard *coeying*, the manner always adopted of signalling in the bush. I entered the rough log hut as there were[1] signs of a thunderstorm just commencing and was not sorry to be asked to take tea as I had had nothing to eat since breakfast on the steamer. A sort of flour cake, plentiful Wollongong butter[2] & weak tea yet formed a good dinner and I was much pleased by the honest, good natured & hospitable manner of the people. They were only settled there six months yet had effected a good deal in the way of cultivating & improving the place.

The rain having ceased, I presented the father with 10 shillings & turned down the road as rapidly as possible, yet it was so late that the sun was now set, and before I had got a mile I had to pick my way out nearly in the dark. I have not described that the roads were most execrable and often or even generally only a mere expanse of furrowed mud which it was impossible to avoid by a side path. Walking in the dark was therefore mere mud larking which I had to continue to the very doors of Russels Hotel since the streets of Wollongong are only the Mother earth, cut up & churned into mud by the traffic of a small town.

I reached Russels, in the dark of night soon after 7, exceedingly fatigued, & wet in the feet as I had been in fact all day. Hot brandy & water, a light supper on fowl and a comfortable bed put me however in a fair way to recovery.

April 11. Saturday. Paying a bill of 8s. for the accomodation & leaving my bag etc behind at the Inn, I started about 10. am along the coast in a southerly direction intending to skirt the lagoon & make towards Dapto. The sandy beach is always composed of 1st a sloping & often highly inclined beach, 2nd a bank a few yards wide of uneven blown sand, 3rd a dense belt of low peculiar & uniform scrub,[3] 4th a flat more or less swampy or under water with sparse gum trees etc. Finding however I had been wrongly directed & was only going onto a narrow spit of land, I left the beach, & crossed over with some

---

[1] Jevons wrote 'was' here.
[2] 'butt' in the text.   [3] 'scub' in the text.

difficulty a wide salt water flat covered by [*blank space*] grass; this was at the head of Tom Thumb lagoon, an uninteresting & very shallow piece of water. This was bordered by a sort of regular bank of alluvial land rising about 20 feet at the least above the sea level. At this bank the alluvial country seemed to begin, extending inland in a pretty level manner except when interrupted by swelling hills founded no doubt on coal rocks. It was lightly wooded & much cleared & cultivated. (This alluvial flat would then appear to be probably analogous to the flats of Double Bay etc formed when the sea was about 40 feet above its present elevation.)

An uninteresting walk through fields, muddy roads, across swampy places, & over hills brought me to the Dapto Road near where a creek runs in a channel of the depth of about 15 feet. Mt Kembla now towered up above me at the apparent distance of 2 or 3 miles but the impenetrable covering of bush was unbroken around its sides, and my only hope of climbing it lay in diligent enquiries for the road. A most magnificent large & symmetrical Australian fig tree stood at the side of the road near the creek, the lower part of its lofty cylindrical trunk being beautifully clothed in creepers, (it is affirmed there to be one of the finest trees in the colony). Near this was the Fig tree Public House, where I not only got full information but a man offered me a ride up a portion of the road in his cart.

The road, I found, leads off to the right close to the Fig tree & winds up the side of the M^t and through the Gully at its rear. After passing a mile or two of execrable road, passing however many fine farming establishments with fine grass paddocks & numbers of the milch cows[1] (those no doubt which supply the famous Wollongong butter) we came upon a creek which flowed from Mt Kembla and I then entered a country the beauty of which I shall never forget. I was was[2] formed of undulating grassy hills or rather short ranges & projections descending from the sides of the mountain (as explained in the case of Mt Keira etc) and down a sort of valley between the slopes of Mt Kembla on the left and those of the main ranges on the right, the creek pursued a winding course. In Australia it was an object of pleasure itself, a stream of pure & deliciously cool mountain water, running & gurgling over a pebbly bed, but the objects that lent the scene its principal charm were the clumps & thickets of bush which in every hollow, bordered it or formed a complete arcade over it. Fine well shaped trees with tall bare trunks formed a sort of scaffolding which besides bearing aloft their own

[1] This district has produced the Illawarra Shorthorn, a noted strain of the milking shorthorn giving a high percentage of butter-fat.

[2] Jevons first wrote 'The country was' then crossed out 'The country' and substituted 'I was'. Presumably he intended to write 'It was'.

spreading branches with a light graceful foliage, served also as a frame work upon which Nature could display to advantage numberless beautiful vegetable forms never seen in less favoured spots. The trunks indeed were hardly visible being generally covered by thick masses of creeping plants the luxuriousness & gracefulness of which could not be exaggerated while the rope-like stems or roots of these plants stretching across from tree to tree in singular sinuous forms or descending straight to the ground from an elevation of some 40 or 50 feet had a very remarkable appce. On the higher parts of the trunks stag-horn or similar beautiful varieties of ferns were flourishing as if placed there by the hand of some skilful gardener, while on the ground at your feet, or rising between the trees on every side of you were further beautiful & remarkable plants such as tree-ferns, cabbage tree palms

The road at times passed through pretty dells formed by some projecting hill or cliff and many times it was necessary to cross the creek by stepping stones. At one part a number of blocks of hard stone were lying at the side of the road which on examination proved to be very excellent specimens of silicified fossil wood, in which the exogenous rings were very plain. There were also pieces of hard ironstone rock containing an infinity of distinct fern leaf impressions.

Continuing the ascent, there were numbers of small farms apparently just occupied since cultivation was very little advanced, and the log huts were of very rude construction. At one point where[1] a considerable space had been cleared there was a very beautiful glimpse of the Ocean, the view being bounded on either side by the undulating slopes of the mountain or the dark bushy ranges, while a number of tall cabbage trees, which are usually allowed to stand formed a very striking foreground with their long thin stems and graceful tufts of leaves.[2]

A little above this the ground was covered by blocks or small pieces of sandstone, in no way differing in appearance from the Sydney Sandstone, indicating that the coal rocks terminated and the sandstone commenced at a little above this elevation which a barometrical measurement gave = 644 feet.

I proceeded onwards as rapidly as the steepness and frequent wetness of the road would allow. The ground became too more steep and more

---

[1] 'were' in the text.

[2] At the end of this paragraph, at the top right-hand side of this page in the Journal, Jevons noted the following calculation:

$$
\begin{array}{r}
298 \\
8 \\
\hline
306 \\
612 \\
1360 \\
\hline
1972
\end{array}
$$

covered by large gum trees I was now[1] just below the Mountain Kembla and was entering the Gully between it and the main ridges. The road followed pretty closely the course of the creek as being the lowest & most level ground, but in many parts much water seemed continually to drain or run into it from the side of the Mountain on the left, rendering it very bad to walk on. I frequently tried the temperature of the water in the creek finding it about 63° and therefore very little below that of the air. Its coolness in drinking was however most delicious. The wetness and richness of the soil here produced here most luxurious bush which together with the large trees forming a continual arched canopy over the road produced a most beautiful scene.

In the narrowest part of the gully I came to a considerable clearing where were[2] two log huts placed a few yards up the slope with some signs of cultivation. But as a good road led forwards I hastened on without stopping in order to reach Fishlockes in good time. But the road now passed through a clump of bush which surpassed in beauty everything else I had seen and which it is in vain for me to attempt to describe. The whole gully was occupied by large & singularly handsome trees (box trees I believe). These had smooth cylindrical trunks rising, straight and unbranched to the height of at least 50 feet above which the light graceful foliage, with scarcely a break between tree and tree formed a sort [of][3] roof or canopy which warded off the, glare & heat of the sun and preserved the space below deliciously cool and shady.

Between the trees the creek pursued a tortuous course running in a clear stream over a stony bed, its gurgling noise impressing one through another sense with the feeling of delicious coolness. But on each side of the creek rose the tree ferns, the spreading leaves of the cabbage tree and the thick masses of luxurious creeping plants which gave the most beauty to the scene. The trunk of almost every tree was clothed to a considerable height by the close green leaves of creepers while the rope like stems of these stretched about in every direction, often rising 50 feet.

The effect of the whole gave the impression of some great conservatory or crystal palace, of which the trunks of the trees formed the supporting columns, their branches and foliage, the framework of the glass which however was the sky itself while in the interior of this true Palace of Nature, no art or expense had been spared to collect the most beautiful collection of tropical plants and to dispose them on every side in the most artistic yet negligé manner, hiding or adorning the bareness[4] columns of the trees by twining plants or stag horn ferns, and covering

---

[1] Jevons first wrote 'for the road now lay' but changed it to 'I was now'.
[2] A word appears to be missing here.
[3] This word is omitted in the text.
[4] Jevons appears to have omitted some words here.

the ground by a profusion of pretty flowering shrubs or herbs. Such was the beauty of this spot that I could hardly[1] on myself to pass it as quickly as the circumstances required. But the road still continued wide & well marked and was yet ascending (at one place the water of the creek had the distinct taste and appearance of *iron*; its temperature was 58°)

All at once I was astonished to find myself among vegetation, as stiff and thinly scattered as the thickets just described being graceful and luxuriant. I had passed again within the limits of a new & poorer soil which allowed only of the growth of the ordinary Sydney bush. The suddenness of the change was however very singular. I was now past Mt Kembla and the road led round a hill which sloped down into a deep gully on the other side of the mountain. Being very tired & hungry and even a little faint, I became anxious and uncertain as to whether the last huts might not be Fishlockes and the road lead onwards in the Campbelltown direction.

At last I determined to turn back, but seeing a lofty summit rock above the road on the right, I climbed up through the bush to it with the greatest exertion, and rested while taking a few observations. The elevation according to these is 1597 feet. The rocks were large & much weather worn blocks of rather coarse sandstone. Though so elevated the bush prevented here as well as elsewhere any extended view whatever, the woody summit of Kembla being alone visible in front.

A quick walk down the beautiful road I have just described, brought me to the huts, the first of which was locked up, but the second contained a family who received me in a kind hospitable manner I shall not easily forget. On enquiring for Fishlockes, the old man, Andrew Moran, a cobbler by trade, informed me that it was a short way beyond the point I had reached, and expressed much indignation at my passing his own cottage without calling in. His wife, a very serviceable but pleasant looking one, first offered me a cup of fine milk, then pressed me to take a little gin for both of which I thanked them more sincerely than is usually the case. Then as there was unfortunately no *bread* in the house she set about making some, and soon had it baking in a flat cake at the bottom of the camp kettle, the process of making being completed by mixing up a little flour and water and kneeding it well. Finally they asked me to stay the night and proceed the next morning to Fishlockes, which the quick and evident approach of twilight obliged me to acquiesce in also.

In time my hunger was appeased by quantities of damper bread and butter with tea but the fare as they said was not the most dainty and did not sit quite easily in my stomach. Besides the cobbler and his wife were present a young woman named Mary Gleeson from Sydney, two young men apparently other relations or else acquaintances of the cobbler and

[1] A word is missing here.

several children. But seated on a rough 3 legged stool by the fire which burned beneath one of the capacious chimnies of a log hut, and amusing myself at the novelty of my lodging and the conversation of the family in which I occasionally joined, I passed a pleasanter evening than[1] I might have done in many circumstances, for instance in a ballroom.

The hut was itself a curiosity being of complete Robinson-Crusoe-like construction. An iron bed stead, looking-glass, a few boxes, pots and pans etc were all the articles of importation and civilization visible for the furniture which Moran had had in Sydney was either sold or lying in Wollongong, its carriage up the mountain being quite out of the question. The table was a sheet of bark, the shelves above it, roughly shaped planks of split wood, the windows holes in the logs closed by rough wooden shutters & unconscious of glass. The cottage had in reality but one apartment a low partition without any door shutting off the part representing the bedroom. About ten oclock I retired to bed, if getting into bed with two other men can so be called, Moran and one of the young men, his brother I think being my bedfellows. His wife and the young woman slept in the other half of the hut on the ground before the fire but even such a strange & novel lodging did not prevent me soon falling asleep.

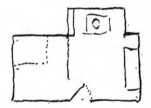

Sunday. April 12th. I found a log hut a decidedly cool sleeping place, as the cold mountain air blew right through the crevices between the logs. I lay awake most of the night listening to the noise of the wind among the trees and the water in the creek, and fancying it rain. When day dawned however and we got up my apprehensions were most pleasantly disappointed as there was all promise of a true Australian fine day.[2] A small piece of very nice pickled pork, (no fresh meat is of course to be had so far in the bush) with potatoes & pumpkins in vast quantities were boiled for breakfast, immediately after which I started (8 am) for Fishlockes, sincerely thanking the old cobbler and his wife for the kind entertainment he had given me & offering him a sovn which however he absolutely refused.

[1] Jevons wrote 'that' in the text.

[2] Here Jevons wrote: '. . . a true fine Australian day'.

A walk through the bush up the gully was again as enchanting as I have before described it and this time I saw it with all the advantages of the freshness of early morning & freedom from fatigue. About ¾ of a mile beyond the furthest point I had before reached, I found an[1] extensive cleared space of pretty level ground. Tall ranges were on the right hand, and two streams of pure water of considerable size formed a junction at the corner of the property. The bush consisted of a forest of close large gum trees with abundant ferns & underscrub, a few tree ferns, palm like plants, etc, wholly different however in general character from the Illawarra vegetation, and more resembling the ordinary bush. In a new well built little barn I found an old man, who on my stating the object of my visit to be the black-lead mine, announced himself to be Fishlocke, and with much evident delight set about showing me all the improvements and advantages of his land. A part of this was covered by a curious red ferruginous earth, which he said had been been pronounced good fullers earth, but however this might be, it seemed to me hardly likely to repay the trouble he was taking in cultivating it. The other portion of the land on the banks of the branch creek had a good black soil and was laid out in a kitchen garden or sown with Indian corn, or with Italian rye grass, all which seemed to flourish. On the bank of this creek a little above the level of the bed was the black lead seam, into which however a hole of only a few feet dimensions each way had yet been dug. It consisted of a bed 2 to 3 feet thick (as he said) of a soft black shaly substance which when dried has much of the appearance of inferior black lead

Its analysis by MacCutcheon[2] is

Carbon	32.3
Clay	63.7
Soluble Iron & Alumina	2.9
Lime	1.1
	100.0

From the large quantity of earthy masses contained I doubt if the more proper name for it is not *Carbonaceous shale*, or whether it will be of much use.

Fishlockes house stood in the centre of the cleared ground on nicely sloping ground. It was a comfortable cottage and showed the same appearance of neat and careful management[3] as I had noticed in every thing also on the farm. His queer little body of a wife insisted on my

---

[1] 'a' in the original text.
[2] One of Jevons's colleagues at the Mint.
[3] Here Jevons wrote . . . 'careful and neat . . .'

having tea and damper which his daughter provided; the latter also quickly sewed up a little bag in which were deposited a few specimens of the mineral productions of the farm. Then I as quickly as possible started again, the poor old man hobbling after me some distance (for he had been lamed by an accident in felling trees) completing his account, which he had commenced on my first arrival, of his family history, his nine brothers who with himself at one time were all soldiers, his visiting the Cumberland lead mines, his buying this farm of 100 acres about five years since, spending much time and money in making the good road I had rather wondered at, and in searching for the black lead guided as he said by the appearance of the trees, his want of money and the small mortgage of £100 on the estate, the disgust of his numerous children at his foollishness as they considered, the elder ones leaving him & settling elsewhere in consequence, and most of all the great importance of the discovery he had at last made, and the attention given to it by numerous great people as well as governments

Leaving this simple old man in his comfortable secluded home (there was only one other farm near that of Moran the brother of the cobbler, which was just a short distance across the stream of the *Cordeaux River*)[1] I hastened back to my former lodgings.

The cobbler and his family had departed for the day down the mountain on a visit but had as kindly as ever left their hut open, a meal ready spread, and my barometer on the table. It was now Noon, and divesting myself of my coat and everything weighty or inconvenient I started to make my way through the bush to the summit of Mt Kembla, my barometer etc strapped on my back. It was steep work, and after passing the first portion of bush which was of the character of that in the gully and therefore nearly impenetrable, there were frequent patches of plants growing with innumerable close straight stems about 4 to 6 feet high, these with an equal number of dead sticks forming a very serious obstacle. The most of the way however the bush was very thin, and in less than half an hour I found myself on the summit. I first settled my barometer on the highest point & in the shade of a trunk, then leisurely rested myself or took observations at the most salient edge of the precipice. Here the view was almost exactly similar to that from Mt Keira, only rather more extensive & splendid from the more central position of Kembla. The character of the mountain was also much the same; an immense isolated rock, with a perpendicular precipice on the south side and extremely steep rocky slopes on every other side but the back part by which I ascended. The fall of a stone down the precipice took the same time 4 sec. as at Keira the height was therefore much the same about 250, but the spirit level showed that the summit where

[1] A tributary of the Nepean.

I stood was level with the foot of the immense precipices of the Shoal-haven ranges so that the summits of these much have been many hundred feet higher.

Two readings of the barometer, carefully compared with Sydney and calculated out gave the elevation

$$= 1795 \text{ feet.}$$

After cutting my name W S Jevons/57 in the rock beside a rude cross formed of two sticks tied together which some former[1] visitor had left I suppose as a memorial, I quickly performed the first part of the

(The rocks were of a very coarse sandstone or rather conglomerate of white quartz pebbles)

descent but unwisely following too much the course of a small streamlet became entangled in a complete thicket of creeper-bush. Long thorny briars, networks of climbing plants, cabbage tree plants with their large sharp pointed leaves, and a confused mass of bush & dead sticks & branches, rendered the greatest deliberation & exertion necessary to advance safely & without injury a single step over the rocky dangerous ground and I was delighted when I suddenly found myself in sight of the cottage & close to the path by which I had ascended. In my hurry however to rest myself after such fatigue, I foolishly plunged right into a thick body of prodigious weeds & nettles which here as at Mt Keira appeared to spring up wherever the ground had been disturbed by settlers. After much trouble I reached the[2] cottage, and leisurely ate[3] my dinner and rested & washed myself. As I could not think of receiving so much from these poor but honest & good natured people without some return I left a half sovn on the table.

The day throughout was delightfully fine & clear, still cool on account of a fresh south wind and the walk down the road through the beauti-ful scenery & country, and the splendid displays of vegetation I have before described formed in my opinion no unfitting occupation for

[1] Jevons wrote 'formed' here.
[2] Jevons wrote 'to' here.　　　[3] 'eat' in the text.

a Sunday afternoon. Whether the minister whom I was surprised to meet with several ladylike daughters, thought so too I rather doubt, as my appearance from exposure to bush & mud was not at all Sunday-like. Though already well loaded I picked up as many specimens of fossil wood as I could carry, obtaining several very nice sections.

I had now completed everything that I desired, excepting to visit the Keira Coalmine for which but about an hour remained before sunset. This might have appeared desperate only that I met, just on reaching the Dapto road, a young boy who soon informed me during a little conversation that he was the son of one of the colliers in the mine. He seemed to have heard from young Brace of my ascent of Keira, and with true Colonial sharpness had an eye immediately to pecuniary profit in leading me up to the mine. With the greatest exertion, for I was now nearly done up, I walked[1] with him about a mile up the Keira road, then turned off along a newly made road to the right, which after a little steep ascent among fine bush, brought us to the lower extremity of an inclined tramway. At the top of this which seemed well constructed, was a gallery, in height about 5 feet cut direct into a splendid seam. It was as yet only about 30 feet long but as soon as arrangements were completed the mining of the coal would be rapidly proceeded with. A measurement gave the height of the gallery = 727 feet. From here there was a fine view as well into the gullies & thickets of bush immediately below, as over the flat country beneath including Wollongong Five Islands. The sun was now setting and this fine & to me happy and well spent day was soon closed in with all the calm and soothing influences peculiar to that time.

To me, however, in my entirely fatigued and hungry state, a nobbler of hot brandy and water, and a very comfortable & neat tea which I got at Russels Inn combined with a soft warm bed were the most acceptable things in the world.

Monday April 13th The following morning however I was far from fresh, these three days work having been probably the most severe I ever did I determined to start by the afternoon steamer at 2 PM. During the morning I strolled a short way along the beach towards Bulli. A sloping sandy beach, forming a sort of continuous elevated *bar* against the ocean, a belt of close scrub trees & on the summit & interior slope of it, with a low wet alluvial flat within formed[2] the country here which stretches about 12 miles in a strip becoming gradually more & more narrow till near Bulli the Ocean advances to the foot of the ranges. In places the sandy bar is broken and the sea water flows into a shallow

---

[1] Jevons wrote 'walk' here.
[2] 'former' in the text.

irregular shaped lagoon of greater or less extent, which forms a great impediment to roads.

May 11th 1857.[1]

*   *   *

'As far as I can see, indiscriminate visiting tends only to a waste of time and a vulgarising of character.' II.175[2]

'Originality is the pearl of great price in literature, the rarest, the most precious claim by which an Author can be recommended.' II.233

'With these fair weather friends (of Miss Martineau) I cannot bear to rank; and for her sins, is it not one of those of which God & not man must judge'?

'Nor can I take up a philanthropic scheme, though I honour philanthropy, and voluntarily & sincerely veil my face before such a mighty subject as that handled in Mrs Beecher Stowe's work "Uncle Tom's Cabin". To manage these great matters rightly, they must be long and practically studied, their bearings known intimately and their evils felt genuinely; they must not be taken up as a business matter, and a trading speculation'. II.264

'A solitary life cherishes mere fancies until they become manias.' I.21[2]

Mozart and Beethoven. 'Mozart struggled all his life with difficulties and was obliged to toil incessantly, not for fame, but for his daily bread. His widow was saved from destitution by her second marriage with a respectable man who became too a father to her dead husbands children. His sister, the celebrated girl who shared the triumphs of his childhood, and whose name is for ever associated with his memory, died a few years ago in old age, and such extreme penury that she was actually supported by charity.

Beethoven lived unpatronized by the great and neglected by the public, barely able to subsist by a life of labour and parsimony, unknown and unheeded among his countrymen even while his great name was resounding through Europe and all because his transcendant genius was unaccompanied by the suppleness of the courtier and the acts of the man of the world'. Hogarths Memoirs.[3]

---

[1] Jevons's diary shows that he finished writing this account of his trip on 11 May 1857. At the end of this entry in the Journal he wrote:

Notes. Distance from Wollongong to R. Cordeaux 10 miles.

    11th 5.40 am. At Morans Mt Kembla.

    Temp. of air = 50°. Of water in stream 61°.

    Showing the water to remain nearly constant.

[2] E. C. Gaskell, *Life of Charlotte Bronte*, 2 vols. (1857).

[3] G. Hogarth, *Memoirs of the opera in Italy, France, Germany and England* (1851) Vol. II, pp. 201–2.

8 Dec. 1861 8 Porteus Road. London [1]

It is now more than two years since my return to London, and I have been during this time almost incessantly working at Philosophical subjects. In leaving Australia I had scarcely hoped to have more than a single year free in this manner, and I now seem to have heights of general learning before me which then seemed unapproachable. The M. A. degree[2] for instance was then quite beyond hope –

Within these two years my tastes have much widened, so that I may almost say I despise no kind of knowledge. Formerly I was unable to appreciate the value of classical & antiquarian learning – or the worth of poetry & general literature. It is only by degrees for instance that Shakespeare becomes quite congenial to me. At the same time the return from the newness of a colony to the venerable antiquity of this old country has given me almost an exaggerated taste for the antique. Thus nothing is more pleasant to me than to make some fresh slight discovery concerning our ancestors,[3] worthless people though they seem to have generally been.

The subjects which had pressed themselves upon me as my proper sphere of employment, viz. pol. econ. – & the Social Sci. seem opening before me by degrees in a manner exceeding my first hopes[4] – But it is of course always true that we can have no idea of what is to be found out & not yet known. I cannot avoid also paying some attention to *philosophy proper*, in addition to what is required for my degree – and I begin to understand things, which were utterly beyond me, some years ago. For a year perhaps I have entertained hopes of performing a general analysis of human knowledge, in which the fallacies of words would be as far as possible avoided – and *phil. would be shown to consist solely in pointing out the likeness of things.*[5]

---

[1] Porteus Road was conveniently situated for the Marylebone Road, leading to Gower Street and University College. Jevons lodged at this address from September 1859, until he left London in May 1863. His two sisters lived with him for most of this time and during the winter of 1861/2 his brother Herbert also lived there.

[2] Jevons had taken his B.A. in October 1860 and had since been studying for the M.A.

[3] A reference to the work he had been doing since October 1860 in tracing the history and pedigree of the Jevons family.

[4] In the early part of 1860, Jevons had 'struck out' what he had 'no doubt' was *'the true Theory of Economy'* (see letter of 1 June 1860 to Herbert, Vol. II, Letter 144). On the basis of entries in Jevons's diary for 1860, Professor La Nauze has claimed that 'young Jevons arrived on one identifiable day, February 19, 1860, at a comprehension of the "true theory of Economy" ' (La Nauze, 'The Conception of Jevons's Utility Theory', *Economica*, xx (November 1953) 356–8).

[5] Jevons mentions the same idea a few years later in his entry for 14 May 1866 (see p. 205 below).

About October 1860 – having recently commenced reading at the Mus. Libr. & met some stat. I began to form some diagrams to exhibit them – the first I think showing Mr Newmarchs Bill circ. research.[1] I hit upon a mode of dividing a sheet of paper into 1/10 inch & then pricking off curves through it when in Sydney, and the square was ready at hand.

After doing two or three diagrams the results appeared so interesting that I contemplated forming a series for my own information – then it occurred to me that publication might be possible – and I finally undertook to form a Statistical atlas of say 30 plates exhibiting all the chief materials of *historical stat.* For the last year this atlas has been my chief employment & I fear to look back upon the labour I have spent in searching all likely books for series of stat. then copying – calculating, arranging, & drawing the diagrams.

Towards the end of last October I had some 28 diagrams more or less finished, in the first copy – & thought it time to arrange for pub. I first wrote to Taylor & Walton, describing my work & wishes, & soon had a talk with Mr Walton, a very respectable old gentleman, who was quite disinclined to undertake the pub^n. but took interest in it, and gave useful advice – he[2] told me to apply to Longmans – to whom I accordingly wrote – receiving a note back from Mr W. Longman I was in much hopes, visiting Paternoster row (I never see Paternoster Row without remembering when I once mentioned to my Father that I had been through it, on my first coming to London, and he expressed his regret, in letter or conversation, I forget which, that I seemed so little impressed with the memory of the great men who had trod that narrow lane with so various hopes & desires).[3] He likewise took a pleasing interest in them, but was equally clear about having nothing further to do with them – He however recommended several map publishers who would most suitably undertake the work, & also gave me an introduction [to][4] Mr Newmarch. My spirits naturally were now [at a low eb?]b but fell still lower on visiting Mr Newmarch, at [the Globe?] Insurance office, a cold, prosperous place, & [a? co?]ld, ugly, man, who looked at

[1] This must refer to William Newmarch's statistical enquiry into the number of Bills of Exchange in circulation and their fluctuations, during the period 1828–47, originally presented to the Statistical Society in 1851. The enquiry was subsequently continued in his publication *The New Supplies of Gold: Facts and Statements relative to their actual Amount; and their present and probable Effect* (1853). (See p. 181 below.)

[2] Jevons wrote 'I' in the text.

[3] In a letter, dated 19 November 1850 (see Vol. II, Letter 5).

[4] There is a small triangular tear in this page of the Journal, apparently the result of three subsequent pages being removed, leaving gaps in the wording on both sides of the page. The missing words are inserted where possible in square brackets.

my diagrams *without interest*[1] & almost without a word so that I soon left him.[2] I took dinner & a glass of ale to restore my spirits & then through crowded Cheapside, Fleet Street & Strand made my way to Charing X to Mr Stanford the map publisher there – a dry sensible man of business, apparently with a liking for maps – [so?] that he seemed pleased with the diagrams; whether [for?] this reason or not he was not disinclined to undertake some risk in pub. them, but talked much of the opinions he would have to obtain upon them and the toadying of the stat. magnates which would have to be done. To this I was so averse that before long I was[3] the work must be done at my own risk – and accordingly asked him to give some rough estimate.[4]

[1] In LJ (p. 162) this part of the sentence has been amended to the following: 'My spirits naturally were now zero, but fell still lower on visiting Mr. Newmarch at the insurance office, who looked at my diagrams without *interest* . . .'.

[2] William Newmarch (1820–82) was in the front rank of economists and statisticians at this time and as he was the leading authority on historical statistics and price movements, the reception Jevons received must have been especially discouraging. Newmarch had collaborated with Thomas Tooke in producing the *History of Prices from 1792 to the Present Time*, and in the last volume (published in 1857) had expressed doubt as to whether the new gold discoveries had caused any appreciation of the general price level. The effect of the increased gold supplies on the standard of value had occupied Newmarch since the early 1850s and he continued discussion of the subject in a series of papers contained in the *Statistical Journal* in 1859, 1860 and 1861. It would, in fact, seem that it was largely through Newmarch's statistics that Jevons himself came to write on this subject, for it was the statistical diagrams which first suggested to him the reality of a fall in the value of gold (see *A Serious Fall in the Value of Gold* . . ., reprinted in *Investigations in Currency and Finance* (1884 edition), page 16). At the time of Jevons's visit, Newmarch was by profession Secretary of the Globe Insurance Company. Largely self-educated and widely experienced in banking and commerce, he was a prominent member of the Royal Statistical Society and of the Political Economy Club and also a Fellow of the Royal Society. Newmarch was one of the leading critics of the Bank Act of 1844 and of the Currency School doctrines behind it.

[3] A word appears to be omitted here in the text.

[4] Jevons was only able to ask Edward Stanford to publish two diagrams, at a cost of £25 (see Jevons's letter of 28 December 1862 to his brother Tom, Vol. II, Letter 168). They appeared in June 1862, entitled as follows: '*1862*: Diagram, showing all the weekly accounts of the Bank of England, since the passing of the Bank Act of 1844, with the amount of Bank of England, Private and Joint Stock Bank Promissory Notes in circulation during each week and the Bank Minimum Rate of Discount. Sheet, 20″ × 30″, coloured. 'This diagram represents to the eye all the useful results of tables, containing about 113,000 figures.'

'*1862*: Diagram, showing the Price of the English Funds, the Price of Wheat, the Number of Bankruptcies and the Rate of Discount Monthly, since 1731, so far as the same have been ascertained. Sheet, 20″ × 30″, coloured. 'This Diagram is drawn from tables carefully compiled for the purpose, and containing more than 12,000 figures. Explanatory Notes and References are appended to each Diagram.'

These diagrams are reprinted, in modified form, in the 1884 edition of *Investigations in Currency and Finance*, edited by H. S. Foxwell, who in his Introduction remarks on their historical significance. Cf. Biographical Introduction, p. 35 above.

6 September 1862. 8 Porteus Road.

My 28[1] birthday has come & gone & I have spent a week in nearly perfect solitude, in the midst of the multitudes of this great city striving to make a start at the work before me.[2] Wishing if possible to earn money by a method which will not carry me away from the source of learning – the Museum library – I am trying to establish a kind of agency for literary research & am advertising in the Athenaeum, Saturday Review etc – But as the days pass by & not an answer that is of any use, comes, my spirits utterly fail – I take to my statistical calculations – but they are long, indeed, & when done what thanks have I; I write an article for the 'Spectator' but ca[nnot?] satisfy myself – let alone R Hutton.[3]

I walk about oppressed with the [   ] own hopes & convictions – unable as [   ]est or convince scarcely any one with eith[er my ex?]pectations or my powers. A year ago I mi[ght?] have said no one – But lately I have found one to whom my works did not seem a matter of indifference & to whom it was a sweet pleasure to speak of what I had never before spoken aloud. But now I am alone again & have not even a letter to console me.

I have hitherto kept pretty closely to my plans & my own mind in the main points has seldom disappointed me. But of outward encouragements I seem to have few – and I almost doubt if God has given me strength to go on long without it.

I attribute all my want of worldy success to my[4]

The diagrams were sold at 3s. 6d. each and proved modestly successful (see Jevons's letters of 18 January 1863 to his brother Herbert and of 27 August 1864 to Harry Roscoe, Vol. III, Letters 169 and 207). Jevons did not in fact publish any work entitled *Statistical Atlas*, though a portion of the data was used in the pamphlet *A Serious Fall in the Value of Gold Ascertained*, published in 1863. (Table, p. 30 of *Investigations in Currency and Finance*, 1884.) On p. 109 Jevons also mentions using his diagrams constructed from Tooke's *History of Prices* and other sources. The outline contents of the Statistical Atlas are given in a manuscript now in the possession of the Royal Statistical Society: see Vol. II, Letter 149.

[1] Jevons was actually 27 on 1 September 1862.

[2] Jevons had left University College after taking his M.A. in the preceding June. He was now living alone, for his sister Lucy had married earlier in the year, Henrietta was away and his brother Herbert had recently sailed for Australia. His brother Tom had entered business in Liverpool.

[3] Richard Hutton had, in 1861, left the *Economist* and become editor of the *Spectator*, a position he was to hold until 1897. Meantime, Walter Bagehot had taken over sole editorship of the *Economist* (see Jevons's letters of 1 September 1862 to Richard Hutton and 14 September 1862 to Herbert, Vol. II, Letters 164 and 165).

[4] The sentence is unfinished, for three pages have been torn out of the Journal here. The following entry begins at the top of the next remaining page. A letter Jevons wrote to his brother a few days later bears on this subject: '. . . Our family have not half enough humbug. One part of our composition with five of humbug would make a first rate character. If I had even a small percentage of H. E. R.'s ways, I should by this time have been soaring

5 October 1862

I have generally taken it for granted that though my style of writing was generally heavy, I might by a little practise make it lighter & thus newspaper writing or magazine contributing was any time within my power. But in writing a couple of articles for the Spectator[1] & an Essay, I get on so slowly painfully & heavily that I almost distrust my former confidence. If my distrust be well founded, I here meet a new obstacle to my present success. Light easy writing is not essential to philosophical subjects – it is perhaps rather prejudicial to ultimate soundness – but of course it is nearly essential to making any money by a literary life.[2]

During the last five days I have been almost wholly occupied in entertaining my Uncle William Jevons,[3] now a bent old man, but filled with the true affection, & the calm clear mind for which he & my father have been remarkable. Two days we visited the Exhibition,[4] one

---

up in the regions of fame ease and fortune, instead of labouring away in obscurity and without a half penny of profit. I quite agree with Shakespeare when he wrote in disgust in one of his sonnets

> "Gilded honour shamefully misplaced
> and right perfection wrongfully disgraced
> and strength by limping sway disabled,
> and art made tongue-tied by authority,
>
> . . .
>
> and captain [sic] good attending captain ill" '

(see letter of 14 September 1862 to Herbert, Vol. II, Letter 165). Jevons refers to this 66th sonnet again in the Journal entry for 25 April 1863 (see p. 191 below).

[1] See above, Biographical Introduction, p. 38.

[2] Jevons makes no mention in the Journal of his 'true theory of economy' which must have been much in his mind at the date of this entry and to which he refers in his letter of 14 September 1862 to Herbert (see Vol. II, Letter 165). He had sent his two papers 'On a General Mathematical Theory of Economy' and on 'Commercial Fluctuations' to be read at the British Association Meeting at Cambridge in October (see Journal entry for 31 December 1862, p. 188 below).

[3] William Jevons, Junior (1794–1873). After studying at Manchester College, York, he became a Unitarian Minister. Being, as his religious writings show, of independent and critical mind, he later left the ministry, and devoted himself to private educational work in Liverpool. His philosophical views, drawn from the Glasgow School, helped to crystallise the economic attitudes of the influential dissenting community here. In his study of these attitudes S. G. Checkland finds that William Jevons, in his book *Systematic Morality: or, a treatise on the theory and practice of human duty, on the grounds of natural religion* (1827) 'typifies the logical economic philosophy of the community to which he belonged'. (See S. G. Checkland, 'Economic Attitudes in Liverpool, 1793–1807', *Economic History Review*, v, No. 1 (1952).) Jevons corresponded a good deal with this uncle, especially in the early sixties (see below, Vol. III). William Jevons's other writings are listed in the British Museum Catalogue as follows: *Elements of Astronomy illustrated by problems on the Globes, etc.* (1828); *The Claims of Christianity to the character of a divine revelation considered*, pamphlet (1870); *The Book of Common Prayer examined, in the light of the present age*, in 2 parts (1872); *The Prayer Book adapted to the age*, pamphlet (1872).

[4] The International Exhibition of 1862 at South Kensington.

day was spent in the City, at Longman and Trübners publishing shops – where he was making arrangements for publishing 'Christianity without Miracles', yesterday we were at the Kensington Museum. Afterwards he left by a train at four oclock. His expressions of affection and satisfaction are so warm, that I must feel pleasure in believing him to be truly pleased. But I never have unalloyed satisfaction in society, especially where I am not perfectly at my ease; for every now & then I unskilfully say things which I regret unavailingly long after. And now especially I am so glum & wrapped up in my serious thoughts, that I can scarcely give any attention to the entertainment of others.[1] Who can say how dift I might have become had my affection for another person not been so abruptly disappointed.[2]

Yesterday afternoon after leaving Uncle W. at the Victoria Station I wandered again to Westminster Abbey of which I shall never tire. Where else can one feel so surrounded & encouraged by the greatness of humanity? After looking over a great many tombs of second rate heros & writers, I succeeded in finding the venerable tomb of Chaucer, venerable in its age & simplicity among the venerable. The crumbling stone has lost its inscription, yet his tales remain not only the well of English undefiled, the first great monument of the greatest of languages, but a mine of true simple poetry & of sound philosophy. Shakespeare excepted he is doubtless the poet that I shall best admire among the English.[3]

December 1862[4]

It was a bold & momentous decision which brought me out of Australia. I shall not regret [it][5] even if my remaining days be spent in poverty. In spite of industry I could not have done much in Sydney. I thought what I did very clever then but it seems foolishness to me now and my first efforts at a theory of economy look strange beside[6] the theory which has

---

[1] Jevons seems often to have exaggerated the poor impression he made on other people and to have had no idea of the pleasure he gave. After his uncle's visit he wrote to apologise for being a gloomy host, explaining how worried he was about his prospects, to which his uncle replied that he had no idea that Stanley had worries of this kind and that he had not found him gloomy.

[2] There is no trace of the identity of the girl Jevons fell in love with.

[3] Jevons left the rest of this page blank. See p. 98 above for further entry for October 1862.

[4] This entry, which has no date heading in the text, was begun on the first of many pages apparently left blank by Jevons during the account of his visit to the Richmond district, written in January 1857. It is followed by the entry for 10 November 1865 (see pp. 99 to 101 above for further entry for December 1862).

[5] This word is omitted in the text.

[6] Jevons wrote 'besides' in the text.

gradually opened upon me. At Sydney I had by me Whateleys logic[1] but had never read it. I scarcely knew what logic meant – After a time however I read John Mills logic, which I perhaps partly understood; & yet on the other hand I admired Whewells Phil. of the Inductive Sciences which now (Dec 1862) seems nothing but fog. I conclude that I knew little or nothing about[2] logic then & never should have done but for the new exercise for my thoughts afforded in my second college course. It seems rather late in life to be learning what logic is, yet it is better late than never. It may prove that my visit to Australia by breaking my college course & giving time to mature my powers did peculiar service.

I left Sydney with many exaggerated notions of my own powers & probable achievements – To spend a year in successful travelling over the globe – perhaps publishing accounts of what I had seen when I got home. This was one of the things I thought worth my notice. I had thought myself so successful in writing flowery letters home – and my letters & papers were so freely printed in the colonial papers & magazines,[3] that I entertained no doubt it would be the same at home. Reviews, & magazines, were fully[4] open to me if I cared to write – and if I found any difficulty in getting money other ways to take to the newspaper profession seemed always open to me. I did not see that one kind of writing & thinking may be inconsistent with other kinds.

21 December 1862[5]

I have had a good deal of disappointment in the last six months – but now the shortest and darkest days are past one[6] may begin to hope for something better – In short my plans are considerably altered and as it now seems to me improved. The notion of struggling on in London year after year until some sort of literary success should at last come, is fairly given up. H E R[7] wants me to go as Tutor to Owens College where I may make £200 & I shall go if all can be favourably arranged.

I do not find that my life passed half at home half at the Museum is

---

[1] Richard Whately, *Elements of Logic, comprising the substance of the article in the Encyclopaedia Metropolitana: with additions, etc.* (1826). The latest edition available to Jevons would have been the ninth, revised (1848).

[2] 'but' in the text.

[3] For a detailed bibliography of the Australian Writings, see La Nauze, *Political Economy in Australia*, pp. 39–44.

[4] 'freely' has been substituted here in LJ (p. 171).

[5] This entry is to be found 33 pages further on in the Journal, following that for 5 October 1862.

[6] 'we' has been substituted here in LJ (p. 172).

[7] Harry Roscoe was now Professor of Chemistry at Owens College, Manchester.

favourable in any respect. As I take up each new subject & get a few new facts about it, my interest & hopes rise so highly & suddenly that I can think of nothing else. Hence most exaggerated notions of what I can do with it. After working a few months at it very hard, the interest of new discovery ceases and the materials have to be worked up & finished A breath of doubt & disgust seems to dispel the illusion & I soon become as much depressed as I was before excited. This is just the history of my work at the subject of the volunteer system in England. I amassed a great quantity of amusing & new facts about the V. In setting to work to write them out in a formal account, I soon grew dis[1]

31 December 1862

Still at the old work and in rather better spirits. Yet I know I shall shortly be in as bad spirits as ever, these changes being regularly periodic with me. Harry Roscoe lately wanted me to go tutor to Owens College and the prospect of more regular work and an income nearly made me give up all London plans. Lucy however sent a vigourous prote.t against it which caused me to think twice, and I shall go on here for at least 9 months.

My atlas of monthly com[1] stat. progresses satisfactorily but my logical speculations give me most confidence. I cannot disbelieve, yet I can hardly believe that in the principle of *sameness* I have found that which will reduce the whole theory of reasoning to one consistent lucid process.[2] I can hardly confess to myself the value of such a work. Surely I ought not to want confidence in following my own plans out regardless of the opinions of others when I may expect such fruit from them. And yet how irksome is it to have everything in the future nothing comparatively in the present.

Of late I have not been altogether wanting in exertions towards correcting some of my greatest failings. For many years I have had such

---

[1] 'disgusted' (LJ, p. 172). The sentence ends here. The rest of the page has been left blank. On 28 December 1862, Jevons wrote to Tom, '. . . You will be enquiring about my volunteer history. This has rather come to grief. For after almost completing the information necessary, I found I had not the light imaginative pen necessary for making a book popular in the present day. The history would have proved little more than a series of historical notes, yet it is a pity to let so many interesting facts go waste. . . .' (see Vol. II, Letter 168). The Volunteer movement started in 1859 because of alarm over the intentions of Napoleon III, Emperor of France. Jevons was an ardent member of the movement. The spare-time drilling and outdoor training were arduous, as some of the descriptions in Jevons's letters show, but he found 'volunteering an excellent antidote to metaphysics' (see letter of 1 June 1860, to Herbert, Vol. II, Letter 144).

[2] This principle forms the basis of his first book on logic, published in December 1863 (see Journal entry for 4 June 1864, p. 197 below).

fear of speaking in public that even in reading in the College classes my voice shook. I regarded it as a physical impossibility. When I had papers to communicate to societies I got Dr Smith or Harry or Clifton to read them & slunk away myself out of danger.[1] This seemed so very foolish & so serious a bar to my advancement that I resolved to try to get over the difficulty by joining the college debating society.[2] On the first night I said a word or two about some inconsiderable matter – I was named by the President to open the debate of the following meeting. Suspended between desire to do the thing & fear of incapability – I at last doubt-fully consented prepared a speech – and did not appear when I had engaged – to the disgust of the society. I willingly paid the fine and bore some little censure & ridicule, and did not give the matter up – In the last few months I have been a pretty frequent attendant making brief remarks & undertaking on one occasion to reply. That I can ever be a good speaker is altogether beyond hope – but to be able to read with self possession is almost sufficient for any position I am likely to have and this I shall no doubt be soon able to do. I am even engaged in getting up a Literary & Scientific Society at College for the reading of original papers, in which I shall be much more at my ease.[3]

In all public life such as I have at College, in the Rifle Corps, in society I feel a constant unreadiness of thought, a want of tact, of practice, of quickness which puts me in awkward positions saying & doing things which cause no little subsequent regret. I have especially an incapacity of remembering persons & their names which is very

---

[1] Dr John Smith had read each of the two papers which Jevons presented to the Philosophical Society in Sydney in July and December 1857 (see Biographical Introduction, p. 25 above); Harry Roscoe had read a paper for Jevons entitled, 'Remarks on the Australian Gold Fields' before the Literary and Philosophical Society of Manchester, on 15 November 1859; Professor R. B. Clifton had read Jevons's first paper to the British Association, in Manchester in September 1861 (see Biographical Introduction, p. 36 above).

[2] Walter Bagehot, R. H. Hutton and Jevons's cousin William Caldwell Roscoe were the prime movers in the foundation of the College Debating Society in about 1843. (Bellot, op. cit., p. 296; see Biographical Introduction, p. 39 above.)

[3] The Literary and Scientific Society was originally formed in 1853 but disappeared after 1855. Jevons was the first President of the new Society which he formed in 1862 (see letter of 19 May 1863 to Herbert, Vol. III, Letter 177). 'It published a volume of papers in 1865, and survived until 1873' (Bellot, op. cit., pp. 297 and 360). Mrs Jevons, in a footnote to p. 175 of *Letters and Journal*, writes: 'The formation of a literary and philosophical society amongst the students was suggested to Mr. Jevons by his friend and fellow-student, Mr. Philip Magnus, who tells me that Mr. Jevons was chosen as president of the new society, and that he contributed a paper on the value of gold, prior to the publication of his *A Serious Fall in the Value of Gold*.' However Mrs. Jevons's statement that this paper was published in a volume of the transactions of the society is an error. Only three of the papers read between January 1863 and May 1865 were selected for publication and that by Jevons was not among them. Cf. *Essays read before the Literary & Philosophical Society of University College, London* (1865).

troublesome. And yet if these are the accompaniments of superior power in other ways I should put up with them contentedly and not be too thin skinned. Though many would say otherwise, I aim at virtues which will make up for many smaller vices. Deficiency in an ordinary virtue is more than made up by proficiency in an extraordinary virtue. I am infernal-tempered to those to whom I should be most kind & constantly mild – I am rather jealous, I dont go to chapel, I am a sluggard in the morning & at many odd hours, I am rather stingy, and have many other faults & vices which no one knows better than myself. And yet a great deal perhaps will be forgiven me if plans known only to myself prove someday not mere delusions.

The year of which only five minutes have now to run seems to have been a long one. It has seen many of my hopes fulfilled, many frustrated. It has made me an M.A. It has seen my theory of Economy offered to a Learned Society (?) & received without a word of interest or belief.[1] It has convinced me that success in my line of endeavour is even a slower achievement than I thought. This year has taken much youthfulness out of me.

It is often a cause of regret to me that my pursuits & my utter want of influence in society prevent me giving any assistance to others even my own sisters and brothers.

*　　*　　*

[1] 'Notice of a General Mathematical Theory of Political Economy' had been read before Section F of the British Association at its meeting in Cambridge at the beginning of October, together with the second paper entitled 'On the Study of Periodic Commercial Fluctuations, with five diagrams'. Both papers were summarised in 'Proceedings of Sections', pp. 157–8, *Report of the Thirty-Second Meeting of the British Association for the Advancement of Science, held at Cambridge in October, 1862* (1863).

For a comment on the total lack of interest in Jevons's 'Notice', see R. D. Collison Black, 'W. S. Jevons and the Economists of his Time', *The Manchester School*, xxx, No. 3 (September 1962) 205–6, in which Professor Black points out that this was the more surprising because Macleod read a paper advocating a mathematical approach to economics at this same meeting. However, as Lord Robbins has said, '. . . there can be no doubt that his great idea, the idea that the origin of the objective exchange values of the market was to be traced to the subjective valuations of individuals, was very revolutionary. However much we emphasize the continuity of analytical tradition, we must admit that the vindication of this idea has shifted the whole emphasis in such a way as to deserve the name of revolution.' (Lionel Robbins, 'The Place of Jevons in the History of Economic Thought', *Centenary Address to the Manchester Statistical Society*, delivered 27 February 1936, p. 5).

Jevons had learned to be prepared for his work being received without interest. On 14 September 1862, he wrote to Herbert: . . . 'I have resolved, however, at last to let out my theory of economy, and have accordingly written a short paper entitled, "Notice of a General Mathematical Theory of Economy". . . . Although I know pretty well the paper is perhaps worth all the others that will be read there put together, I cannot pretend to say how it will be received – whether it will be read at all, or whether it won't be considered nonsense. . . .' (See Vol. II, Letter 165.) The paper on commercial fluctuations similarly failed to create the slightest interest and it was only printed completely posthumously as Item I in *Investigations in Currency and Finance*. The *Theory* was printed in full in the *Statistical*

1 January 1863

How gladly would I brighten their lives – how could I enjoy a pleasant house a well filled purse a power of aiding & pleasing others each hour of the day – What would I not give to inspire Herbert again with that energy & hope which can alone make this life tolerable – How I fear that he has lost them for ever – & that Australia promises to him little more than Minnesota. How gladly would I return Hennys forgetfulness of self – & constant devotion to the good of others by such return as could be made, instead of keeping her in an uncomfortable lodgings & in uncertainty. But all this it seems I must suffer & regret in quiet, & with but faint hope that I shall be justified by the result.[1]

During the year now begun I hope that I may not falter & distrust even my highest hopes of doing good in my own peculiar way. In action, social influence etc I am nothing – never shall be of the slightest consequence. In many kinds of mental excellence I am nothing – no imagination – an imperfect memory, no classical or mathematical scholar, a heavy writer. I have but one slight thread of hope, a capacity of seeing the sameness & difference of things – which if history & the sayings of experienced men are to be believed is a rare & valuable kind of power. Let me set the single purpose before me of developing & properly using it, not pretending to what I am not & cannot be, in order that I may be what others seem incapable of being.

A week or two ago when H E R proposed my going to Manchester I took a violent dislike to the Museum – & thought my escape from it would prove a turning point in my life. Now I am again nearly caught in the toils of Literary dissipation. I intend fairly to try my plan of Literary agency, although I am somewhat ashamed of it. To send circulars & hire out ones time at 3sh per hour seems rather *infra dig.* but perhaps it is false pride and I ought not to stick at anything short of moral wrong.[2]

Journal, xxix (1866) p. 283 and as Appendix III to the fourth edition of *Theory of Political Economy*.

[1] The feeling behind these thoughts can be appreciated when one recognises the financial sacrifices which Jevons had imposed on his two sisters by leaving his job in Australia. Henrietta was still single. Lucy had married but Jevons was not relieved of anxiety on her account. Her first child had just been born and her husband, whose financial circumstances were precarious, already had five children by his previous marriage (see Biographical Introduction, p. 11 above). Herbert had landed in Australia the preceding October but had not yet found any kind of employment.

[2] A copy of the circular reads:

'Mr. W. Stanley Jevons, M.A., Medalist (London) gives his attention to procuring Information for Literary and Scientific purposes from the Libraries and Collections of the

8 Porteus Road *March 8, 1863*

Dear Tom

. . . There has been nothing talked about here for many days but the Princess, and the whole of London has been quite wild about yesterdays proceedings.[1] The Queen's turned out about 1000 strong and assembled near the Duke of Yorks Column. Thence about 2 pm we marched in grand array up Pall Mall, St James Street and Piccadilly to Hyde Park. All the club houses & Mansions were just filled with their crowds of visitors, and together with their decorations presented a very brilliant appearance. What with volunteers and soldiers and bands and balconies & stands full of elaborately dressed ladies with flags, garlands and decorations innumerable, and a dense but enthusiastic mob, the streets looked as perhaps they never looked before In Hyde Park we were drawn up in two immense long lines stretching out of sight the rabble being kept at a very respectful distance by railings.[2]

25 April 1863   8 Porteus R[d].

For several months before Christmas I was often in low spirits – since Christmas I have hitherto felt buoyant in spite of every apparent obstacle. Now that I have returned from Manchester with a reasonable prospect of a comfortable living – I find myself again falling into dejection. High hopes must it seems be succeeded by the opposite. It is peculiar too that as long as I am going on with any work I am happy;

Metropolis. He finds that he may thus be of occasional service to Authors and others not at the moment within reach of works or objects to which they may need to refer. In the Library of the British Museum he has access to almost any English or Foreign work of note, and to large collections of newspapers, periodicals, transactions of Societies, maps, drawings, engravings, music, parliamentary and official publications, catalogues, indexes, bibliographical and genealogical works, etc. He will also consult some parts of the Manuscripts. When requisite he will extend his services to other accessible libraries and collections.

'MR. JEVONS will at once decline any inquiry in which he believes he cannot give satisfaction. Care will be taken to render the information exact and reliable by giving the original text as far as possible, and supplying full references.

'Terms will not exceed three shillings per hour for the time actually occupied in the inquiry. A limit may be agreed upon.'

On 18 January Jevons wrote to Herbert, 'I . . . as yet have had only one job, and that not the right sort. I am much inclined to fear it will not do. It is regarded as too dubious and irregular an occupation, as is apparent from the notes of the few who have applied to me . . .' (see Vol. III, Letter 169).

[1] A reference to the ceremonies held to mark the arrival in London on 7 March of Princess Alexandra, for her marriage to the Prince of Wales which took place in St George's Chapel, Windsor, on 10 March 1863. (See letter of 12 March 1863 to Tom, Vol. III, Letter 172).

[2] Jevons left the rest of this page blank.

when it is done I collapse, hate my work, & feeling my best efforts useless life seems useless & better away. This is no doubt unreasonable, but how avoid it? Now I suppose I am low because my Essay on Gold is out, & as yet no one has said a word in its favour except my sister who of course does it as a sister.[1] What if all I do or can do were to be received so – In the first place one might be lead to doubt whether all ones convictions concerning oneself were not mere delusions. Secondly one might at last learn, that even the best productions may never be caught by the breath of popular approval & praise.

It would take infinite time & space to write all I have thought about my position lately. As I have ever thought myself in many ways a fool – I am in no way surprised to find that many notions which I have had are ridiculous – At last I fairly allow that the one great way of getting on in this world is to get friends & impress them with a notion of your cleverness. Send them about to advertise your cleverness, get their testimonial like so many levers to force yourself where you wish to go. How well did Shakespeare see through all these things when he wrote his 66th sonnet.

It is quite obvious to me that it is useless to go on printing works which cost great labour much money [and][2] are scarcely noticed by any soul.[3] I must begin life again & by another way, ingratiating myself where & when I can – only after long years of slow progress can ones notions be brought out with any chance of being even examined by those capable of judging of them.

Faulty as I am in so many ways – I yet feel that my inmost motives are hardly selfish. I believe they grow by degrees less so. Sometimes I even feel that I should not care for reputation wealth, comfort or even life itself if I could feel that all my efforts were not without their use. Could I do it all anonymously, I perhaps might consent to it. And yet

[1] *A Serious Fall in the Value of Gold Ascertained and its Social Effects set forth, with two Diagrams* had been published on 16 April by Edward Stanford, Charing Cross, London (reprinted in *Investigations in Currency & Finance*, edited by H. S. Foxwell, 1884). 'My pamphlet . . . has as yet sold very badly', Jevons wrote a few weeks later to his brother, 'and has not been noticed by more than one or two papers. R. Hutton has given me an article or part of an article, and warmly adopts my view of the question . . .' (see letter of 19 May 1863 to Herbert, Vol. III, Letter 177).

Lucy's approval of the tract was without doubt due to her exceptional discernment and not just dutiful praise, and was soon to be confirmed. See entry for 9 January 1864, p. 192 below; also Biographical Introduction, p. 39 above.

He had written to his brother Herbert on 18 January 1863, that his diagrams of prices had led him 'to observe the great rise in prices of nearly all things since 1851, which is obviously due to a fall in the value of gold . . .' This, he continues, 'I am now trying to ascertain and prove in a conclusive manner, which will, of course, be a very important and startling fact . . .'

[2] This word is omitted in the text.

[3] Jevons had published *A Serious Fall in the Value of Gold* at his own expense, the total cost being £43. See his letter of 24 July 1863 to Herbert, Vol. III, Letter 187.

the condemnation of friends & all you meet is hard to be borne, & their praise or admiration must be sweet.

I am convinced that at any rate it is best to clear out of London. I make no progress here – Quite the opposite. I may do better elsewhere. I must go upon a different tack.[1]

9 January 1864

Though still capable of taking a very gloomy view of affairs, there is much on which I may congratulate myself. My first college term has convinced me that I can be a lecturer, a passable if not a good one. One intolerable fear & weakness, that of public speaking is removed from my way. Morevoer my pamphlet on the gold question has had a degree of success that must surely be allowed to be beyond my highest hopes.[2]

I often debate with myself & have cause to debate, whether it is better to lead a solitary laborious life given up wholly to study & writing, or whether it is not better to do as others do – involve myself in the pleasures of society & of a family, & trust still to find time and opportunity sufficient to my other work. There are many instances of the highest men who have remained unmarried – and two of them Locke & Newton are the very two that one might take as almost perfect examples But Locke, if never married, was yet a man of great social powers, & far from being the morose awkward creature to which I have a great tendency. Newton again though he lead a close college life for a

---

[1] This entry was written just after Jevons had returned from a visit to Manchester during which he had arranged to take up the tutorship at Owens College.

[2] The first person to realise and draw attention to the importance of the pamphlet was J. E. Cairnes. The support Cairnes gave Jevons from the end of May 1863 onwards (see Jevons's letter of 31 May 1863 to Lucy, Vol. III, Letter 179) is examined in detail by R. D. Collison Black in his article, 'Jevons and Cairnes', *Economica*, xxvii (August 1960) 214–32. 'There can be no doubt', he concludes, 'that the transformation from potential failure to actual success was due in the first instance to the interest which Cairnes took in Jevons' work and the support which he gave it.' Jevons was also much indebted to Cairnes's friend, Henry Fawcett, who gave considerable prominence to the pamphlet when he quoted from it in an address to the British Association in August 1863, 'On the Effects of the recent Gold Discoveries', a subject on which he had written several previous papers. Fawcett's views were of weight; his *Manual of Political Economy*, a popular exposition of the teachings of Mill, had been published early in 1863 with great success and he had subsequently been appointed Professor of Political Economy at Cambridge. His speech caused considerable discussion in the Press (see Vol. III, Letters 191–4) and caused Jevons's findings and reputation to be generally confirmed. The significance of the tract in the history of applied economics was discussed by both Keynes and Robbins on the occasion of their papers commemorating the centenary of Jevons's birth. Professor Robbins has pointed out that the value of the pamphlet has remained permanent, for its methods have contributed to the whole development of the technique of measuring price changes. See J. M. Keynes, 'William Stanley Jevons, 1835–1882', *Essays in Biography* (1951); Lionel Robbins, *Manchester School*, vii (1936) 1–17.

long time, was probably not the better for it. It seems very likely that he rather overworked himself, & injured his mind, & he indubitably wasted a great part of his vast labours.

Should we not be always striving to correct our worst faults, our weak parts. We should not indeed place ourselves in a place[1] where those faults may do us special harm, but if possible let us place ourselves where they may be corrected as far as possible. Then our better parts may be almost left to develope themselves.

I begin to think that I am too much wrapped up in my own thoughts & prospects; too constantly dwelling upon congratulating myself on my own supposed excellencies, This cannot be good. I should get quite as much work done without thinking so much about it. And if I had some [one][2] to love & care for no real interference with my other work need be apprehended.[3]

23 May 1864

The above is quite true. Everything convinces me that I should utterly reject all thoughts of a solitary & gloomy life.

Yesterday I walked with Tom & Will Jevons[4] from St Michael's Hamlet to Allerton & the neighbourhood. We walked in the fields near the hall, & in every way it was an hour of pleasant feeling to me.[5] I could not but reflect upon those from whom I come. I could not but feel the hope that I may do my duty & use my powers as well, and l was filled with the beauty & cheerfulness of the scene around.

As we were coming away Tom examined the trunks of a fine row of ash trees running south from the road to Garston. Many initials & dates were marked upon them, several of which such as F. J. R.[6] seemed to belong to some of the family. But we noticed also the letters $^{RJ}_{1845}$ There can be no doubt I think that they were carved upon the tree,

[1] 'position' has been substituted here by the editor of LJ (p. 194).

[2] This word is omitted in the text.

[3] It is not possible to throw any definite light on who was causing Jevons to debate the question of marriage at this time.

[4] His brother Tom and his cousin William Edgar, son of Timothy Jevons, whose family lived at St Michael's Hamlet in the south end of Liverpool, adjoining Dingle.

[5] Jevons's mother had been brought up at Allerton Hall, the home of William Roscoe from 1799 to 1816. For a photograph of Allerton Hall in this century, see Chandler, *Liverpool*, p. 161; also Sir H. E. Roscoe, *Life and Experiences*, pp. 2–3.

[6] Jevons's cousin Francis James Roscoe (1830–78), youngest son of William Stanley Roscoe (1782–1843) and brother of William Caldwell Roscoe, B.A., University College, London, 1850; clerk at Messrs Anderson and Hunt, Austin Friars; 1862 emigrated to Victoria, Vancouver Island; 1864 married Letitia le Breton; 1874 M.P. for Victoria Island in the Parliament of the Dominion of Canada.

the second of the ash trees, by my excellent but unhappy brother.[1] In 1845 his genius must have been developing itself, & his intellect was yet unclouded. I could not but feel the place endowed with tenfold interest. Under the very trees, where my mother had strolled & read & reflected in her happy & well spent youth, there my brother had been when hopes of usefulness & greatness were filling him. And there I now was an humble admirer of my brother.

I have of late occasionally read portions of Roscoes diaries & poems which have happily fallen to my care in safety, through the care of others.[2] I have hardly perhaps read them all, for I can hardly bear to read much at a time. But the more I read the more I am convinced that he was as great in soul as he was good. Every sentence he wrote is full of a fervid feeling of duty, of religious faith, & of innate love of intellectual greatness. His all absorbing desire was to be a poet, one whose thoughts aptly & beautifully expressed should dwell in other mens minds[3] & lead them also to beauty & to truth. His love perhaps in his then early youth was even more of the beautiful than of the simply & barely true; his emotions were even more elevated than his intellectual capacities. But his skill in mathematics & mechanics showed the latter were of no common quality.

My personal recollections of my lost brother are unfortunately scanty. I played & worked under him as a younger brother. I admired him & the things he made. I have some few of them yet, for instance the little set of grain weights, which he[4] constructed for his chemical balance. The latter was ingeniously made of wood with a common knife edge; the movement & pans & weights were all complete, & he was able to make quantitative experiments with considerable exactness. Our workshop was an old coach house & stable which yet stands, in front of the house in Park Hill Road, though I fear it will not long stand.[5] There how many hours did he work. I remember too the galvanic battery he made with metal plates & rivets & a hammer & anvil that my father procured for him. Many old tools, & some things made by his hands were long mine & I regret that they have in my

---

[1] Roscoe Jevons.
[2] These have not survived.
[3] Jevons wrote 'mind' in the text.
[4] 'his' in the text.
[5] At the time of the publication of *Letters and Journal* (1886) the house at Park Hill Road, Toxteth Park, was being used as a Sunday School belonging to the Unitarian Chapel in Toxteth Park Road, in what had become a poorer part of Liverpool. The house is no longer standing.

For H. E. Roscoe's account of how he worked with Roscoe Jevons in this old stable see Biographical Introduction, pp. 7–8 above.

distant travels & changes been dispersed. But I yet use the drawing instruments that he used; I have used them till they are almost worn out; but they will I hope long be used yet. I have not a few of his books, chiefly mathematical with his own handwriting in them. They shall long be kept & used. And I have his own diaries which reveal to me what he was. They are something almost sacred. They are sent to elevate my hopes & feelings & purposes.

What he hoped & was not permitted to do, that may I hope & do. May I aspire sincerely to follow out & complete somewhat of the work that must have filled his mind. I am indeed deficient of his probable powers. At his age I had not the like clear & powerful feelings as far as I can remember. They were comparatively vague & weak. And of his poetical powers I am entirely deprived. But I may inherit some of the same logical & mathematical[1] and carefully developed they may lead to much.

But I do not unreasonably fear his fate. I am long past the age at which his feelings were overstrained. Perhaps my worst years of that are lately past, and there are some promises of success that encourage & lighten my spirits. And then I am awake to the danger of overworking my mind. I know the symptoms of mental fatigue & do not disregard them. And as far as in me lies I will use all remedies for the overstraining of my thoughts.

The last thing almost that I remember of my brother before his misfortune, is a gloomy incident. He was sitting in the back breakfast room at the Park & telling me a half thoughtless younger brother how much he had disliked his life at the foundry, & yet how he had been determined to go on with it uncomplainingly because my father wished it, & *it was his duty* to do as his father wished. And then he asked me as I can clearly remember whether I did not think he did right. I little understood the full melancholy meaning & result of his thoughts but yet I remember that the question placed me in a painful dilemma. Would that I could have comforted him, & lead him back to cheerfulness & hope! But I was a child some 12 years old, & with child like straight forwardness I said he was not right, but should have told what he felt. How much pain may I not have caused to his mind so filled with regard to duty & so sensitive.

O that I may be enabled to fill in some degree the place that was to be his! I will show imperfectly what he would have been more perfectly. I will try to bear some fruit worthy of the saintly spirit of my mother, & the upright & humane goodness of my father.

[1] A word appears to be omitted here in the text.

4 June 1864

This day the working session ends at Owens College and as I have nothing to do with the examinations my college work is at an end. I shall stay however another week in Man^r having to give three lessons to a pupil Capt Blundel, to get some price diagrams drawn for the Brit. Assoc^n.[1] & to wind up my affairs for the session.

I have for at least a month now been in good and what is more equable spirits. As the session drew to an end the intense discouragement my work often gave me was lightened. Having sent in a report & proposals which were approved by the Professors, I have a reasonable prospect of better success next year. Convinced that I received great detriment from my want of sociality, I resolved to do what was possible to throw it off. It was indeed like resolving to throw off nature itself & become somebody else, so habituated have I long been to shyness, retirement & consequent awkwardness in all strange society. Even now no doubt I must not hope to become more than in average degree social. A long existing fault can hardly be changed by any exertions into its corresponding excellence but I think it is quite possible that the fault itself may be removed, and that is a great thing. I could hardly have hoped so much had I not in a previous instance achieved a like measure[2] of success. I have learned to speak with some composure in public, a thing which for many years seemed beyond the bounds of possibility.

Few could form any notion of the state of agitation into which at first the mere thought of having to speak in public threw me. My heart beat wildly & strongly, my blood rushed all about my body, I seemed turned into moisture & warmth; worst[3] of all my ideas either left me altogether or fell into confusion beyond all control. This is just what happened the first few times I ventured to speak at all, so that what I said bore no proportion whatever to what I might have had to say. But now by taking such opportunities as present themselves I am acquiring some composure; last evening I spoke twice at a dinner given by our students; it was the first time I had ever spoken at a dinner. Though what I said was no doubt wretchedly poor, I was satisfied to get off passably, & do better on a future occasion. And when ideas are not deficient, speaking is so much a matter of practise that I may almost hope to become a good & fluent speaker.

So may I not hope to become passably social? May I not hope by making myself better known to those around me to use my acquirements with better advantage, & gain position which I desire more as a means

---

[1] See p. 197 below.   [2] 'manner' has been substituted here in LJ (p. 199).
[3] 'most' has been substituted here in LJ (p. 199).

than an end. And may I not even find in the society of ladies & friends generally a relaxation from my own devouring thoughts much needed if I am to avoid all chances of a breakdown.

The last few days I have been making some exertions towards this end. On Wednesday night[1] Henny & I had a small party, our first, with the assistance of course of my aunt.[2] It included four students, Miss Smith, the sister of one, & Miss Boyce, & went off just passably considering the limited means of entertainment in our small house. The next night I was at a similar but larger entertainment at Cliftons except indeed that Mrs Clifton was the only lady. On Friday we had the college boat race, & the dinner in the evening. Lastly today I have been to make my first calls, in company with Henny.

I am looking forward to several considerable steps in my onward progress. I am on the point of getting myself proposed & perhaps elected a fellow of the Statistical Society, as the use of the title, F.S.S. the use of the library, & possible acquaintance with other statisticians will be of high advantage to me. As my analysis of prices since 1782, too, draws towards completion, a most long & tedious piece of work indeed, I have formed the notion of reading the results at the next Brit. Assoc.

It will require some courage but perhaps if I undertake it, I shall get through all right.[3]

Lastly I am going to spend nearly four months in London, in continuous work upon the coal subject. I shall throw my whole energy into the work, & strive to form a piece of statistical reasoning on the subject which may in some degree approach one's abstract notion of what it should be. I will do my best & I almost hope that I may be favoured with success.[4]

When I look back for a year or more I cannot deny that I have made some advance – that I have published two small works, one with a success it does not deserve, the other perhaps deserving a success greater than it has had;[5] that I have also commenced a new profession & earned sufficient money by it to pay my way without inroads on my capital. And when I look back to my notions in Sydney, they seem almost

---

[1] 1 June 1864.

[2] Mrs Henry Roscoe, at whose house at 9 Birch Grove, Rusholme, Jevons and his sister were living.

[3] Jevons was elected a member of the Statistical Society in November 1864. The results of his analysis of prices were read to the London Statistical Society in May, 1865 (see letter of 25 May 1865 to Herbert, Vol. III, Letter 217), since he was unable to complete the work in time for the 1864 British Association Meeting. The paper was entitled 'The Variation of Prices and the Value of the Currency since 1782' (reprinted in *Investigations*) and Jevons's object was to test the conclusions reached in his pamphlet on gold by studying price changes over a longer historical period.   [4] Cf. above, Biographical Introduction, p. 43.

[5] The pamphlet *A Serious Fall in the Value of Gold ascertained and its Social Effects set forth* (April 1863) and his first book on logic, *Pure Logic, or the Logic of Quality apart from Quantity with Remarks on Boole's System and the Relation of Logic and Mathematics* (December 1863). By

ludicrous. My faint hopes of a degree, BA at most, MA being a height beyond my view; my wondering respect for whole regions of knowledge then a blank to me, now not quite so; & especially my respect for the position & name of a *statistician* – Now I have already been[1] called by reviews of authority, a *competent statistician*, & have been said to treat a statisticians subjects with[2]

10 November 1865.[3] Birch Grove Manchester

At intervals success rewards me deliciously but at other times it seems but to oppress me with a burden of duty. More & more I feel a lifelong

---

August 1864 only four copies of the latter had been sold (see letter of 27 August 1864 to Harry Roscoe, Vol. III, Letter 207). Jevons attached high value to his work on logic and to the 'principle of *sameness*' which formed the basis of this book.

[1] 'be' in the original text.

[2] The sentence ends here as the next page of the Journal has been torn out. On the page following this entry, a press cutting and a ticket of admission have been pasted into the Journal, and on the reverse side is pasted the letter from Mr A. Macmillan mentioned by Jevons in his entry for 5 March 1866 (see p. 202 below). The press cutting is the official announcement of Jevons's appointment in May 1865 as Professor of Logic, Moral Philosophy and Political Economy at Queen's College, Liverpool. The ticket is for admission to his Introductory Address on the evening of Monday, 2 October, on the subject of 'Reading and Study'.

Although Jevons was in fact appointed to two distinct professorships at Queen's College, Liverpool – Logic and Moral Philosophy in April, and Political Economy in May 1865 – his duties only required attendance at the College on one day in the week. In the session 1865–6 he had four day and eight evening students in Logic, five day students in Moral Philosophy, and two evening students in Political Economy.

On 5 June 1865 the Council of Queen's College resolved 'that it would be well if at the opening of the next session a well-considered address were delivered by one of the Professors, and they suggest that if the Faculty have no objection Mr. Jevons be requested to undertake this office'.

Jevons served as Professor at Liverpool for only one year, resigning on 7 June 1866, on his appointment to the chair at Owens College. (See Minute Book of the College Committee, Liverpool Record Office, 373/INS/1/12/2.)

Queen's College, Liverpool, was incorporated by Royal Warrant in May 1857 with two Faculties, Arts and Law, and Medicine. It was in fact a department of the Liverpool Institute: most classes were given in the evening and attendances were generally small. In 1881 the title 'The Queen's College' was dropped and the classes were amalgamated with those existing in the Liverpool Institute. See H. J. Tiffen, *History of the Liverpool Institute Schools* (Liverpool, 1935).

[3] This entry is to be found 49 pages further back in the Journal from the end of the previous one. During the interval of 17 months between making these entries, Jevons wrote and published *The Coal Question* and after reading his paper on prices in May, resumed his work on logic. He constructed 'a reasoning machine or logical abacus' (see letter of 25 May 1865 to Herbert, in which he first mentions work on this, Vol. III, Letter 217). During the summer vacation that year he became deeply absorbed in his logical work (see Journal entry for 17 December 1865, p. 201 below) and as he told Herbert in a letter of 18 November 1865 he was engaged in 'getting my reasoning machine into a true machine form, it having previously been an abacus or counting board, not a machine' (LJ, p. 213; see also letter of 4 November 1865 to Lucy, ibid.; and Journal entry for 28 March 1866, p. 204 below).

work defined beforehand for me & its avoidance impossible. Come what will I cannot but feel that I have faculties which are to be cultivated & developed at any risk. To misuse or neglect them would be treason of the deepest kind.

And yet the troubles are not slight which such a high & difficult work brings upon me. One duty too seems to clash with others. My ideal seems to involve contradictories. I would be loved & loving. But the very studies I have to cultivate absorb my thoughts so that I hardly feel able to be what I would in other ways. And above all poverty is sure to be my lot. I cannot aid others as I would wish.[1] Nor in a money making & loving world is it easy to endure the sense of meanness and want which poverty brings. And if I could endure all this myself I could not expect nor hardly wish for a wife nor any relative to endure it. Half my feelings & affections then must be stifled & disappointed.

It is when I have such feelings as these that this book serves me well. I look back to my former confessions & my former resolutions. *I find I have too long pursued a straight & arduous course to think of swerving now.*[2] I must choose the greater duty – the higher work, where work or duty would seem to clash. I must cultivate indifference to other persons' opinions where I cannot rightly hope to gain it. I must work like one who is a servant not a master – must execute the orders he so plainly receives to the best of his ability; & feel no anxiety for the result – it is not in his hands nor on his responsibility.

3 December 1865. Sunday Evening

My changing moods of hope & depression, of long sighted resolution, & of present prudence are strangely marked in these successive paragraphs. Now I am no longer inclined to brave the worst hardships of a poor authors life and strive to earn its deserts & honours as my only reward. I have often thought in reading or hearing of the lives of the great but unfortunate, that a little prudence, now & then, a slight relaxation in the ardour of pursuit, would have yielded far greater results. It is not poverty and overwork, and hopeless anxiety surely that will raise the powers of mind to their highest. It is mere asceticism to prefer the harder & more straightened life if a happier & perhaps more useful one offers.

Have I not sufficient or more than suft ardour in the pursuit of

---

[1] A reference to the worry Jevons felt in being again unable to assist his sister Lucy and her husband, whose business was in serious difficulties.

[2] In the Journal, this sentence is underlined in pencil. As it was Jevons's practice throughout to underline in ink words he wished to emphasise, it is possible that this underlining was done neither at the time of writing nor by Jevons himself.

discovery and knowledge? Have I not in the last few years seriously overstrained my head, once at least, and may I not justly fear that some day my strength will prove unequal to the labour that my position may demand.

I have shown how much I would risk where it must be risked – It would be fool hardiness to refuse the easier & happier life if it were in my reach.

I confess I can hardly bear the thought of a solitary life of unrelieved labour. The happiness of marriage may not be the only happiness the only good I aspire to; but am I excluded from the one because I hope for the other.

It is at times truly depressing to work for future appreciation only. Money, rank, manners social position, or at the best brilliant talents, carry off all consideration at the moment.

The work of the thinker & inventor, may indeed prove for ever futile & mistaken – but even if it be in the true & successful path, it is not and perhaps can hardly be recognised at once. At least it is not. One of my chief reasons for the little love of society is that in most company, my hopes & feelings seem snuffed out.[1]

14 December 1865

Yesterday, by a curious coincidence, I enjoyed two of the greatest & truest gratifications of which life is capable. The one needs & can have no writing down. It was the satisfaction of doubts. The other was a letter from Sir John Herschel,[2] approving in the most complete manner of my Coal Question, which I lately had sent to him. Long periods of labour & depression have to be repaid in brief moments of such satisfaction as that letter gave me – perhaps I may say amply repaid. If the book which was to me a work of intense interest & feeling, is read by few & understood by fewer – it has at least the endorsement of one scientific man whom I should perhaps of all in the world select as the most competent judge of the subject as a whole. I may almost say that I feel the work is not a slight one – to my self I cannot help but say it. When I set about it, the subject inspired me to make exertion, & treat it worthily if possible. And at least labour was not wanting – for I worked throughout one vacation at it, often writing for 5 or 6 hours at a stretch

---

[1] Jevons added here 'like the clear but struggling light of the distant stars, when the strong beams of the nearer sun break out' but crossed it out. He substituted 'strong' for 'rude'.

[2] Letter of 23 November 1865. See Vol. III, Letter 227.

scarcely leaving my seat. No wonder I was somewhat the worse when college work came on in addition to the work of completing the book. I may well be glad, it did not destroy my powers.

Now it is indeed pleasant to be assured that I was under no mistake.

17 December 1865

My mother says in her Diary 7 July 1822[1] – 'The habit or the power of giving your attention strongly to any object of attainment is a most difficult acquisition and childhood is the time when it can be best attained – afterwards it is a task of no common difficulty – to resist every temptation around you'.

I believe that by long practice ever since my childhood I have acquired no inconsiderable power of this time.[2] I am seldom troubled now by not being in the humour. Even in composition I can sit down almost any time and work at what I want. I can thus give one day to one subject or work – another to another or can portion out my work as is desirable. Or I can carry on different kinds of work, from time to time passing from one to another without the least difficulty. My danger is somewhat the other way – I can concentrate my thoughts upon a subject at almost any time till everything else vanishes out of view – But if I am once interested or excited about a subject I cannot always dismiss it.

In the autumn at Clynnog[3] I got involved in Boole's probabilities[4] which I did not thoroughly understand. I thought & wrote about it hard for a week or two until I found I could not dismiss the subject. The most difficult points ran in my mind day & night till I got quite alarmed. The result was considerable distress of head a few days later & some signs of indigestion.

I feel that some degree of inaction and laziness is now a virtue rather than otherwise. Ease & freedom from work is as pleasant to me perhaps as anyone, & it is no small privilege to enjoy the reaction from hard work.

---

[1] *Literary Diaries of Mary Anne Roscoe*, Volume for 1819–22, unpublished. The quotation is from the entry for 8 July 1822.

[2] Jevons probably intended to write 'kind' here, which has been substituted by the editor of LJ, p. 217.

[3] Jevons had spent the months of July and August 1865 at Clynnog in Caernarvonshire, where his sister Lucy (Mrs John Hutton) was now living, the family having moved from Beaumaris.

[4] George Boole, *An Investigation of the Laws of Thought, on which are founded the mathematical theories of logic and probabilities* (1854).

1 March 1866

Even though the deepest disappointment should come upon me, give me strength, O God, to be thy brave and true servant.[1]

4 March 1866

How can we doubt that there is a God when we feel Him moving in us? In the midst of anxiety & disappointment & sense of failure such as I have seldom had to feel before, I spent a morning of calmness & hope, almost inexplicable. I went to chapel, & prayers, hymns & lessons seemed written to inspire me with confidence. In the sermon Mr Steinthal[2] seemed to interpolate sentences directed at me. I believe he did for he might easily see that I was moved, & could hardly maintain my composure. Whence is this feeling that even failure in a high aim is better than success in a lower one? It must be from a Higher Source, for all lower nature loves & worships success, & cheerful life. Yet the highest success that I feel I can worship is that of adhering to one's aims, & risking all.

5 March 1866.

Such were my thoughts yesterday. Today I have reassurance which seems to me nothing less than providential. The following is a copy of a letter forwarded me by Mr Macmillan.[3]

[1] It seems most probable that the disappointment feared by Jevons was the possibility that he might not get the new professorship in logic, mental and moral philosophy and political economy to be established at Owens College, because it was to be publicly advertised. See Journal entry for 14 May 1866, p. 205 below; also letter of 24 March 1866 to Herbert, Vol. III, Letter 239. The causes of the deep depression Jevons went through at this period are discussed in the Biographical Introduction, p. 46 above.

[2] The Reverend Samuel Alfred Steinthal was minister at Platt Chapel in Rusholme, the district in Manchester where Jevons was living. His name is an honoured one amongst Unitarians for his work for the abolition of slavery, domestic missions and other social causes. See G. E. Evans, *Vestiges of Protestant Dissent* (Liverpool, 1897); also R. V. Holt, *The Unitarian Contribution to Social Progress in England* (1938).

[3] The original of the letter from A. Macmillan is pasted into the Journal on a page further on in the book: the full text is given in Vol. III, Letter 233. Macmillan advised Jevons to write to Gladstone – see Letters 241–3.

Windsor Castle
Febr. 24 66

My dear Sir

I am not certain whether I owe to your kindness, or to that of Mr Jevons, my early opportunity of perusing his work on coal: but I have perused it with care, and with extraordinary interest. It makes a deep impression upon me, and strengthens the convictions I have long entertained, but with an ever growing force, as to our duty with regard to the National Debt.

I think it a masterly review of a vast, indeed a boundless subject.

But I feel that I have not the Scientific knowledge which alone could make me a competent judge of the grave conclusions involved: and I shall look with the utmost interest for other and weightier opinions upon this remarkable product of the English Economic School.

Pray take my thanks as intended both for you and for Mr Jevons, and believe me I remain faithfully yours

W. E. Gladstone

I find the opinions of *Ecce Homo*[1] which I regard as the best and weightiest concur in regarding it as a work of extraordinary powers & of high & useful aim.

A Macmillan Esq.

11 March 1866

I seem to have more clearly before me by degrees the position to which I would aspire. Accepting the progressive triumphs of physical science I would aid in the reform of abstract science and in the establishment of moral & political sciences. But I would also join science to morals & religion. I would try to show that they are not antagonistic.

24 March 1866

I have lost & shall lose many of the most exquisite & true pleasures of life, but I can look upon their loss without much regret when I feel that I

[1] J. R. Seeley's controversial life of Christ, which Macmillan had published in 1865.

am following something above even such pleasures. But there is one thought which fills my soul with dread. It is the thought of

'that one talent which is death to hide
        lodg'd with me useless.'[1]

It is a fearful trust for one to have who feels he has not judgment, and the worldly means & qualities which would enable him to use it with effect.

28 March 1866

I cannot forget or omit to record this day last week. I was sleeping as usual for the night at St Michael's Hamlet.[2] As I awoke in the morning the sun was shining brightly into my room. There was a consciousness on my mind[3] . . . that I was the discoverer of the true logic of the future.[4] For a few minutes I felt a delight such as one can seldom hope to feel. But it could not last long – I remembered only too soon how unworthy & weak an instrument I was for accomplishing so great a work, & how hardly could I expect to do it.

12 April

This morning the advertisement appeared opening my coveted professorship to public competition.[5] I have toiled and I have fought my weaknesses. I have hardly left anything undone which in my poor judgment would secure success. Surely the result is not on my hands.

[1] From Milton's sonnet, *On His Blindness*.

[2] Jevons stayed overnight at the home of his uncle, Timothy Jevons, at St Michael's Hamlet, Liverpool, when he lectured one evening a week at Queen's College, Liverpool. See letter of 18 October 1865 to Herbert, Vol. III, Letter 226.

[3] Here Jevons reaches the end of a left-hand page in the Journal. The top line of the next page has been cut off. See note 2 to page 205 below.

[4] Jevons's mind had for some time past been engaged on logical problems, in particular with his invention of a logical abacus, and shortly after writing this entry he read a paper to the Manchester Literary and Philosophical Society, on 3 April 1866, entitled 'On a Logical Abacus' and exhibited the abacus he had constructed. On 19 March he had given a similar account to the Liverpool Literary and Philosophical Society. See letter of 24 March 1866 to Herbert, Vol. III, Letter 239; also entries for 23 May 1866 and 19 November 1867, pp. 206 and 211 below.

[5] The advertisement reads as follows:

> OWENS COLLEGE, MANCHESTER (in connexion with the University of London). PROFESSORSHIP of LOGIC, MENTAL and MORAL PHILOSOPHY, and POLITICAL ECONOMY. – The Trustees of the College invite Applications from Gentlemen desirous of offering themselves as Candidates for the above Professorship. The Trustees propose the allowance to the Professor of a fixed Salary of 250l., in addition to a proportion of the fees to be paid by the Students attending his Classes. It is requested that Applications may be accompanied by Testimonials or References, and that each Candidate will state his Age, Academical

15 April

The one thing requisite to me is invincible determination & perseverance – When I think what discouragement I have gone through I feel sure that the greatest of disappointments cannot permanently shake me.

20 April

What is this poor mind of mine with all its wavering hopes & fears, that its thoughts should be quoted & approved by a great philosopher[1] in the parliament of so great a nation? Do not grant me intellectual power O God unless it be joined to awe of Thee & thy Truth, & to an ever present love of others. For two whole days I have hung about old Westminster[2]

14 May 1866

The matter of this professorship will be settled by the end of this month. Disappointment gloom & despair may often or always be my lot but I must try for the highest which I feel myself capable of. At the worst it is but one poor life lost – and it may be a great stake gained. If anything should go wrong with this prof[n] I have the notion of undertaking a work on the limits & nature of knowledge generally directed to set at rest the discussions between Mill and Hamilton.[3]

Degree, and General Qualifications. Communications addressed 'To the Trustees of the late John Owens, Esq.,' under cover to the Secretary to the Trustees, Mr. J. P. Aston, Solicitor, South King-street, Manchester, on or before the 14th of May next, will be duly attended to, and further information will be furnished if required. It is particularly requested that Applications may not be made to the Trustees individually.

J. G. Greenwood, Principal.
April 11, 1866.   John P. Aston, Secretary to the Trustees.

The establishment of a separate professorship for the teaching of Logic, Philosophy and Political Economy marked the official recognition of a division of subjects which had already come into being, for Jevons was acting as substitute professor of both Political Economy and of Logic and Philosophy. In October 1865 he had taken over the duties of the professorship of Political Economy from Professor Christie, who had combined it with the chair of History and Jurisprudence, and the duties of the professorship of Logic, and Mental and Moral Philosophy from Professor Scott, who had combined it with the professorship of English Language and Literature.

[1] John Stuart Mill.

[2] The sentence ends here, at the bottom of a right-hand page. The top line of the page has been cut off. On turning over, the newspaper cutting of the advertisement of the professorship is pasted into the Journal at the top of the page, presumably at the end of this entry.

[3] Jevons possibly had in mind J. S. Mill, *An Examination of Sir William Hamilton's Philosophy, and of the principal philosophical questions discussed in his writings* (1865). He continued this sentence, '. . . & be to the present time what —— was to a past century' but crossed it out.

The last week or two I have had enough of newspaper fame. I know it is no slight thing to be quoted in the Budget of a Minister[1] when he announces a change in the policy of the country he leads. But what poor mortals we are! I feel as if I would readily give it all for a few kind words from a loving girl. I may some day be rewarded with happiness such as it seems to me others could hardly feel – & if not there is such a thing as working without reward.

14 May

When I read different parts of this book & compare them with each other, recent thoughts or feelings with those I had 10 or 12 years ago I cannot help saying how strange it is. What led me to work to an end I knew not, & to hope where there was nothing to hope? And I cannot but ask is the future to be constant as the past & favoured by the like aid from I know not where? What I do cannot be my doing for I feel too weak for it.

23 May

After so many entries in this fragmentary record when I was anxious and dispirited I should not omit to say that today the professorship is practically mine the committee of Trustees having yesterday decided to submit my name only to the general meeting who will no doubt at once appoint me. I shall now have about £300 a year from the College & nearly £100 from my own money – what can I not do with it?

I should not omit a brief mention of my late visit to London. I had a pleasant meeting at U C L. with old students & others & gave an account of my Abacus. Prof Hirst[2] made an interesting speech & seemed pleased. De Morgan also a day or two afterwards saw it & allowed that it achieved very well the exclusion of contradictories. My visit to Gladstone[3] however was the striking event – which I shall not easily

---

[1] Gladstone had introduced his Budget on 3 May.

[2] Thomas Archer Hirst (1830–92), Professor of Mathematical Physics at University College. On the resignation of De Morgan the following year, he became Professor of Pure and Applied Mathematics (Bellot, op. cit. p. 311).

[3] The visit, which Jevons mentions in a letter of 21 May 1866 to Lucy (see Vol. III, Letter 257) took place shortly before Gladstone introduced his Terminal Annuities Bill on 24 May, to implement the scheme he had proposed in his Budget Speech for reducing the National Debt. It may be presumed that he wished to see Jevons beforehand. The relevance of coal exhaustion was to the fore in the long debate but it is noticeable that Gladstone on this occasion was cautious in referring to the coal argument (Hansard, CLXXXIII (1866) 1220–78). Jevons records a further meeting with Gladstone in 1877 at the Political Economy Club in a letter of 16 December 1877 to his brother Tom, see Vol. III, Letter 507.

forget. As an author to meet a great minister in the height of his power.
Some pleasant hours, partly with MCJ.[1] in the exhibitions theatres
&c filled up my time.

I am too much rewarded – may I strive doubly hard to use aright
whatever power is granted to me.

31 May 1866

This afternoon I was finally and positively appointed Professor of logic
and M & M Phil. & Cobden Professor of Political Economy in Owens
College, by the Trustees in full conclave. Mr Greenwood asked me into
the room and the chairman in a short speech informed me of the
appointment & explained why rules had prevented their making the
app^t earlier. I replied in a short but I suppose suitable speech &
the thing was done.

4 June

I cannot be sufficiently thankful that I have never yet suffered any
conspicuous public failure – on the contrary I have enjoyed almost
uniform success. I feel as if I had escaped untold dangers.[2]

I cannot be too thankful for the happiness that seems to have been
given me.

1 November 1866

My Introductory lecture to the course of Cobden lectures, has brought
some little criticism from the Radicals upon me.[3] I am often troubled

[1] Mary Catherine Jevons, his cousin.
[2] The rest of this page is taken up by a newspaper cutting which has been pasted into the
Journal, announcing his appointment to the professorship:
'OWENS COLLEGE. – The Trustees of Owens College, at their meeting, on Thursday,
elected Mr. Adolphus W. Ward, M.A. fellow and assistant tutor of St. Peter's College,
Cambridge, to the professorship of the English language and literature and of ancient and
modern history; and Mr. W. Stanley Jevons, M.A. fellow of University College, London
(whose treatise on the exhaustion of our coal-fields has recently attracted much attention
in parliament and elsewhere), to the chair of logic, mental and moral philosophy, and
political economy. The vacancies were occasioned by the death of Professor A. J. Scott,
and by the resignation by Professor Christie of the subjects of history and political economy,
he retaining the professorship of jurisprudence. Advantage was taken of the vacancies
occurring at the same time to re-arrange the duties of the two chairs; and for the future
history will be united to the English chair, and political economy to that of logic.'
The next page of the Journal has been torn out. The text on the subsequent page continues 'I cannot be too thankful etc.' and there is no way of knowing whether this was
written on 4 June or at a later date.
[3] *An Introductory Lecture on the Importance of Diffusing a Knowledge of Political Economy*, delivered
in Owens College, Manchester, at the opening of the session of Evening Classes, on 12th

and now more than ever to know how to reconcile my inclinations in political matters. What side am I to take one – the other – or can I take both? I cannot consent with the radical party to obliterate a glorious past – nor can I consent with the conservatives to prolong abuses into the present. I wish with all my heart to aid in securing all that is good for the masses yet to give them all they wish & are striving for is to endanger much that is good beyond their comprehension. I cannot pretend to underestimate the good that the English monarchy & aristocracy with all the liberal policy actuating it, does for the human race, and yet I cannot but fear the pretensions of democracy against it are[1] strong & in some respects even properly strong. This antithesis & struggle perhaps after all is no more than has always more or less existed but is now becoming more marked. Compromise perhaps is the only resource. Those who rightly possess the power in virtue of their superior knowledge must yield up some that they may carry with them the honest but uncertain will of those less educated but more numerous and physically powerful.[2]

4 December 1866

Some few days ago I began thinking about logic again seriously. I was determined to try whether I could not graft on to my system as already printed some extensions which may render it more perfect. After a day or two I suddenly met with what seems to me the great and universal

---

October 1866, by W. Stanley Jevons, M.A., Professor and Cobden Lecturer in Political Economy' (1866). A condition of the endowment of the Cobden Professorship was 'that the professor deliver each session a course of weekly evening lectures, to which any of the public primary school teachers engaged within the boroughs of Manchester or Salford should have free admission' (Thompson, op. cit., p. 288). As Professor of Political Economy Jevons therefore became Cobden Lecturer on the same subject. The object of the lectures was to qualify these teachers to teach political economy to the working-class boys in their schools from the age of about eight years of age and upwards (*Introductory Lecture*, p. 4).

The lecture was a public one and Jevons therefore felt at liberty to make some political remarks about the growth of trade unions. 'There is,' he said, 'one great disaster, almost the greatest that I can figure to myself: It is that our working classes, with their growing numbers and powers of combination, may be led by ignorance to arrest the true growth of our liberty, political and commercial' (loc. cit., pp. 12–13). In the *Manchester Examiner and Times* for 18 and 20 October Jevons was attacked by correspondents for criticising workers' strikes and for discussing the political objections to them and to the enfranchisement of the working classes. In a letter dated 19 October, Jevons explained and defended his position. See below, Vol. III, Letter 268.

[1] 'and' in the text.

[2] Jevons reflects here general public concern with the questions of democratic government and the extension of the franchise to the upper working classes. The defeat of Gladstone's Reform Bill the preceding June had intensified popular agitation for reform.

principle of all reasoning that same things may be treated identically or that whatever we may say of one member of an identity we may say of the other. All logical processes seem to arrange themselves in simple & luminous order in ones mind the moment it is allowed as self evident that if we start from the same beginning & pursue similar paths we must get to similar results. It would be worth while to spend years in developing a system of logic on this basis.

But can I ever finish such a work? My health seems not to be what it was.[1] I have had indigestion gradually coming on & I fear to engage in the work I so much love. I am ready I hope at any time to yield myself up to Him from whom alone can come the power to achieve any worthy result.

I fear again, lest I may be mistaken in other dear hopes which I entertain perhaps too much.[2]

Sunday, 20 January 1867

My notions of a new logic become clearer and clearer as I think about the subject now & then. By working gradually and steadily I know not at what I may not arrive. For six years I have thought about it & my thoughts have gradually penetrated. Give me strength for all that seems before me in no long period of years, if these be granted.

11 February 1867

I have now fully decided on commencing at once a complete work on logic. It is indeed only putting into form the notions I have had for seven years or more, but the work will require several years of hard thinking reading & writing. I should wish to produce a work which will not only embody a new & luminous system but will be readable & read by many. For this purpose it must be devoid of formality & teeming with illustrations. A strict logical sequence must be disguised under a

[1] Some entries in Jevons's private notebook for 1865–6 show his concern about his health. There is a series of pulse readings and on 26 August 1866 the following 'Rules for the Preservation of Health': Walk at least five miles every day, use no omnibuses, no work on Sundays, to bed at 10 p.m., plenty of sleep, no stimulants, no work after 9 p.m., general care in eating and dr'. He wrote to his brother Herbert, '. . . Sometimes I think I have a tendency to the kind of health you used to suffer under viz, low pulse, weak digestion and general depression, but I take great care of my health now, having for some years given up working at nights' (see letter of 28 December 1866 to Herbert, Vol. III, Letter 277).

[2] The next two pages have been torn out of the Journal and without them it is impossible to say in regard to whom Jevons entertained 'dear hopes'. The following page contains the entry for 12 March 1867 but the two next entries are to be found further on in the book.

tempting variety of subjects. The best years of my life now coming may well be given to such a work.[1]

12 March 1867

Sometimes I am in low spirits now and distrust my future – £900 of my money are profitless & in jeopardy[2] – moreover I am unsociable, ill-tempered & feel that I deserve no more than a hermits life of self denial & labour. But if I can do so with any safety to my health I will labour hoping that the success hitherto accorded me in a less important field will not be wanting in a greater. I excuse myself for writing in this book because I sometimes find it a wonderful comfort to read over the record of my past hopes & despair, & observe how my hopes have been almost constantly better founded than my despair.

21 May 1867

I cannot describe in words the soreness of the conflict of[3] in my mind. I have long ago exhausted my own judgment in trying to decide the right course. Such indecision is unmanly and yet the conflict of duty, of feeling, of prudence is more than I can resolve. May I be guided to the right!

19 November 1867

a great change has come over my prospects and I cannot express sufficiently the thankfulness I have felt at my happy prospects of

---

[1] This book was to be *The Principles of Science*, published exactly seven years later in February 1874. Jevons meantime published a sketch of the fundamental logical doctrine embodied in this book in his small work *The Substitution of Similars, The True Principle of Reasoning, Derived from a modification of Aristotle's Dictum* (1869). In the preface to this, his second book on logic, he writes: 'All acts of reasoning seem to me to be different cases of one unifom process, which may perhaps be best described as the *substitution of similars*; this phrase clearly expresses that familiar mode in which we continually argue by analogy from *like to like*, and take one thing as a representative of another. The chief difficulty consists in showing that all the forms of the old logic, as well as the fundamental rules of mathematical reasoning, may be explained upon the same principle; and it is to this difficult task I have devoted most attention.' Jevons's application of the Law of the Substitution of Similars in economic theory in the form of the Law of Indifference has been noted by Dr W. Mays in his article, 'Jevons' Conception of Scientific Method', *The Manchester School* (September 1962) p. 248.

[2] It would appear that this sum comprised £600 invested in the North Wales quarry company of his brother-in-law, John Hutton, and £300 in the Liverpool Shipping firm of Booth & Co. (Unpublished letters of 17 May 1865 and 9 July 1868 to Jevons from his brother Herbert.) [3] Jevons appears to have left out a word here.

marriage.[1] I know now how right I was in thinking that the love of a wife & the tranquillity of a home were needful to me if only to enable me to work better than before.

I always feared that I could hardly marry without sacrificing objects which have hitherto almost filled my soul. But to my delight Harriet is far from jealous of 'my old love' my work; she promises to aid it to join in it, to esteem it as her own, & to find a pride & gratification in it. Her good sense is surpassed only by her affection. From the bottom of my heart I thank my God for what seems to me sure to fill up my cup of usefulness & happiness in this world. Now indeed I have much to work for. It is new to me to feel that anothers happiness is in my hands & that I can make her happiness. I have not hitherto felt that the greatest efforts at kindness & sociability which I could make appreciably added to others happiness. With her it is far otherwise.[2]

I have not much else to record. My mind was so unsettled during the summer that I found myself almost incapable of work. I spent the vacation first in London in intolerable solitude – then for 10 days at the Paris Exposition;[3] then in Holland & Belgium for a week or two.

On getting back to Manchester I set rather hard to work at my new logic reading a good deal for it, & advancing well. I also commenced the final designs for my reasoning machine & advertised for its construction.[4] Just before the commencement of the session, irresistible circumstances led me to the happy step which I hope will bring about my marriage this day month.[5] Since then I have had a press of engagements not unnaturally to add to which I found it necessary to undertake a new course of lectures on Political Economy & Statistics to raise my afternoon class to more fair proportions in which at great cost of trouble I have partially succeeded having now 7 students in place of 2 or 3 in previous years. This has led me temporarily to substitute statistical for logical work. My machine has struggled forward as best it could under

---

[1] Jevons had become engaged to Harriet Ann Taylor at the beginning of October 1867 (see Biographical Introduction, p. 47 above). Writing to his brother Herbert on 23 October 1867 Jevons said: '. . . I have to tell you of my engagement to marry Harriet Ann Taylor, the sister of Fred's wife. You have more than once advised me in your letters to take a step of this kind; and the fact is that, for some years past, ever since I had a fair prospect of an income, I have felt myself impelled towards it by every motive that ought to influence me. I have always been, more than anyone, I think, in need of a wife and a quiet domestic life; and, to all appearances, I have now secured these great benefits. . . .' (LJ, p. 237.)

[2] 'different' has been substituted here in LJ, p. 238.

[3] The Paris International Exhibition, 1867.

[4] At the end of September Jevons had 'found a young clockmaker in Salford, who has begun to work for me at thirty-five shillings a week'. See letter of 25 September 1867 to Herbert, Vol. III, Letter 280.

[5] The marriage took place on 19 December 1867 at the Presbyterian Chapel at Altrincham near Manchester.

constant interruptions & I much fear now that much of it must be reconstructed before it can work properly.[1]

19 March 1869

This book has long been closed and is opened but that I may record the death of my best & noblest of brothers Roscoe.[2] He it was who inspired me with whatever love of knowledge and of labour I may have. Why was the work given to the weaker hand? Why was his life a living death when his place could not be filled? The more I think of past times the more I cherish the slightest memories of him; the more I love to read the broken record of his secret feelings & to find therein companionship.

Happy beyond measure, successful more than I ever dared to wish, with life and a life long work yet before if God still grant it to me, it is a deep sorrow to me that he should sink to death through such a clouded life. Why should he be taken thus & I left? But if it be the will of God I will fill his place as far as strength of body or of mind will serve me.

His was the saddest of lives. It is a mystery how such thoughts of virtue as filled his mind could spring so early & so strongly.

[1] In June the following year Jevons began a new machine. He wrote to Herbert, '. . . I have been very busily engaged, the last two or three weeks, on my logical machine, having begun a new one altogether. I have now got it to work fairly . . .' (see letter of 23 June 1868, Vol. III, Letter 300). This machine was completed in September 1869. See letter of 1 September 1869 to Lucy, LJ, p. 249.

[2] Roscoe Jevons died on 18 March 1869, aged 40. This entry, the last in the Journal, was made about three-quarters of the way through the book, overpage from the previous chronological entry.

APPENDIX

Diary[1] of a Journey to the Gold Diggings at Sofala
March 9th–March 23rd, 1856

9 March Sunday

The weather to be expected this morning had been an anxious subject but it turned out most encouragingly.

To the S E, a handsome storm cloud rose high above the horizon with immensely tall piled cumuli, but in fact more handsome than threatening while soon after a few scattered flying traces of cumulus further convinced us we were to have a fine day for the first at all events.

About a quarter to nine oclock we started, fully equipped, reaching the New town station after a hard walk by nine. Here was all the decorum & app^(ce) of a town life to be encountered with which we were little inclined to agree

From Sydney to Parramatta the country is of a poor rough valueless app^(ce) being covered with gum trees & low scrub or bush, the only variations being in the height & thickness. In one place old half dead stumps, with twisted bare arms, surrounded at their base by low bushes & young gum tree saplings, at other places close tall well conditioned trees. Fire too has also in many places bared large spaces tall blackened poles alone remaining until a new growth shall have sprung up, but from this part Sydney has to be supplied with fire wood and while money is to be made, trees will never in Australia be spared for mere ornament, so that large tracts are being gradually cleared & left ugly & barren, as other parts near Sydney already are.

Just before entering the town of Parramatta from the station we reached the Penrith road which we were going to follow.

Parramatta is a pleasantly situated little town being on a sort of flat between undulating hills among which runs the Parramatta river. It is very squarely laid out & with decent regular buildings, generally of red brick, and a proportion of gardens & trees throughout can be said to have a cheerful & happy app^(ce). Of the Penrith Road to describe 100 yards is to describe the whole; after passing a little bush it is a good

---
[1] This account is written in a notebook approximately 7½ in. by 4½ in.; the first 14 pages contain meteorological records.

straight road, fenced with interminable three rail fences and running over continuously & nicely undulated land very lightly timbered. Care has here been taken to cut down the old & useless trees alone, so that what remain are of more uniform size & better app^ce.

12.15 Then on top of ant hill in sun just covered with earth 137°.5

Camped during middle of day in piece of plantation like ground, lighting our fire, making tea &c for first time. Tea though made of thin muddy water not to be despised.

About 4 PM recommenced journey with difficulty passing a creek on which is situated a small village Toongabbee formed chiefly of neat comfortable little inns. Passed at once into a thick wood of different character from all before in which scrubby ill-formed trees of singular app^ce almost predominated over gum trees. Here we soon lighted our second fire, which I may say is so easily done that it is like lighting up the ground; one or two handfuls of dry leaves commence the blaze, and the dead rotten sticks of which enough generally lie within one or two yards circumference soon burning entirely & give a fine heat. It is singular to observe the good feeling or at least friendly behaviour of people to each other as they are out of towns & living in the woods. One felt quite surprized at the number of good mornings & good evenings received & people seeing your fire at night shout you a good night from a distance most likely without seeing those it is intended for.

The night was clouded often I think with cumulus & some light drops of rain fell at one time. I did not sleep well the first night being more in a sort of dose than sleep, but getting up in the morning before it was yet light I found myself fully refreshed & none the worse.

My dry & wet Bulb hygrometer I had missed the night before & could not now find.

March 9th We continued our way along the same straight road, our loads lightened however for M^r O Connel left behind his carpet bag, & the provisions I carried were diminished. The road, is in almost a straight line and over a continual succession of low hilly ranges running at right angles to its direction. In every hollow we generally found a pool or creek of water so that it could not be said to be scarce, but this no doubt is owing to the recent rain. The country here may be said to improve in app^ce as well as in reality every mile you go; the grass being richer & forming a little closer cover to the ground, which as far as one could see is deeper in soil & does not contain ironstone gravel. The gum trees though as monotonous as ever are more gracefully & thinly disposed and often large square portions of land at the road side are cleared & either bearing crops of nearly ripe Indian corn or garden produce or used as pasture.

11 PM We nearly reached Penrith before camping. The Blue moun-

tains now give a little variety to the scene, which would otherwise remain exactly the same except that the hills & dales are wider between as we proceed. Other high ground seems to lie between us & the Mountains.

2m fr Penrith. A quarry on top of hill from which road metal *had* been taken. Rock is a sort of shaley hard dirty-greenish sandstone, appearing to be *bedded* & to cleave in a very irregular manner. In many points resembling both the shale & sandstone of Sydney but very much harder.

Section of country

Between Toongabbee & Penrith in a fine flat open space pleasantly surrounded with woods is St Mary's a newly settled nice looking town, the houses one storied verandah cottages often of brick arranged as in all the other villages along the road for the distance of about a mile. The number of decent little inns is surprizing: here are a few general shops.

5 PM River Nepean 30.105 87°7
       Temp. of Water 778   Air 758

There are a few points worth observing about the River Nepean. It is a fine stream of water about 120 or 130 yards across, running or rather lying, the current being little observable between steep banks of very deep alluvial earth. Where an approach to the new bridge had been cut a section of 10 or 15 feet was exposed & no doubt the earth, which was of fine soft substance & brown from organic matter must have extended considerably deeper. It was perfectly pure & its richness was proved by the appearance of the fields & gardens on each side.

In advancing, however through Emu[1] plains, the soil dwindled away in thickness, very low hillocks or other beds showing themselves where the ground was penetrated. Immediately beneath the soil was a layer of fine brick red clayey earth the colour very bright, the thickness of this was very uncertain & it rested on large deposits of large gravel in parts almost consisting of small boulders. These were of a size from 1-6 inches & composed of granite[2] and other hard rocks. This gravel has been quarried for road metal.

The beds just described, causing evident poorness in the land above which remained as a sort of common about Emu, running N & S

---

[1] 'Ema' in the text.
[2] Jevons then wrote 'Gneiss?' in brackets, but crossed it out.

parallel to the continuous hilly range which rises abruptly out of Emu plains. This we ascended for a short distance but tired turned off the road to the left. Searching for a sleeping place we got into the top of a little gully with evident signs of a recent stream. Following it down therefore we soon hit upon several pools some of which lying in crevices of sandstone rock contained beautifully sweet & pure water. Other ponds on the clayey bottom, I could not avoid noticing retained a large muddy sediment which had not subsided as among rocks.

On looking about us, the spot about the pools struck one as the most beautiful camping place conceivable. In a narrow crushed gully on the side of a steep hill shut in so as completely to exclude all notice or interruption, it was adorned by graceful gumtrees thinly placed, & by flowering bushes (similar to those near Sydney) which spread a pleasant odour all about. In the centre of a circle of these we camped, the pools affording me a bath, as well as water for tea, & the bushes a partial shelter from dew & wind.

About 5 PM it became evident we were to have a thunder storm.

Large masses of cloud spread out & moved |60 much more of a cumulus & cirrous character, But loftier & more to North were branches & streamers of $\searrow$ reading past zenith. The scroll like edge was sometimes visible an evap^n of the foremost cumulous portions. Rainfalls in various places, one *very heavy* shower of small & definite area, remaining nearly stationary about a mile off, for some time. A few drops fell on us, & occasional thunder near & almost overhead was heard accompanied with one or two flashes sufficient to be observed. The storm cloud advanced furthest to N. where a singular cumulus mass. To South a distinct row of cumuli, flat & terminating in a distinct line parallel to mountains Afterwards flattening to a stratous shape, sky otherwise clear but a line of small regular or in parts large flat cumuli parrallel to coast, and possibly over sea.

Clouds afterwards clearing off entirely leaving bright sky.

During storm very loose scud very evident moving rapidly |320 beneath crown of storm cloud & almost through rain falls.

Aneroid barometer readings

29.440	677	First turn of road above Emu
29.368	69	DB 640 WB 640
		(657)?

Mist among the trees.

Pilgrim in 29.259   70 Temp 64°

10 March

At camp above Emu passed an uneasy night in spite of the convenience of the place; not getting to sleep till after midnight. Night was very undisturbed, the occasional notes of the birds with the croakings of frogs & a screech of some animal now & then being the only sounds heard.

Awakened a little before six and a little before seven had had breakfast dressed & packed up.

During the night much mist had collected over many parts which rising formed about this time & quite complete then uniform covering which while we were ascending the high ground gradually broke up.

At about 7.30 The mist was rising from off Emu plains & the river Nepean, and presented a singular resemblance to flat loose cumulus clouds as seen in the atmosphere. Stratous forms could scarcely be distinguished. Above Emu the road rising very steeply the gullies & heights of King's tableland. The first ravine with nearly perpendicular sides still covered everywhere by the ceaseless gumtrees now varied by a few different varieties & trees of different order presented a pleasing contrast to the dull succession of flats & undulated hills which we had passed[1]

These mountains are entirely composed of sandstone, generally reddish & a little coarse; the beds appeared to dip to the East or perhaps S. of E. The road which wound round the sides of ravines or followed the tops of the ridges was exceedingly well made being no doubt the work of numbers of convicts sent to labour on the roads. It was indeed a well finished work with water channels strong railings & one bridge. As we proceed higher, we reached a layer of mist lying among the trees which were dripping with wet, but I do not think this was any distinct vapour plane. The road rises continually over these ranges and it was very interesting to watch the gradual sinking of the Aneroid barometer as higher regions of the atmosphere were reached.[2]

The manner in which mist lay among the trees in these gullies was, portions seeming to lie hid, & afterwards rise in loose detached clouds. Early in the morning a nearly uniform covering had been formed of

---

[1] Jevons wrote 'Lapstone Hill' in the margin at the left-hand side of the page beside this passage.

[2] Jevons recorded the following observations at the top of this page in the notebook:

Hill 1 mile fr 17 Mile Hollow

5407.	28.018	793	
10.10.	11th March		
Vapour plane reached			
27.117	64	558	558

risen mist, but this soon broke up, & evaporated am In attempting to take the direc. of some loose masses I found that above the range on which I was the clouds around had every various direction from Nly E to S.

Regular detached cumulus then above remained, in small quantities About noon heavy drops of rain began to fall very unexpectedly. This increased and continued for about a quarter of an hour as an exceedingly heavy shower but very little cloud appearing overhead (is this from slanting fall of rain) & blue sky in most parts of sky except West (this shower is most probably like that seen at distance yesterday) There were at the same time a few *rattling* thunderclaps.

Soon after various thunder clouds passed rapidly over from W, known by their curled curious edges, but their form would not be made out distinctly.

During the afternoon we had a fine walk over ranges gradually rising but not otherwise differing from those passed. From one part a fine open view of the country was obtained, appearing to be beautiful flat planes, over which hung a cumulus see fig P29[1] which for magnificence & beauty I have not seen surpassed.

Its summit rose distinctly into a quantity of hazy cirrous cloud. Other piled masses of cumulus were visible & the sky was clouding over in many parts in a threatening manner.

[1] See sketch reproduced above.

About 6 PM it became evident that a thunderstorm lay to the W fast approaching. We therefore put up at a small roadside in at 19 Mile (24 mile?) Hollow. The cloud was not remarkable but a singular red light was cast under it for some time at sunset. About 8 PM the storm was overhead; though not hearing I observed several splendid flashes one I believe trifurcated as in figure a fig b was a remarkably brilliant flash.

After passing the frequency of the flashes increased an immense number seeming exactly over same spot in an extraordinarily quick succession.

the[1] inn at which we were was kept by a comfortable old man who did nothing but sit at his door & gossip. He had a family some of them very nice children

About their manner of living in these solitary places there seemed a great deal of simplicity. Their manner of getting supplies is also very simple; for meat they take several sheep or a bullock from any passing flock or herd going to town, for which they pay the shepherd on his return at Sydney prices. The best meat is thus obtained & the owner no loser.

To judge by the tea & breakfast which we got for 2s each, things must be very plentiful here. A bed also is 2s Oconnel & I being in one bed in a small room, & a drayman in the other

In the morning March 11th a complete foggy cover lay over everything About 7 it broke up a little wind being from 200°, but only disclosed a thick stratous veil, of very threatening appee above.

We continued ascending ranges similar to those of yesterday, the covering becoming more threatening until at last we reached a true vapour plane where everything appeared enveloped in very thin mist.

[1] Jevons began this sentence with 'In' but crossed it out.

Soon after rain began & very fine, indeed quite drizzling but at times falling a deal more heavily.

We passed several Inns situated at distances of about 3 miles & being the only habitations on these mountainous parts. At one place called Weather Board, there was no accommodation but a few huts upon a space of the dreariest app^{ce} possible having been apparently [laid] bare of all vegetation & of most [of]^1 the soil by recent floods

We continued walking through rain & mist till we reached Blackheath where we engaged a room at the Inn The weather at this time surpassed all I have seen for dampness & coldness; a very cold & quite saturated wind was blowing from ESE filled with watery particles half rain half mist or cloud. A still more singular thing was mist seemed continually to rise from the ground & road being blown along with the wind giving it the app^{ce} of *steaming*. The coldness was surprizing & most miserable to us who were anything but dry.

The rock about here though still continuing sandstone has changed in app^{ce} being in parts filled with small quartz of less than 1 inch diam. In parts layers appeared almost to be called conglomerate; the stone also was much more ferruginous, hardened veins running through it.

Mount Victoria Inn

27.345　71　64°　Had no rain at all here, only mist and dew (The landlord of Kings Arms Inn 24 m Hollow informed me that 10 Months ago, a horse standing in front of the inn was struck dead by lightning, a servant at the same time being stunned.

At Pulpit Hill on 11th I heard a stroke had fallen near on previous night, a loud report of thunder being simultaneous with flash.

After passing 17 m Hollow Tollbar *Spring water* was found especially in a well made by the road makers possibly. I saw a blue slate^2 looking stratum in sandstone at level of water, which was of excellent quality

March 12th Encamped in hut, in Convict village 5 m fr Bowen^{fels} This morning got breakfast at the Blackhut Hotel with Mr Woods driver of the luggage van and a wild black looking digger with whom had some talk

Started along a road not differing for a long way from that passed. On the whole it descended and it was in much better condition for travelling. Weather was same also thick & foggy & very threatening.

We now approached the part of the mountains called Mount Victoria, though this name does not appear to me to be given to any particular emminence. The sandstone became very ferruginous, (or pos-

---

^{1} Jevons omitted these words.　　　　^{2} Jevons wrote 'slat'.

sibly a little manganeseous too) & we came to a bed of either white
hardened shale or (limestone?) also red & other hardened shales & a
little conglomerate. The ridges became by degrees more precipitous
till we reached a large valley surrounded by remarkable Mountain
masses of sandstone of peculiar form the fig. being one very characteristic & singular. We were now descending rapidly into a fine wide
valley beautifully wooded in the centre of which lay a small village,
Little Hartley. Now too, a few boulders of granite gave notice that

the sedimentary formation had been suddenly exchanged for primary
rocks. An alpine stream ran over granite boulders down the middle of
this valley. The land became rich & of cheerful beautiful app^ce. The
trees too about thus changed the gums having long narrow & very
drooping leaves instead of still cordate ones; the app^ce is far more
graceful

A few miles further on we passed through the township of Hartley
consisting of Courthouse Chapel, several neat inns & a few houses
beautifully situated on the side of the stream among picturesque granite
hills covered as everywhere by trees. The road passed these hills in a
totally different manner to the sandstone ranges of the Blue Mountains
winding round their sides & descending valleys instead of following
continuous ridges. Proceeding, the sandstone, now very ferruginous
appeared again slightly even forming tall rocky hills.

A mile before Hartley we stopped to eat dinner at an old womans hut where we had seen the following notices.

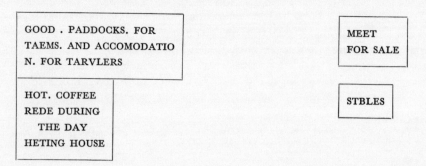

| GOOD . PADDOCKS. FOR TAEMS. AND ACCOMODATIO N. FOR TARVLERS | MEET FOR SALE |
| HOT. COFFEE REDE DURING THE DAY HETING HOUSE | STBLES |

However she gave us a pretty good dinner at the usual rate of 2ˢ, but we had gratis a deal of talk about all her own concerns, & how she had settled on the spot 16 years ago & lived there her husband being a Government man

She had a man staying there & working for his *keep*, of fine handsome & intelectual app^ce but who had fallen short of money & could not get to the diggings. He talked very sensibly about gold digging and at him as well as many other diggers I have met I have been astonished at for their intelligence, & respectability, nothing about them appearing *low* We proceeded through a straggling but pleasant village Bowenfels, the rocky hills assuming a constant picturesque & singular shape as thinly wooded all over but so as to allow fine rich grass to grow between,

the land now becoming suitable for pasturage & inhabitation. The rocks beneath varied much being often of disintegrated granite, the feldspathic small crystals of which formed a sort of quartz. The road was often cut through masses of soft granite.

Turning off the Sofala road we rather injudiciously entered upon a long solitary portion of road (4 PM) the nearest Inn being 5 miles.

The scenery became finer & finer at each turn, with steep lofty ranges of hills & fine valleys traversed by streamlets. The rock became a hard slate breaking into parallelopic portions. Becoming very tired we looked about for a camping place though the weather was very cold &

threatened rain. I espied a small stone erection & upon ascending a bare slate hill we found a number of roughly built slate fire places which had evidently at some time belonged to houses forming a regular village. This was no doubt a convict settlement, & the deserted, wild, dreary app^ce of the place brought to ones mind forcibly the circumstances in which they had been built & inhabited & the character of the inhabitants and we found one more complete than the rest which had no doubt been used for camping many a time before and after 1 or 2 hours and[1] roofed it in a little with boughs collected fire wood & settled ourselves for a cold night in the best manner we could.

March 13th Convict settlement

Bowenfels 4 miles. On awakening at sunrise we found ourselves none the worse for a night in the mountains; & even quite comfortably warm. The night had been very fine & clear, & a few cirrous & stratous patches were all the cloud now visible. A little mist was rising from two or three places. Numbers of black & white Australian magpies were flying about, or perching on the ruined huts trees & the scene was wild & remarkable.

We pushed on along the road which presented little novelty in any way. The land was somewhat descending quite uninhabited & consisting of wild timbered hills of slate rock, the cleavage & bedding in places very distinct. The sky gradually clouded with ordinary cumulus.

After a few miles we reached Rydall, where was a small public house & a little cultivated land. Here the road at once commenced a steep ascent & for some miles it ran with an uninterrupted rise winding round & nearly over the summit of a lofty hill, I believe Honeysuckle Hill. From the high point I obtained the finest distant view I had had, looking South over the fine wide beautifully wooded valley beneath with small spaces of cleared & cultivated land & beyond & to the east over a succession of hills & ranges, the more distant ones distinguishable by their shape & app^ce as of different character from the nearer. I climbed

---

[1] Jevons completed this sentence three pages further on in the book.

a short way to the summit of the hill where I took my highest barometer observ. The rock I am not sure of, but was very likely of the
same slate. The descent was as long & tiresome nearly as the ascent,
but we had evidently entered a new region of country. The land was
irregularly undulating & richer than any we had yet seen.

Large spaces now appeared to be cultivated and there were several
small villages of log huts This in fact I think must be one of the best
tracts of country. When very thirsty I got a drink of a pint of milk
for 3^d, such as I have never tasted except in the country at home.

We pushed on after dinner till past sunset arriving just before dark
of an inn beautifully situated at the foot of the last hills bordering the
plains of the Macquarie The general app^{ce} of the place most rural &
pleasant. The road had been somewhat uninteresting, quartz now
appearing the greater distance to be the surface rock. The landlord of
this 'New Inn' was a specimen of a perfect blackguard such as I should
be sorry to meet often again. In app^{ce} resembling Mr Forbes of Sydney
notoriety, drunk & swaggering, & wishing to pass himself off as a much
greater rogue than I think he would have the heart to be, he bored us
all the evening with accounts of his life & future, a mixture no doubt
of as much lies as truth. However we slept comfortably there, and were
well entertained at the same rates.

14 March

In the morning I found my feet very sore from blisters and it was with
great difficulty that I could proceed.

The road passed through land slightly undulated & gradually descending into the plains of the Macquarie. The trees began to thin off in
a surprizing manner, the gums too appearing to be poorer. It lay I fancy
on quartz rock

At last we suddenly reached the plains, the app^{ce} of which at once
strikes a person as extremely remarkable & a contrast to all we had
passed. The woods & bush terminate at an almost well defined line all
along the eastern boundary of the plains, which are seen extending in
gentle slopes, out of sight to N & S, & to the foot of further barren
ranges to the W. The ground may be said to be absolutely bare of trees,
excepting a very few acacia trees standing out with their dark green
foliage against the unvaried greenish brown of the plain, upon which
they are scattered in twos & threes at very distant intervals. The depth
of the earth appears generally very great, perhaps 5 feet, strongly resembling in this & other features the Emu plains. Here we meet a fact
strikingly illustrative of the Australian climate. The Emu plains were

covered with a cheerful green sward, the Macquarie plains were more like the floor of an empty barn, covered with loose short hay, for on account of excessive dryness & heat the grass had lost its green & appeared quite scorched up. We were informed by a Colonial born girl who had scarcely been beyond these plains in her life and in her communicativeness & ease was quite a character, that there had been no rain for a long time. That during hot winds the heat is most excessive here, and is increased almost to stifling by the bush burning all round, & by the very grass of the plains catching fire & burning over large extents.

Through the plains a distance of about 8 miles the walk was the more severe I ever remember, there being no shelter from the direct rays of the sun, except under two acacia trees near the house where the girl lived from who we got a water melon & some peaches for refreshment

In nearing the Macquarie river to which the plains slightly descend on both sides, but irregularly so as to form creeks & branches in the hollows, thick beds of coarse gravel were to be seen formed entirely of quartz pebbles in this way both resembling & being distinct from the Emu plains.

The ground the natural surface of which seemed always to have formed the road, was of such surprizing hardness & dryness as to be easily mistaken for solid rock. It must now have been intensely heated causing very distinct refractions, as well as preceptibly hot & cold gusts of air.

With the Macquarie river I was greatly disappointed. Its bed was broad, nearly as wide as the Nepean, rather flat at the bottom & with perpendicular curiously worn banks of earth. But a little water however ran in it, covering a small portion of the bottom. The tributary creek too had much the same form.

Crossing the river by an excellent bridge, we reached the town after ½ miles walk, and being excessively fatigued went into the first inn that appeared. We found we missed the comfort plenty & simplicity of a country inn & country people, for a low public house, where was nothing but drunkennous and swearing.

In the afternoon we wandered for an hour about the town which requires but a few sentences to describe it. It is a portion of the plane laid out in rectangular streets, half filled up in a very straggling manner by a succession of red brick houses & stores presenting scarcely the best app^{ce} of ornament or variety. Several square blocks in the centre seem to have been reserved by Government forming a sort of[1] large 'Place', one end of which is partly occupied by two ugly red brick churches, & by a gaol the most prominent & noticeable building in the place.

[1] Jevons wrote 'a' here.

Around this Square it must be said there were extensive & well furnished stores & shops, one bank, (the Union) and a house or two but beyond there everything was most second rate. The people too appeared to be of but one class, a hard money getting utterly unintellectual race of gold diggers & tradesmen. It is the centre of all business of division of N.S.W. in which it stands, & it is indeed a mere exchange & market & seems not to suggest a thought of what is not strict business & money getting. In my life I never passed through streets with less interest & pleasure & in the people, untasteful situation & everything the feeling was fully borne out. I bought a shirt & socks as cheaply as they could be had in Sydney.

Weather

Early, patches of cirrus & stratus were alone to be seen, somewhat wavering during morning regular cumulus beginning to form moving |NW. In Afternoon accumulated heavily to S with some masses of frilled cumulus, & other thundery signs.

6 PM Heavy fall of rain from large cumuli, topped with cirrostratus & with stratous signs, over hills to Eastward, & causing very distinct scraps of rainbow.

8 PM A storm of forked lightning to East. Afterwards clearing off.

Over Macquarie plains I saw a large cumulous cloud overhead the lower side of which reflected an unusual brownish light, which I think must have been the actual reflected colour of the plane naturally lighted by the suns rays.

Sunday 16 March

Very much disliking our lodging at the Bushman's Inn Bathurst, we preferred walking on to staying over Sunday for the Mail. The characters we met at the inn were indeed of the lowest sort, especially the female, and if as I understand the same is the case in most others the place must indeed be a low one.

To get out of Bathurst we had to undergo 3 or 4 miles of the same detestable broiling plains as we crossed in coming into it, & the heat nearly knocked O Connell up who began to complain of dysentery. When we reached the edge of the plains there was still some miles of the same sort of land but slightly undulated, absolutely devoid of water and with ordinary gum trees so thinly scattered as to afford no shelter. Walking over this sort of land is indeed quite a torture. At last the turn of a hill brought us in sight of a rocky hill which seemed immediately to relieve us & inspire us with fresh spirit. At the foot of this range of hills ran a beautiful creek containing plenty of water to quench the intolerable thirst which seizes you before you have gone a mile.

At this spot granite rock appeared as a very coarse red stone containing which[1] quartz crystals. We proceeded along the road a few miles further over undulating hills running between low hilly ranges forming a sort of valley between. The lower parts of this valley seemed generally rich & were much cultivated.

We put up early in the afternoon at a little newly formed village Peel, placed on the edges of a flat through which runs a creek. The accomodation here was the worst we had encountered. For beds two sofas were assigned us with a few sheets & blankets, but finding the fleas intolerable we soon made beds of our own on the floor. This place & the characters we met there were on the whole uninteresting, with the exception of 'Corbow' an Aborigine belonging to the tribe of this district and a better specimen of the race than is to be met with in Sydney. This one had a serious cut on his head from the tomahawk of another black but it seemed to trouble him little and his only want was 'rum'.

Monday 17 March

On account of waiting for breakfast we did not start till about nine & then got on very slowly M[r] OConnell being anything but well.

The road was over rocky lightly timbered hills, & undulating land, occupying the valleys & presented little new interest. The rocky formation was altered but I do not know the names or characters of many of the rocks passed over. The commonest was a finely laminated shistose sort of mineral of greenish grey colour. Gravel & rough fragments of quartz were found everywhere.

We dined at the Wyagden Inn, an extraordinary wooden construction of considerable size, inhabited almost entirely by a number of females, in a way not easy to understand the reason of.

Here we were told that the nearest diggings were four miles off, & at 5 oclock in the evening we determined to push on there to the nearest Inn. For a mile or two the country was the same as we had passed through becoming more picturesque, but just as the twilight was ceasing we reached an immensely steep & high hill not to be equalled throughout the journey to difficulty of ascent, but to cut the account of a long walk short, after successive disappointments, misdirections, and a mistake, of the best road it must have been nearly ten oclock before we reached an inn, which was only 3 miles from Sofala, being at the end of the Wattle flats nearest that town.

The Public house was a rude wooden[2] but entering it, the scene somewhat surprised me even on the diggings. About half a dozen diggers

---

[1] Jevons probably intended to write 'white' here.
[2] Jevons appears to have left out a word here.

it being St Patrick's day had thought proper to get fairly drunk, and between their app^{ce} & their drunken performances seemed more like a set of devils & they seemed for some time to find amusement in teazing us two[1] strangers until the landlord, a mild, decent & probably honest man took us into his rude kitchen where he had got us ready a very good supper of the usual dishes with tea to drink. He seemed indeed quite kindly disposed towards us but having all his beds full of these drunken devils we were obliged to turn out afterwards & seek a sleeping place in the bush. Being excessively tired the choice of the place was a matter of no difficulty, and under a bush, among hard sharp rocks, we spent a good night better indeed than we had had on the floor of the Peel Inn, 'The Golden Pippin'

Tuesday 18 March

The night before I had collected a number of dry *clumps* of wood, and a nice little fire which I had made with them kept alight all night. We were much refreshed in the morning, and for a wash I descended the gully on the side of which we had slept, finding it a deep one with the bed of a torrent at the bottom running over large smooth hard rocks (of bluish colour, like road metal) with veins. At present there was no stream but only pools of clear water.

For breakfast we again visited our friendly host at the public house, where we had a comfortable private breakfast. One of the drunken devils of the previous evening was washing himself & now[2] when sober looked like a steady, almost quiet man

While breakfast was preparing the landlord walked down with us to a few diggings near, which being the first of what we have heard so much about, we looked upon with great interest. It was a dry diggings meaning

one not upon the sides of any constant stream or river, the water for washing being obtained occasionally from rain or a supply kept in water holes.

It was along the bottom of a hollow, the holes being sunk perhaps

---

[1] Jevons wrote 'to' here.   [2] Jevons wrote 'no' here.

generally 10 feet through earth & clay containing pebbles & very various small boulders.

But 2 or 3 holes were being worked at this time the rest being old ones, & the landlord told us that the only diggers staying here were men with families who had built themselves houses, & so settled down with gardens &c that the gold was almost a secondary thing.

I was surprised to meet such a respectable man as our host in such a place; His wife too seemed a nice person, and his family of girls & boys chiefly young were modest & nice looking. About the house were also some slight signs of refinement & education such as are generally nowhere to be seen hereabouts.

The road to Sofala (Sŏfălă) lay over steep & very picturesque hills only half covered with trees. On advancing into a valley of more than ordinary beauty we unexpectedly discovered the town & renowned diggings in a flat on the side of the Turon river which lay with very winding course at the foot of the principal range of hills to the north of us.

The town struck one from the first with great astonishment & amusement. It was indeed a queerer place than I could have thought even the diggings, consisting of two parallel streets very close to each other, irregularly lined with the most curious collection of huts tents & weatherboard houses. A few stood out from the rest for size & finish but these & two or three buildings which seemed to be churches & chapels resembled most in space & app^ce childrens toy houses & had poles & small flags before their doors to attract attention & show their superiority. We looked for a busy scene of gold digging, the scramble for the previous metal, but saw only a solitary man here & there in the distance, and the place altogether seemed without animation.

After resting some time in a deserted wooden house above the town we descended into it, & walked along one of the streets with some degree of interest. Our dinner however was of the most interest at present so we selected a quiet looking public house, near the extremity of the place & applied for dinner, which was shortly given us in a back kitchen. This house was of heterogeneous construction, logs, bark, & boards being employed besides a quantity of calico & other stuffs.

The landlord here too was a decent pleasant man, rather young, and we had much conversation with him about digging & such things. It happened that at this very time three diggers were adventuring a hole in the yard of this house, the landlord no doubt having a share of profits. They had sunk a shaft 30 feet deep, & were not yet on the bottom & were therefore in suspense as to success. The next day we were informed that the rock was reached at 33 feet & gold found but not in sufficient quantity to pay for carrying the stuff to the river to wash.

Soon after dinner I left Mr OConnell to rest himself, & set off on my first inspection of the diggings. I passed Westward along the main & lower Street, booking myself at the Sofala Inn for the Bathurst mail on Thursday; I then went on over the hills & along the banks of the river in the same direction. The river as it is at present runs between low rounded hills; these are sometimes formed of the basement rock, a hard, red slaty? rock, but generally are vast & rather singular alluvial deposits. Several of these latter seemed to have been the richest spots, & their whole surface was rooted up, turned over in rough large heaps, & tunnelled under. The present banks of the river, for the whole length were almost entirely excavated & disfigured by all sorts of working and the flat gravelly bed of the river even was dug up channelled or covered with large heaps of gravel & coarse sand & mud, the tailings of the

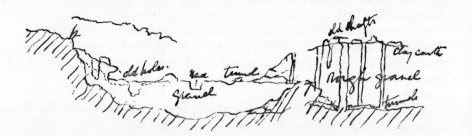

working for the Gold that had been gained in the past five years The figure gives some idea of the general section of the river.

I had some conversation with several diggers who were at work, and they generally appeared to be good humoured and communicative. They[1] all represented the place as being *worked out*, the parts which

[1] 'the' in the text.

alone were known to pay being so cut up by old shafts, tunnels, &c; that a new claim could scarcely be chosen without the chance of hitting on some old workings. Many men worked now only the pillars formerly left standing to support the roof, replacing them with wooden pillars. In general they said they were only earning moderate wages of 10 or 12 shillings per week, & if it were not that they had huts & gardens here, that they would soon move away.

The *stuff* to be washed is a very coarse gravel with sand and clay, with often also fragments of the basement rock, chipped of for the sake of any gold that might be lodged in their interstices. The general mode of

washing is by the cradle which consists of 1st a perforated plate iron sieve on which the stuff is thrown & washed with water ladled from the river or hole, in order ro wash off all the finer portions containing the gold dust, & 2nd of a system of washing boards & ledges against which the gold lodges & accumulates. The whole is on rollers so as to rock like a cradle & a quick motion is communicated by a handle. It is a rude uneconomical way, a deal of time being lost in continually filling & emptying the sieve.

After the days work or oftener the gold dust & dirt is washed out of the ledges into a washing pan and the dust soon obtained perfectly clean.

Much better ways of washing were employed wherever a continuous stream of water & a fall could be obtained, these processes being called *sluicing*. All that is used is a slanting board with several ledges & sometimes a sieve. Immense quantities of stuff may be washed by means of

sluicing but a considerable outlay is necessary in making a race, that is a channel running for some hundred yards evenly on a level along the river to convey water so as to abtain a fall of some feet at the lower end.

The river bed all along is I believe rich in gold generally coarser than that in the banks, but in order to work holes in the bed pumps must be kept continually going to remove the water which drains with great rapidity through the gravel.

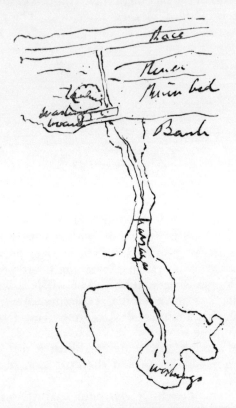

In one large concern this was done by a small portable engine & fire pumps; in other cases by men working Californian pumps

It appeared to me that though two or three men working together & poking into a small hole, may not make more than small wages, that a public company of large capital might be able by a tunnel to deflect the water of the river between two close bends, and then take out & wash bodily the bed of the river ensuring a large weight of gold.

After going about a mile down the river, beyond which point the ground seemed to have been less rich, I slowly returned examining whatever I saw worth notice. Returning to the Public House, I accompanied M^r OConnell in the other direction along the river i.e. up. Here there was even less activity, & all the washing done by the cradle. Parts of the banks however seemed to have been very rich & these were entirely undermined.

At one house we saw a beautiful bird, of the crane tribe probably standing about 4 feet high & of extraordinary tameness; it was called the Native Companion and was walking about quite free.

The Man at the Public House not being able to accomodate us took us next door to the Gas Hotel a much larger but equally singular wooden structure. Here we had a large long room partially to ourselves with a small bedroom leading from it. The walls and ceiling were lined with calico; the floor was the natural earth. We were however well & civilly served and at prices even less than those on the road, so that we could not say much as to dearness of things at the diggings

The weather these few days was very splendid, and I never remember to have seen the sky freer from all cirrous or stratous clouds, regular rounded clouds of the ordinary day cumulus being alone seen

Wednesday, 19 March

The mail not leaving before Thursday morning, this day was unoccupied except in walking about the place which I had for the most part seen yesterday. I was quite bilious during the morning but notwithstanding walked down the river with M^r OConnell who was determined if possible to get employment on wages. The only offer he had was one to pump incessantly for 8^s per day, but the work being the hardest possible & all other circumstances disadvantageous, he of course did not accept it.

In the afternoon I strolled about and up a part of the hills on the other side of the river. From the latter place I attempted a sketch or so of the diggings. The scenery it must be acknowledged is fine & romantic and with the additional interest attached to the place on account of its celebrated diggings, I shall not easily forget these two days.

Strolling about till evening I met M^r OC. returning from an unsuccessful search for employment, & returned with him: We had another tea in the singular shaped room, & I went to bed early in order to be in time for tomorrows mail.

20 *Thursday*

Breakfast was done in good time & everything packed up for the mail. At about nine oclock the Royal Mail app^d, a light sort of drag with back seat, the whole only holding 3 passengers & the driver. I sat behind, the other passengers being a young woman whose husband had run away to Port Phillip after selling his dray & team with which he had gone down to Sydney as a carrier. We jolted out of the town with the least ceremony possible, and soon lost sight of the wooden huts of Sofala.

To Wattle Flat we proceeded chiefly at a walk as there are not many yards of level road, and a considerable part even I used my own legs instead of the horses. At the Flat we went the road leading through the main portion of the diggings, which I found very intensive & apparently rather in better condition. The diggings were along shallow hollows or dry creeks, extending several miles through flat, timbered country. Diggers tents & huts were scattered without order throughout the place generally among the trees a short distance from the holes; and the whole was a somewhat picturesque colonial scene.

After seeing the last of the digging but little of interest occurred up to Bathurst. The Wyagden hill appeared more formidable than ever, and the driver who keeps his head going down must run the risk of his life every other day. At the Inn, we had a wretched dinner & the landlady filled up the vacant seat to Bathurst.

Arriving about 3 or 4 pm, I engaged a bed at the Inn we stopped at as at any rate preferable to our last place. The rest of the afternoon I spent in the Court House where the assizes were going on; if everything was done in the colony with as much uprightness as is the administering of justice, there would be no need of complaint.

For tea I found myself at the general table, among a miscellaneous collection of snobs & others, eating in consequence with little satisfaction Among them were a number of actors or at all events performers of some sort; one of them occupied the second bed in my room & seemed a decent young man. The evening I tried to while away by wandering through the streets which however did not strike me as any more agreable than before. Pianos were to be heard sounding in the houses of the richer store keepers who are[1] pretend to be fond of accomplishments & luxuries in their houses

[1] Jevons first wrote here 'fond of a pretension' but crossed it out.

Good Friday, 21 March

I awoke early & was dressed in such good time that I had half an hour or more to spare. So taking my barometer I walked quickly out of the town & down to the River Macquarie in order to take a[1] the altitude of its bed more exactly by an additional observation. I walked along its bed for a short distance; the slightest pretension to beauty or picturesqueness this river & the country immediately adjoining cannot make in the least degree. It is flat, bare, & hideous, but is somewhat interesting when one thinks of the strange nature of these Australian rivers, with their square broad channels only filled during floods which occur at intervals of many years, and running with a most unsatisfactory sort of progress through hundreds of miles of almost unexplored country at last all unite in the main river of SE[n] Australia the Murray.

We had breakfast before starting in the same disagreable public manner as at tea the night before, with a lot of impudent girls making tea &c.

The Mail[2] to Harteley was larger & different from the Sofala one which returned loaded with the actors & others. It was like a short break, holding one passenger next the driver & 6 in the body in the room that 4 would occupy in any other case. Fellow passengers were M[rs] Keegan & Child, a sober old tradesmanlike man and his wife & *Andrew* an essentially colonial young man. The travelling was moderately easy and with the increased number of passengers more cheerful. The driver formed quite a *type* of character; evidently a first rate & most likely steady fellow, good humoured as long as things went well and always ready with a sort of worn-out jocular wit. After quiting the fearful Macquarie plains the country was certainly a pretty one to ride through and more resembled English scenery than any other we passed through. I got however frightfully hungry & consequently inclined to bad humour; at *Durants* Inn nothing was ready for us and when we got to Rydall Solitary Creek, there was no meat & we had to dine on eggs potatoes tea &c. This inn seemed to have a deal of accommodation as far as space goes, and was kept by an old convict who had been on one of Sir T Mitchells Exploring Expeditions[3] & thus obtained his pardon.

On getting near Bowenfels & Harteley, I was again & ever more

[1] Jevons first wrote 'barometer reading here' but crossed it out.

[2] Most of the following page in the notebook had been torn out but Jevons wrote on the remaining portion 'Travelling in the Mail I had expected better attention & accommodation than before, but found it quite the reverse. The price however was uniformly raised 25 p.c. i.e. a bed or meal 2.6 instead of 2s as before.'

[3] Sir Thomas Mitchell (1792–1855), appointed Surveyor-General of New South Wales, 1828. Carried out four major expeditions into the interior of Australia between 1831 and 1845. See his *Three Expeditions into the interior of Eastern Australia* (2 vols, 1838) and *Journal of an Expedition into the interior of Tropical Australia* (1848).

powerfully struck with the genuine beauty of the place produced no doubt by the abrupt junction of the sandstone & primitive formations.

We stopped at the further extremity of Great Harteley at the Commercial Inn, an[1] excellent & most comfortable house, chiefly because the bar was distinct from the accomodation part

We waited tea for the Sydney Mail which at last we heard coming down Mount Victoria with a deal of blowing of trumpets

The tea included our own passengers the two *drivers* & Mr Long Stock Auctioneer from Camperdown & a few other Sydney passengers. I was in a good humour and the beauty of the place with the calm delightfulness of the weather & the moon light, made a very pleasant impression on one. I slept in a comfortable room on the main floor with Mr Long, but went to bed with great misgiving about awaking in time for the mail at the absurd hour of 4.0 am.

March 22nd. Was awoke most unmistakeably by a loud long continued blowing of horns in the yard below ones windows, a most effectual way of waking us whether that were the object or no. Mr Long was most apprehensive of missing his up-mail & we were both of us soon out, but only to stand shivering outside in the still dark night & the extremely chill mountain air.

Our conveyance today was a still larger one than yesterday but of the same form; it was on its first trip, 'rejoicing in the name of the Mountain Plumb' but had received some severe injuries about the region of the pole & front wheels which suggested impassable roads, smashes[2] & other dangers.

After it had been up the town to get the mails we started at 4.30 at a good pace along the roads for the present tolerable and as cheerily as the cold air and a very natural inclination to sleepiness would allow. We stopped at Little Harteley and had to wait a little for the mails not that anybody was likely to sleep much considering the noise the driver didnt fail to make with the same horn, and seemed to think a very amusing proceeding.

The drivers I may say remained each time with this coach so that each continually drove the same portion of the road. Our new [one][3] was just like the last and entertained us; or at least intended to do so with jokes songs and general display of humour.

The drive up Mount Victoria just at the break of day was indeed romantic & interesting.

The suns beams could be seen gradually creeping down the sides of the rocks & ranges into the beautiful vales (the Vale of Clwyd is the larger one I believe) where thin *local* sheets of mist were yet lying and

[1] 'a' in the text.   [2] 'smashs' in the text.   [3] Jevons crossed this word out.

could be watched gradually spreading at a small height generally above the ground or among the trees, or afterwards breaking up under the suns influence & rising in loose detached portions a short distance before evaporating. Overhead & about the sky were some light portions of cumuloid cloud which from the dull but exquisite violet or purplish tint which it has under diffused light, became suddenly of a singular & nearly pure red, perhaps to be described as brick-red, when the suns light fell on it. This colour became in a most distinct manner gradually more mixed with *yellow* as the sun rose, presenting a succession of phenomena nearly the reverse of those at sunset.

I was again much struck with the cliff like form of the rocks of Mount Victoria & the slanting mass of *debris* reaching with an evident horizontality to certain height & there sharply terminated. The form is singular & must point to some particular or interesting deduction. Can these be ancient sea cliffs; if the debris were found to terminate at the same level at distant parts it would prove it pretty conclusively.

We proceeded on with but little interruption to Blackheath arriving there between seven and eight. The weather now was very different from what we experienced on our way up, being delightful & clear, and the place accordingly had a much more cheerful aspect. I observed there an old convict settlement, or Commisariat stores as the Government people call them similar to the ones at Solitary creek where we passed the night.

After nearly an hours delay during which we had breakfast we again started with an additional traveller viz Capt Scott the Superintendant of these roads. He was an affected but not disagreable man, but without much appearance of fitness for this place as indeed the state of the roads might lead one to suppose. We stopped again to change horses at Blue Mountain Inn, from which, on account of the clearness there was a view of several of the loftiest peaks of the Moutains a short distance to the Northwards; they were very picturesque & precipitous but still appeared entirely clothed with gum trees to the very summit.

The road between here and Pilgrim Inn was at places in a most frightful condition and though I had seen this on my way up, I now felt it and no mistake. Mail travelling in the Australian mode, is never anything but most uneasy & fatiguing owing to the cramped & overcrowded space, & the awful jogging on the roads, but about this part it became quite insufferable except indeed for its novelty and absolute ludicrousness.

Who in England could imagine a *Royal Mail* scarcely larger than a gig, slowly picking its way along a track (of a road it has no appearance) in which the ruts are often 2 or 3 feet deep and where the passengers are continually called upon by the driver to lean over for their lives so as if possible to preserve the otherwise very uncertain equilibrium of the vehicle. Portions indeed were in such a state that it had been thought worth while to clear a new track along side the old one the surface of the virgin earth forming an incomparably better road; thus there were often sorts of arc – branches of the road.

We pushed on all day as well as we could the driving indeed being quite a feat of its kind but at *Springfield* we received a change of *Crack* horses with which to enter Penrith with a dash. These being less manageable at once took us right against a stump at a place where the passable road was not an inch over on either side.

A stump of a tree being a most unyielding obstacle a smash of the splinter bar ensued, but an axe was soon procured a sapling cut down & fitted and in a marvellous short time we were again off. We arrived in Penrith safely but after being very apprehensive of danger in descending Lapstone Hill with such horses, where the slightest fault in the driving might have sent us to the bottom of the gully in spite of the strong railing.

No coach went onto Sydney till Sunday morning, and though at the Commercial Inn Penrith where we had tea, they tried every dodge to induce us to stay the night, I determined to walk on with Andrew – a passenger to Sydney.

He was the son of a publican in the Haymarket Sydney but I was surprized to find him a *decent* & *feeling* though colonial born fellow. After walking till late at[1] night he giving me accounts of colonial & country experience we lay down to sleep in a wood and waking early on Sunday morning, proceeded leisurely to Parramatta. By the 10 am, the first train I then easily reached home where my appearance, hungry tired & worn, covered with dust and in a strange Sunday costume must have excited some surprize.

This journey from Harteley to Sydney perhaps 50 miles of the execrable jolting in the mail & 30 miles of walking in little over 24 hours altogether, including a few hours sleep, is the greatest amount of fatigue I ever underwent, & I experienced no bad effects worth mentioning from it.

[1] 'a' in the text.

FAMILY TREE OF THE JEVONS FAMILY
(unless otherwise stated, surname of Jevons throughout)

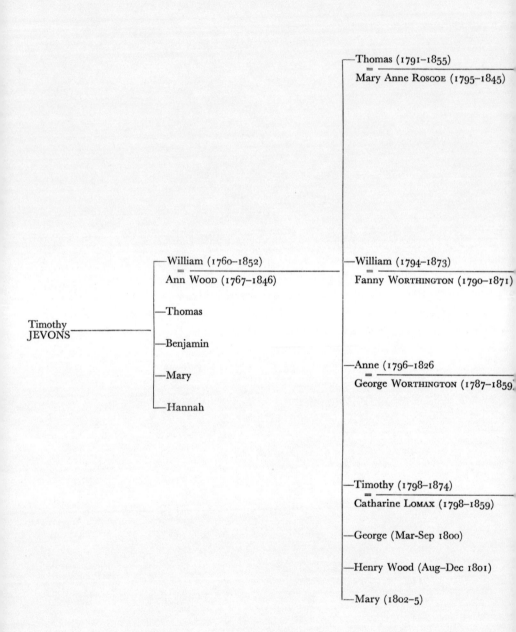

Timothy JEVONS
- William (1760–1852)
  = Ann WOOD (1767–1846)
  - Thomas (1791–1855)
    = Mary Anne ROSCOE (1795–1845)
  - William (1794–1873)
    = Fanny WORTHINGTON (1790–1871)
  - Anne (1796–1826
    = George WORTHINGTON (1787–1859)
  - Timothy (1798–1874)
    = Catharine LOMAX (1798–1859)
  - George (Mar-Sep 1800)
  - Henry Wood (Aug–Dec 1801)
  - Mary (1802–5)
- Thomas
- Benjamin
- Mary
- Hannah

—Jane Emily (Jan–Apr 1827)
—Stillborn son (Nov 1827)
—Roscoe (1829–69)
—Lucy Ann (1830–1910)
  =
—John HUTTON (1824–94)
—Herbert (1831–74)

— —Charles Thomas⎱ Apr 1832–May 1833
   Mary Emily ⎰
—Edward Griffiths (May 1834–June 1835)
—**William Stanley** (1835–82)
  =
  Harriet Anne TAYLOR (1838–1910)
—Henrietta Elizabeth (1839–1909)
—Thomas Edwin (1841–1917)
  =
  Isabel (Isabella) SETON

   ┌—Thomas Grindal HUTTON (1862–75)
   └—Mary Josephine HUTTON (1867–1910)

   ┌—Herbert Stanley (1875–1955)
   ├—Harriet Winefrid (1877–1961)
   └—Lucy Cecilia (1880–1952)

   ┌—Marguerite (b. 1871)
   ├—Reginald (1872–1907)
   ├—Thomas Seton (b. 1874)
   └—Ferdinand Roscoe Talbot (1876–1967)

┌—George (1818–1905)
│ =
│ Elizabeth THORNELY (1820–83)

   ┌—George Walter (b. 1854)
   ├—Fanny (b. 1856)
   └—John Daniel Thornely (1861–67)

—William Alfred (b. 1820)
  =
  Eliza Augusta REES
—Fanny (b. 1821)
—Annie (1825–1905)
—Emma (b. 1829)
—Caroline (b. 1831)

   ┌—Mary (b. 1855)
   ├—Annie Helen (b. 1857)
   ├—Eliza Augusta
   ├—William (b. 1860)
   ├—Rowland (b. 1861)
   └—Francis (b. 1863)

—┌—George WORTHINGTON (b. 1825)
  └—Anne Frances WORTHINGTON (b. 1826)

—Henry (1825–1914)
  =
  Susanna THORNELY (1830–1915)
—Mary Catherine (1827–1908)
—James Edward (1828–60)
—Arthur (1830–1905)
  =
  Catherine Castle DAWSON (1826–1906)
—Eliza (b. 1832)

—ALFRED BARHAM
—Frederick (1834–1916)
  =
  Sarah Acland TAYLOR

—William Edgar (1836–88)
  =
  Mary Ann TAYLOR
—Anne Jane (1836–46)

   ┌—Catharine (b. 1854)
   ├—Elizabeth (1855–1921)
   ├—Thomas Henry (1856–95)
   ├—Wilfred (1858–95)
   ├—Mary (b. 1859)
   ├—Helen (1859–87)
   ├—Susan (b. 1862)
   ├—James Edward (b.&d. 1866)
   ├—Annie Jane (b. 1867)
   ├—Harold (b. 1867)
   ├—Harold (b. 1869)
   └—John Francis (1872–1904)

   ┌—Frederick (b. 1867)
   ├—Mary Catherine (b. 1870
   ├—William (b. 1873)
   └—James Edward (b.&d 1875

FAMILY TREE OF THE ROSCOE FAMILY
(unless otherwise stated, surname of Roscoe throughout)

William ROSCOE (1753–1831)
=
Jane GRIFFIES (d. 1824)

—William Stanley (1782–1843)
=
Hannah Eliza CALDWELL (d. 1854)

—Elizabeth (Jun–Dec 1783)
—Edward (1785–1834)
=
Margaret LACE (1787–1840)

—James (1787–1829)
=
Jane Douglas McGIBBON (1789–1829)

Robert (1789–1850)
=
Martha WALKER (1798–1884)

—Thomas (1791–1871)
=
Elizabeth EDWARDS

—Richard (1793–1864)
=
Mary Ann HODGSON
(nee BARDSWELL) (1801–88)
—Mary Anne (1795–1845)
=
Thomas JEVONS (1791–1855)
—Jane Elizabeth (1797–1853)
=
Francis HORNBLOWER (1812–53)
—Henry (1799–1836)
=
Maria FLETCHER (1798–1885)

—Elizabeth Jane (1820–46)
—Mary Ann (1821–52)
=
Richard Holt HUTTON (1826–97)
— —William Caldwell (1823–59) ——————————— Elizabeth Mary (b. 1856)
= —William Malin (b. 1857)
Emily Sophia MALIN (1830–86) — Margaret Henrietta (b. 1858)
—Arthur (b. 1825)
—Thomas Stamford (b. 1826)
—Francis James (1830–78)
=
Letitia LE BRETON

—William (1810–13)
— —Margaret (1812–52)
—Edward Henry (1813–66)

—James Griffies (1819–95)
—William (1820–71)
—Maxwell Archibald (b. 1822)
— —Edward (b. 1824)
—Mary Jane Douglas (1825–63)
—Anne Letitia (1828–30)

—Emma Jane (1820–87)
=
Rev. DUNSTAN
—Henrietta (1821–69)
=
Timothy Smith OSLER (b. 1823)
—Eliza (1823–97)
=
Richard Holt HUTTON (1826–97)
— —Martha (b. 1825)
—Laura ('Poppy') (b. 1828)
=
James THORNELY (1822–98)
—Henry (1830–99)
=
Eliza WALKER (b. 1840)
—Robert (1831–46)
—Richard ('Dick') (1833–92)
=
Honora WORSLEY (1837–79)
—Clara ('Patty') (b. 1836)
—Alfred (1841–62)

—William Henry
—Arthur
—Edward
— —Mary
—Eliza
—Jane
=
Horace Roscoe ST. JOHN (1832–88)
—Julia

—See Jevons Family Tree
— —William Stanley JEVONS

—Henry Enfield ('Harry') (1833–1915) ——————— —Edmund (1864–85)
= — Margaret (b. 1866)
Lucy POTTER (1840–1910)
—Harriet (b. 1835)
=
Edward ENFIELD (1811–80)